Falconry

Its Claims, History, and Practices – Hunting with Birds of Prey

By Gage Earle Freeman

PANTIANOS
CLASSICS

Published by Pantianos Classics

ISBN-13: 978-1-78987-084-8

First published in 1859

Contents

Preface

The history of this work may be very concisely told in the words of an extract from Messrs, Longman's "Notes on Books" for last May: — "The papers of which it consists were originally written by "Peregrine" for the *Field,* with the view of making British gentlemen familiar with all the details of a sport once so general, though now neglected and nearly forgotten. The papers have been carefully revised; and, in preparing them for the press, the author had access to occasional Notes drawn up by Captain Salvin, and was also indebted for many valuable hints to the experience of that keen falconer, who now shares with ' Peregrine ' the responsibility of this publication. ... To the 'Falconry' are added some remarks on the training of the Otter and Cormorant, from the pen of Captain Salvin, who writes from his own practice."

To my old and kind friend, Mr. Brodrick, to whom I was indebted, many years ago, for a knowledge of the rudiments of the art of Falconry, this book owes something; and I take this opportunity of thanking, in the name of Captain Salvin and in my own, Sir Molyneux Nepean, Bart., Mr. Newcome, and others, for the kind interest which, at the cost of some trouble to themselves, they have shown in our undertaking.

The long letter from an officer serving in India has been gratefully received, and I am sure will be found most interesting.

"Falconry in the British Isles," with its numerous and masterly drawings, is out of print; but the present work, although it does not follow its predecessor in giving a figure of each species of hawk used in Falconry, contains several plates from the excellent and well-known pencil of Mr. Wolf, some of which illustrate the implements necessary for the practice of the sport.

The very great kindness which I have received from a considerable number of readers during the last few years emboldens me to unmask; but I still hope to be recognised in the *Field* under the old *nom de plume* of "Peregrine."

In saying one word on the character of this book, it may not be unwise to remind some of those who may care to observe in what manner our subject has been treated, that I wish "Falconry" to come before them, not only as a *sport* which is slowly making its way among the gentlemen of these islands, but as a gallant venerable *friend,* whom our forefathers loved with all their hearts, — who, like all his kith and kin, left his impress upon the character of our race, — and whom, in the last stage of his destitution, we have just agreed not utterly to forget or ignore.

I may add to this, that the following pages have been written with reference to the *Natural History* of the birds of which they treat, as well as with the intention of showing the process of their training, and the method of using them in the field.

It will readily be granted, I think, that a falconer has more opportunity than any other man of observing, not only the "manners and customs," but the characters of hawks; and few will disagree with the Rev. J. Gr. Wood when he remarks, in that excellent little work of his, "My Feathered Friends," that the true object of Natural History is "to bring forward the character or life of the creature, which is, in fact, its essential being."

This opinion, indeed, recommends itself at once; and I hope it will be found in this treatise that, not only have I given the character of each species by writing directly upon it, but that I have also incidentally illustrated and exemplified it whilst my pen has been more pointedly employed upon the leading object of these chapters, — viz. the training and management of hawks, — or, in other words, the "practice" of Falconry. In giving the character of any kind of hawk, one is, of course, obliged to treat it as it appears when the bird is in a semi-captivity, and as it is developed by training. Indeed, there can hardly be any other circumstances than those belonging to the domestic state, under which the dispositions and tempers of these, or any birds, can be exhibited. We understand them better in friendship than in enmity,— near than at a distance; for it must not be for a moment imagined that hawks lose their specific or individual characters when they become our friends and servants; these are surely retained, and no falconer wishes to destroy them; he only takes care that they are kept under command; and, generally, that they are rendered subservient. It is true that when, for instance, we say a species or an individual is "docile," we speak of a part of its character which is, in a certain sense, artificial and acquired; but we must remember that there was a foundation on which alone the superstructure of "docility" could have been built; and, therefore, from the ease with which we tamed or trained the birds in our possession, we argue correctly concerning a certain, though a latent, character which is resident in their unreclaimed brethren. There can, therefore, be hardly a Naturalist in the world who, whatever he may think of the sport in the abstract, will not allow that Falconry is at least a devoted and faithful servant to one branch of ornithology, — the great family of the *Accipitres.*

G. E. F.
("Peregrine.")

Wild Boar Clough Parsonage,
Cheshire: August, 1859.

Chapter One - Its Claims

I AM conscious of using an expression which is not, perhaps, very definite, when I speak of the *claims* of Falconry. The claims which field sports generally, and in the aggregate, have upon country gentlemen, are frequently discussed; their importance is gathered easily and at once, and few people indeed are found to gainsay them. Thus, "national character," "resident landlords," "health," "good spirits," with an infinite number of small sprites attending upon these great genii, are perfectly familiar to us all. We, very properly, take them for granted, receive them in right of their privileges, vaunt them to our neighbours, and then, excellent as they are, we hunt, and shoot, and fish, without any immediate reference to them at all, but simply because we like hunting, shooting, and fishing.

The claims of any individual sport might probably be made to appear distinctly and with effect by comparing them with the claims or characteristics of some sister amusement, especially with those which should seem weak or objectionable. To do this, however, in any other way than by an incidental comparison would be ill-natured; and, as the choice of a favourite sport is, after all, very much a matter of taste, it would be absurd. Therefore I shall simply make this chapter a vehicle for placing Falconry before the public in a light which I know its friends will approve, a light reflected entirely from its own history and its own merits. — Not that I trust to an introductory chapter in any great degree as a means of making proselytes; that office I assign to detail; I assign it to the incidents of the sport, which will be found in their proper places in this book; but, above all, I assign it to those gentlemen who have land and hawks, and means to boot, and who can excite more enthusiasm, in a couple of hours, by an exhibition of falconry in the field, than I can hope to create by a whole work on "Its Claims, History, and Practice."

Antiquity! — I can scarcely hope that all who may read these pages will care for it, or perhaps, to speak more correctly, I can scarcely think they will *confess* that they esteem it of consequence. I am sorry for those who despise antiquity, because I think they lose half a life by living so utterly away from the past. It is no business of mine to defend the middle ages here — I have no inclination to defend them entirely; but perhaps we all know where we shall most readily find "that generous loyalty to rank and sex, that proud submission, that dignified obedience, that subordination of the heart, which kept alive, even in servitude itself, the spirit of an exalted freedom." The natural mood of a mind wandering back to old times is certainly sober and respectful; sometimes indeed there is the light and warmth of a genial and generous enthusiasm, and the consciousness of a charm which it is difficult to explain or even to understand. Look at the pride — the honest noble pride — of ancestry! I will engage to say that there are few men of cultivation who, in reality, despise the circumstance of a long and honourable descent. The true affectation is to disparage, not to confess, its value. Gibbon says that the family of Confucius is the most illustrious in the world, — not only as they are "the lively image of the wisest of mankind," but because they "have maintained above *two thousand two hundred years* their peaceful honours and perpetual succession." What a wonderful chain! And yet fancy each link with its bobbing pig-tail, or flat nose, or pinched limping horse-shoe foot! Only conceive the long line of tea-pots! Think of the oceans of nectar which so many Celestials must have consumed! Make the matter, in short, as absurd as you may; and then confess, after all, that the reverence paid to the representative of that mighty house is scarcely to be numbered among the follies of the Chinese people.

So much for antiquity, and its value! My own opinion is, that few men exist who do not, so to speak, take off their hats mentally to so respectable an acquaintance. A friend of mine, it is true, once told me that his love for the sport of Falconry was perfectly independent of any feeling for antiquity and the middle ages, for which he cared nothing; but I believe he was mistaken. If I could have twisted the γνῶθι σεαυτὸν into a wand, and touched him with it on the heart, he would probably have discovered a light leash that bound him to the bells and jesses of another age.

Falconry is certainly of high descent, if that be considered a recommendation. It boasts a long line of ancestors, and has claimed and received homage from the chivalry and beauty of many centuries. To *what* date it can be traced we shall consider in the proper place. I can only here express my strong desire that some ultra game-preserving nobleman, who orders every hawk on his property to be slaughtered, could have a few minutes' conversation with that great grandsire of his of whom he boasts so much. Perhaps the dialogue would run somewhat after this manner: —

Ancestor. — A set of arrant rascals, coward knaves!
Robert, my son, art quick, and dost thou heed?
Art in the flesh? — E'en as I pass'd the gate,
Nigh the portcullis, by the bastion-wall,
I spied, with rotten fitchews, pies, and crows,
All daub'd with filth, the falcon-gentle tied,
Pierced with a nail, — a rusty villain nail. —
Wert blind? — Or didst thou from our turret hang
The knave that slew the bird? —
Descendant — Really now, my dear Sir, — aw! — You are. so dreadfully severe. You allude possibly to a "flying vermin:" they infest the manor, and we trap them: caught alive, — hung by the leg a few days, — serve him right, — kills grouse, — wrung his neck, — aw! —
Ancestor. — A hawk, and hang!— Out, recreant, dotard, out!—
But hold! — I do thee wrong, it cannot be!
SS. Nisus! — Palumbarius! — Peregrine!
All to my aid! — How oft, with loving hand,

Have I the *Pelt* [1] for Falcon-gentle held! —
Then, fed, she *rouzed* [2] and *mantled;* [3] and anon
Feaked [4] on my glove, while I did smoothe her *mailes,* [5]
Her *petty-single* [6] with a soft plume touched;
Meanwhile, with right good will, she *pruned* [7] herself. —
Full oft I told her of a Hern *at seidge;* [8]
Then were we friends; and when the drowsy night
Talk'd to the world of stars in its bright dreams,
I loved to deem she *jouketh* [9] well in it.
Descendant — My *dear* Sir: What singular gibber I mean — beg pardon, — aw!

[1] *Pelt* is the dead body of any fowl the hawk hath killed,
[2] *Rouze* is when a hawk lifteth herself up and shaketh herself.
[3] *Mantleth* is when a hawk stretcheth one of her wings after her legs, and so the other.
[4] *Feaking* is when the hawk wipeth her beak after feeding.
[5] *Mailes* are the breast feathers.
[6] Petty-tingles are the toes of the hawk.
[7] *Pruneth* is when the hawk picketh herself,
[8] *Hern at seidge* is when you find a hern standing by the waterside, watching for prey, or the like.
[9] *Jouketh* is when she sleepeth.

The Gentleman's Recreation, 1677.

Here I am quite sure the old gentleman would get so outrageous that I dare not proceed — especially as he speaks in such dreary blank verse.

I have a word to say presently on the extermination of the nobler falcons; but before that point is touched, we will glance at claims apart from those of antiquity.

I really do not think it too much to assert that many hundreds of people, and not all of them sportsmen, have lately become interested in the art of falconry. This conclusion is arrived at in many ways, and in no trifling degree from the numberless letters which I receive from strangers for advice and assistance. And, as public opinion just now cares for the sanction of antiquity least of all earthly things, I conclude that the excellence of the sport itself has not been without its influence in the revival. Falconry came to me accompanied by a charm and a romance which I could not resist; but I like it for itself, and am quite willing to give the second place only to pedigree and a name.

It has been too much the habit to assume that a falconer is a falconer, and nothing else, — that he never shoots, and never throws a fly. It is no such thing. A falconer, to my knowledge, may be as good a shot and as fond of shooting as the man whose whole mind has been forced down the barrels of his gun. I wonder what they would say in Norfolk, for instance, in answer to the charge that a falconer is *only* a falconer!

As for exercise, and intense though healthy excitement, if they are not found in falconry they are not found in anything. This is the coursing of the air; — it has the ethereal properties in itself; it is the very fairy-work of sport. And yet it is practical enough: one does not come empty-handed from the field in game hawking; a single goshawk will certainly keep a family. A flight with falcons may last for forty minutes, or it may last for four; all depends upon the quarry flown at. But there is riding or running, and the absolute essence or concentration of excitement in all. The quarry is viewed; and *à la volée!* or *hooha, ha, ha, ha!* is shouted, and taken up by the field. All are at full speed in an instant: they cheer to encourage this hawk or to honour that stoop; — "Was there ever such a stroke!" they say; — "Money should not buy 'Nemesis;' she is the best falcon of the year! "The quarry is put in, but the good hawks wait above: down they come as it is flushed; "Who takes it now?" — and so on to the end.

One very great "claim" will, I am sure, be admitted at once: ladies may, and do now as of old, join in the sport. I am half jealous of the bow and the target nevertheless; why should they take so many? Archery is a nice quiet elegant amusement; and to shoot as Robin Hood did in ancient, or as Mr. Ford does in modern, times, must require consummate skill and practice. But I shrewdly suspect that a becoming dress and attitude, close companionship, the opportunity of instilling axioms without which fair fingers could do little, run a race, and win it too, with the greatest score and the best gold. There is at least often a very little bow that strikes something better and warmer than the bull's eye, and does not count for nothing. I honour archery for its antiquity, and admire it for itself — but look at a picture, seldom seen, which I think to be better still. The canter of two or three horses; the scamper behind them of as many spaniels; the gleam of a green habit; the sombre of a grey; a hat clasped with a buckle and heron's plume; the red and white of a hood; the quiet hawks as they swing by to the easy motion of the horses; the silver bells and silver voices; the freshening colour; the hopeful eye: — Fly "Blackjesse!" Good hawk! Fly well this day, if you ever flew! For the picture will take deeper colours still when *these* are flying across the plain.

In alluding to the rapid extermination of the nobler falcons, I must urge the "claims" which the sport professes to possess, rather on the forbearance of country gentlemen, than on the time which they devote to amusements. It is said that the peregrine and the merlin are destructive to game on the grouse moors. "With regard to the latter hawk, I pledge my long practical knowledge of its habits, that it is utterly unable to kill an old *uninjured* grouse; but the strongest females may occasionally take wounded or diseased birds, and, I fear, possibly a few backward young ones. The peregrine, however, is considered the more serious culprit of the two, and is persecuted accordingly. If we are to believe some accounts, he takes a grouse a day: and calculations, remarkable chiefly for their ingenuity, have been made to prove, on the plan, I think, of compound interest, how many head one pair would cause to be destroyed in the course of a year. I am not denying that a cast of peregrines on a moor, or moors, of many thousand acres, will kill many grouse; but I object altogether to the doctrine that they will perceptibly lessen the bag of the sportsman. I will go farther: I am not sure that, in the end, they will not increase it.

Of course an assertion of this kind, so contrary to received opinions, requires explanation. Let us investigate the matter. And first, as to the probable havoc made by the falcon: the amount of it must depend upon his opportunities. This bird takes his prey on the wing, not on the ground. Now, it has been remarked, not only by falconers, but it is notorious, that game take wing with very great reluctance when a peregrine is above them. In such a case it is sometimes necessary to hunt or beat them up: they dread ta trust themselves in the same element with their enemy. It was owing to the knowledge of this that the artificial hawk was invented. Neither, as every one knows, is it the *habit* of game-birds to fly much; their time is spent chiefly on the ground, either basking or feeding. Man, dog, or sheep may frighten them, and they rise: the sun on a hill side, the absence of wind there, the abundance of food, with other causes, will induce them to move, even if they are not disturbed; but, in comparison with almost all other birds, how very seldom are they on the wing! So long as pigeons, rooks, magpies, crows, &c, pass over the moor, the grouse are in comparative safety. I admit that in the utter absence of such birds as pigeons, and also the egg-stealing birds I have mentioned, some game must be taken by hawks; but, if an old building could be found in the centre of the moors which could be turned into a large dovecote, — or if a rough substantial place, ornamental or otherwise, were set up for the purpose, — the pigeons, which would remain faithful to their home even when a few years had rendered them wild, would, in my opinion, save every *healthy* grouse from the peregrine falcon. But this perhaps could only be done in the neighbourhood of *grain.*

But there is yet another and a very important light in which this subject must be viewed. All hawks, when they have a choice, *invariably choose the easiest flight.* This fact is of the last importance in the matter before us: I confess at once that I give it the chief place in this argument. Who has not heard of the grouse disease? It has been attributed, sometimes respectively and sometimes collectively, to burnt heather; to heather poisoned from the dressings put on sheep; to the sheep themselves cropping the tender shoots and leaves of the plant, and thus destroying the grouse's food; to the tapeworm; to shot which has wounded but not killed; and perhaps ta other things beside. It may be, I doubt not, correctly referred to any or to all of these. Of this, however, there appears no question, that, from whatever cause it spring, it is *propagated.* A diseased parent produces a diseased child. Now I say that when every hawk is killed upon a large manor the balance of nature is forgotten, or ignored; and that Nature will not overlook an insult. *She* would have kept her wilds healthy; destroy her appointed instruments, and beware of her revenge!

10

Leave the peregrine unmolested amongst diseased grouse, and he will kill them nearly all before he touches a healthy bird, — simply because he can catch them better.

I do not at all intend to recommend "leather" alone for your fortifications; I do not affect to announce a panacea for the grouse disease. What I say with regard to it is simply suggestive. For having given a correct description of the habits of hawks I will be answerable; and my readers can judge of the probable effect of those habits as well as I can.

I fear egg-collectors will scarcely hear me. Should any of them purchase this book in the hope of discovering the positions of the eyries, or the range of hills that hold the eggs, of the peregrine falcon, I imagine that they will be slightly disappointed. My coadjutor and myself beg to bow over this page, — respectfully indeed, but in silence. We beg to assure them, in the language of young ladies, that we shall ever esteem them as brothers, but we decline a nearer intimacy.

Surely all the purposes of natural history can be served, and a cabinet made perfect, by the purchase of eggs from a dealer. These are frequently foreign, though there is no variety in shape, colour, size, or in any other particular; they are absolutely the eggs of the peregrine falcon. They may not be taken from our cliffs; their abstraction may not have tended to make the noblest British bird more scarce in Britain; it may not have left an anxious scientific sportsman for a whole year without the materials to work upon which are essential to his craft; but possibly the broad elegant drawer, with its neat partitions, may look none the worse for that; and I am sure, to some people at least, there will be a satisfaction in knowing that they are not, in these islands, taking the fruit, — for ages national as the acorn, — while it is yet unripe; not quenching life while its spark is just kindling under the Great Hand of all; not attacking Nature in the sacred hour of her privacy, when alone she is suppliant and defenceless.

Applied to taking the eggs of *any* bird, I am quite ready to allow that this is all a rhapsody. With a certain innate horror, I confess, of slaying the *foetus* under any circumstances, I do not grudge the schoolboy his string of trophies; nor do I at all dread one of the ingredients of to-morrow's pudding. I am writing against *extermination,* and especially against extermination in a form which a peculiar instinct of our nature teaches us has some latent elements of cowardice and cruelty.

Were I permitted to address the landed proprietors, and those holding extensive manors, in some parts of England, in Scotland, and in Ireland, on the subject of not warring against the peregrine to extermination, I might perhaps speak to them as follows; and in so doing, I should give something like a summary of that portion of the present chapter which I think is the more important: —

Gentlemen, — It is said that the peregrine falcon destroys so many grouse that an owner or occupier of moors has no option but to kill him. This subject

11

(of the mischief done by the peregrine) has long been one to which I have given much thought, and applied considerable investigation; and without at all laying claim to infallibility in the matter, — but at the same time pledging my honour that I speak, not only as an advocate, but upon sincere conviction, — I assert my firm belief that the peregrine falcon is often wantonly, and frequently excessively, slandered when he is attacked as a game-destroyer. The accusations which reach you are generally indefinite, or palpably exaggerated. Thus you hear of grouse being *picked up*, which are said to have been killed by the peregrine; as if a hawk might be convicted on evidence which is not even circumstantial. Or you are told, as the result of a calculation, that such and such a number of grouse *must* have been taken by this hawk in such and such a number of days. Who are your informants? If you knew how anxious I am for the proper preservation of game, you would not accuse me of wishing to do an injury or injustice to gamekeepers; but I am bound to remind you that they have every possible motive for exaggerating the injury (if there be an injury) done by any hawk. The more destructive a bird of prey is, the more they will deserve for killing it; and the master who sees half a dozen hawks nailed against a wall, while he is addressed by his servant upon the extent and enormity of their depredations, and assured that they represent hundreds of rescued game, naturally perceives his hand going down into his pocket, while the keeper rises up in his estimation; and finally he goes home to tell his friends that Joseph Trapper is a very angel, while the peregrine falcon is the absolute reverse. Even the honest keeper has a temptation to exaggerate in this particular; and for the dishonest keeper, what can possibly be more convenient to him than to explain the absence of game which he ought to have protected by the passing presence of "flying vermin" which he cannot always destroy?

Again, are those who attribute so much destruction of game to the peregrine, *naturalists?* Do they know the falcon from the hen-harrier? Are they sure that they catch the real culprit?

Well, gentlemen, there are some of you who still disbelieve me; you think I am an enthusiast, and in error. Then to you I would say this: — The peregrine falcon is pre-eminently a type of speed, strength, and courage; he has, as long as these islands have stood out of the ocean, made his home on their crags; from time immemorial no link has been broken in the chain of his existence here; your ancestors, for the very purposes of "sport" (in whose name he is now destroyed), protected and defended him; "auld lang syne," and the traditions of other days, have no influence with you, who yet boast a good race and ancient blood: you coldly calculate how many grouse you may save for your bag by the extermination of the noble fellows who claim from you the hospitality which your fathers were honoured in according them: you are wrong even in your arithmetic: you are at fault in adding up your gains: this destroyer of a few head of sound game kills the diseased birds, and saves your moors from an unhealthy progeny: *he,* too, destroys the destroyer, for he strikes down magpies and hooded crows: — for all this, I know you will banish him, but I entreat you to do so mercifully; save his life and his limbs! There are now hundreds of your brother sportsmen who would accept an uninjured peregrine as a very handsome present. Your object cannot be revenge on a dumb creature — I am sure it is not cruelty: let me ask whether it cannot be changed altogether, and turned into a kindness.

Or, look at the matter in another light: — was not this bird evidently intended for the service of man? Is not the fact that it *is* trained to be his servant, easily and effectively, some evidence? Point out any other "vermin" — to use your own expression — with such a "claim" as this! The admission of all time is, that an animal trained to field sports — I don't speak of an individual, but of a race — ceases to be *vermin*. Again: — You encourage the fox in your own woods and in the coverts of your neighbours; you proscribe, as heartless, and worthless, and vulgar, any who dare to destroy him save in *one* way, which some of you have made orthodox. For his food you provide; rabbits — which (in order that, satiated with these, he may not seek a more dainty dish) you preserve, possibly to the injury of -some of your tenants. He *does,* however, seek this more dainty dish after all: you know he takes your pheasants — your sitting pheasants — and those of your neighbours: he is the most cunning, treacherous, destructive *running* vermin that infests these kingdoms. Well — you preserve him; you *kill* him, it is true — but you love him in life and in death. You do well; and if the pen of "Peregrine" were worth the weight of its. own feather in your estimation, or if I thought it were, I would tell you that I believe there is not a single argument set up against fox-hunting, nor a single injury that the preservation of foxes produces, which are not outweighed or compensated for a hundred times by the impress which that brave sport leaves on our national character. I grant — I assert — this with all my heart. Far distant be that bad, ill-starred day for England, when all shall be left to figures and the plodding brain; when nothing shall be left to the strong right hand — nothing to the heart; when the nerve shall be no more strung, the intellect no more braced, by the *practice* of daring courage — by the many incidents of "flood and field" which challenge the judgment, which compel rapid decision, which teach men, in the very glory and school of their sport, how they shall deport themselves, when there is something more glorious indeed, but no more tuition, and no more play!

Falconry, unlike fox-hunting, is not a national sport here at this time; but it *was* a national sport, as I have already reminded you, when those lived who have sent you down, through generations, your horses and hounds. The peregrine is part and parcel of a sport practised by your fathers, — and now sought to be revived by some of their children. Without it. the play has no Hamlet. But your keepers, who rightly preserve the fox of a well-established sport, which is more than powerful enough to shift for itself, have your orders to search out and destroy the creature which, *par excellence*, is neces-

13

sary to the revival and spread of falconry. I only ask for the gallantry and self-denial which one body of sportsmen are ever wont to show another. Notwithstanding the very considerable devastation which follows the existence of the fox, the loss of game through him is accounted as nothing, because the result more than justifies it. I know what would more than justify the moderate (only moderate) preservation of the peregrine falcon. I know what would justify the *toleration* (if you will) of these "*flying* vermin" — the pleasure of pleasing others who love the chase as well as you do; the satisfaction of giving a helping hand to a cause which needs help; the pride of restoring to its place and position in this country a sport so thoroughly national; the knowledge one day may be even amongst yourselves — who have already in such entire subjection the "beasts of the field" — how glorious a thing it is also to have "dominion over the fowls of the air."

Chapter Two – Its History

Of course this chapter lays me open to a charge of plagiarism. I may regret the inconvenience, but cannot avoid it. Nay, I have a great mind to turn testy, and ask how people dared to anticipate me in attempting to collect and arrange materials for an account of the progress of falconry. I would rather have done it myself. Still I beg to say that I *have* added some new chattels to the store; perhaps that circumstance may help me with the critics.

In writing such a history as that contained in the present chapter — or indeed, perhaps, in writing any history at all — a man must derive most of his information from books of some sort. I cannot possibly tell what was done a matter of 3000 years ago, unless I *read* up the subject; for it can scarcely be supposed, even by the most virulent critic, that I was there and saw it. "True," it is said, "but you must read it up in a particular way; it will never do for you to look into some modern author, and simply reproduce all that he has accumulated by painful and diligent labour: *that* will be unscrupulous and foolish in the last degree." I allow this; but it is rather hard, too, in my peculiar case. For of all the subjects I have had to "get up" for any purpose, I think the "History of Falconry" is the most tiresome. Let me explain — I look into every likely and ancient work I can lay my hand on; I write to some of the best scholars of the day, some strangers, some my intimate friends; I amass what I humbly conceive to be a very respectable amount of information; I begin to turn it about a little, and put it into shape, when lo! I discover that some learned but infatuated individual has beaten most of the ground before me, and that if I produce my treasure at all, all the world will declare I stole it. This is distressing and discouraging. It is what one ought to expect, perhaps, in such a clever world. I had to do my work, and have done it — badly, but not without labour. I have done my best.

It is, of course, impossible to give anything like a positive *date* to the invention of the art of falconry — I mean to its rise in the world; but still some little investigation of its antiquity may not be uninteresting. An important reference is made, in "Falconry in the British Isles," to the second volume of Mr. Layard's "Nineveh:" that gentleman, it seems, found in the ruins of Khorsabad a bas-relief, "in which there appeared to be a falconer bearing a hawk on his wrist;" and the judicious comment upon this is that, "although the hand of time had weighed heavily upon this record of the past, in all probability so accurate an observer was not mistaken in his surmise." I quite think that the *great* probability lies with the correctness of Mr. Layard's notion; it would be presumption indeed, especially for one who has not seen the relic, to say anything less; but it may be worth while to remind my readers how frequently, as Mr. Layard has shown us, the hawk's head occurs in Assyrian sculpture. He quotes a fragment of the Zoroastrian oracles, preserved by Eusebius, in which it is said "God is he that hath the *head of a hawk;*" and it is now more than conjectured — asserted, indeed, upon almost certain evidence — that Nisroch, worshipping before whom Sennacherib was killed by his sons, was an *eagle*-headed idol. "Thus," says Mr. Vaux (Assistant in the Department of Antiquities, British Museum), "in Hebrew, Syriac, Ethiopic, and Arabic, the word *nisr* means either an eagle or a hawk, and appears to be derived from an unused root, meaning 'to tear in pieces with the teeth.'" Again, "in the earliest sculptures from Nimroud, the king only is seen in adoration before one symbol of the deity" (not Nisroch this time), "the figure with the wings and tail of a bird," &c. Such seem to have been very frequent. In fact, it is not, perhaps, a very great exaggeration to say of Assyrian sculpture, that it was half made up of wings, with a very fair sprinkling of hawks' or eagles' heads.   Figures also have been found, not only bearing the fir-cone and basket, &c, but also (in the *hand*) living animals, such as the fallow deer or the gazelle. I run through these matters only to show that, unless the bas-relief has a tolerable distinctness, we must not assert *absolutely* that it represents the figure of a falconer. The immense weight of Mr. Layard's opinion, however, should make our conviction little short of certainty; and I must say, at any rate, that the matter is of very great importance to a writer struggling to make out the earliest history of falconry, and to a reader concerned and interested in his progress. For, if this bas-relief be really what it is thought to be, twenty-five centuries *must* have passed away since the art first took its rise, while the fair inference remains that it flourished 3000 years ago, among a nation of princes, palaces, and temples — a nation perhaps at once the mightiest and most luxurious which the world ever saw.

Articles on the history of falconry, as well as those on many subjects of antiquity, often give a seemingly imposing list of authorities, whilst they contain few dates, and scarcely any valuable *minutiae.* Would many people object to own that they know little or nothing about Ctesias? He might have been a soldier, priest, or statesman; perhaps a philosopher or a fool. At any rate they would, most likely, give up his *date* altogether. And yet I find him mentioned (as a witness to the antiquity of falconry) in a quotation in Blaine's article — as well as in the eighth edition of the Encyclopaedia Britannica — without the faintest reference to the century in which he was born, the country which claimed him as her son, or the class to which he belonged. His *testimony* is, that "foxes and hares were hunted in India by means of rapacious birds." What it is *worth* may be gathered from the following account of him (enough of which may be seen by a glance at Lemprière): — He was a Greek historian, seems to have dabbled in medicine, and was descended, in some way or other, from Aesculapius himself, date, B.C. 401. He wrote on Assyria, Persia, India; but I regret, for our sakes as well as for his own, that he did not adhere very strictly to the truth in his Indian history; indeed, that production has been said to be "full of fables." Cuvier, however, apologises for him, and declares that the fantastic animals of which he speaks were not *imagined* by him, but he fell into the mistake of ascribing an actual existence to hierographic figures, &c. &c. This innocent, perhaps, but not very trifling "mistake" induces a sort of shyness on our part, at which his shade ought not to be surprised; and, although I think his testimony in the present matter well worth having, I cannot positively press it upon my readers.

Aristotle (born B.C. 384) is, of course, a well-known worthy. He was born at Stagira, was a pupil of Plato, and private tutor to Alexander the Great, who seems in after years to have been very kind to him, and to have made him a present of rather more birds and beasts than would stock the Regent park gardens. We may rely, I think, both on Aristotle's veracity and acquirements. He was such a clever lad at school, that Plato had a knack of saying in his absence — may-be, when he played truant — "Intellect is not here;" a remark, by the way, which, as an expression of honest conviction, was no doubt creditable to the elder philosopher, but not flattering to the other students. However, it is a great pity that so small a portion only of Aristotle's fifty volumes "on the history of animated nature" are extant; for it is difficult to suppose any ancient testimony to our subject more valuable than his. We know that he *does* say, however, "When the hawks seized a bird they dropped it among the hunters." This quotation will be found in Blaine's article. I confess I have not yet had the opportunity of verifying it; but there is no reason to doubt its correctness. Again, we find in a work ascribed to Aristotle, and evidently written about his time, something like this expression: "Hawks appear when *called.*"

Let us consider, then, for an instant to what point we have arrived. I think it may be fairly said that the great sport existed, at least in Asia, several centuries before the Christian era. The philosopher, the historian, the bas-relief, have each their separate testimony, strong, though perhaps not certain when it stands alone; but their cumulative evidence appears to me irresistible; and I might, without much difficulty, give it even further support.

We shall take up the next link of our chain in the first century; and I only wish that something could be clearly made out as to the practice of falconry by the Romans at this period. The late lamented Professor Blunt, with a courtesy which is not always the companion of great learning, took the trouble to write a letter to me on the antiquity of falconry, reminding me, amongst other things, of a passage in Pliny (lib. x. c. 8), which, however, as he hinted, is generally known, to the effect that in a particular part of Thrace men and hawks prey together, — the men beating the woods, the hawks pouncing on the birds they disturbed. This testimony, even if it can be relied upon at all, as proving the existence of the art of falconry, and the use of *trained* hawks (which I doubt), is valuable in our present immediate consideration, rather as fixing a period than directing us to the customs of a people. Indeed, it is an uncertain witness altogether; and the Professor, in his letter to me, speaks of it only as showing an "approach" to the art. He goes on to say, that "it is impossible to believe that the art itself was then known, and yet Pliny not take notice of it on this occasion."

All this, then, is unsatisfactory; but I once thought we might collect a ray or two of light from the epigrammatic poet Martial, born A.D. 40., about thirty years later than the Pliny of whom we have spoken. I borrow the following lines of his, which have already been quoted in an Essay on our subject: —

"Praedo fait volucrum, famulus nunc ancupis idem,
    Decipit, et captas non sibi moeret aves:"

and which I take the liberty of translating thus: — "Once a plunderer of birds, now the servant of a bird-catcher, he snares birds, and grieves that they are not caught for his own benefit." *Decipit,* however, looks sadly like *decoying* birds; and my coadjutor has suggested, correctly I am convinced, that the little owl (*strix passerina* of Linnaeus) is here intended. It has been for ages used on the continent to lure up small birds for the nets, &c.

We are told that the ancient Britons had a taste for hawking; but of course no proof is given of this assertion. "The short Roman sword," however, of which they decidedly had a taste, must have turned their attention to other matters; but, if it could be proved that they practised the sport before the Roman conquest, we might suspect that their masters learned it from them.

That trained hawks were flown in Britain before the Heptarchy is very clear. I copy the following from Turners "History of the Anglo-Saxons," vol. iii. c. vii. p. 65; and just remark, by way of introduction, that this was the time of the famous King Pepin of France, whom indeed Boniface crowned; and therefore Ethelbert, who is probably the "King of Kent" alluded to, must not be confounded with the Ethelbert of 860, king after the union of the Heptarchy, and with whom we are more familiar: — "Hawks and falcons were also favourite subjects of amusement, and valuable presents in those days, when, the country being much overrun with wood, every species of the feathered race abounded in all parts. A king of Kent begged of a friend abroad two falcons, of such skill and courage as to attack cranes willingly, and seizing them to throw them on the ground. He says he makes this request, because there were few hawks of that kind in Kent who produced good offspring, and who could be made agile and courageous enough in this art of warfare. Our Boniface sent, among some other presents, a hawk and two falcons to a friend; and we may infer the common use of the diversion from his forbidding his monks to hunt in the woods with dogs, and from having hawks and falcons." And then, speaking of a somewhat later period, he says: "An Anglo-Saxon by his will gives two hawks and all his staghounds to his natural lord. The sportsmen in the train of the great were so onerous on lands as to make the exemption of their visit a valuable privilege. Hence a king liberates some lands from those who carry with them hawks or falcons, horses or dogs. The Saxon Calendar, in its drawings, represents hawking in the month of October. Hunting and hawking were for many years favourite diversions in this island. In the tapestry of Bayeux, Harold appears with his hawk upon his hand."

Passing for a moment from England to the continent of Europe, we may gather something from Spelman's "Glossarium Archaeologicum" — a work written in Latin, with occasional English equivalents. He (writing in 1629) says, "that the art was invented more than a thousand years before," and quotes "Lex Salica," tit. 7. § 1: "Qui acceptorem de arbore furaverint," &c, *i.e. from the nest,* or (more properly perhaps), as we say in English, a brancher. Ibid. § 2: "Acceptorem de perticâ," *i.e. a hawk of the perch.* § 3: "Acceptorem intra clavem repositum," probably *a hawk in the mew.* In Leg. Ripuarior., tit. 36. § 11: "Acceptorem domitum," *a reclaimed hawk;* "Acceptorem mutaetum," *a mewed hawk.* In *Leg. Frisonum:* "Qui canem acceptoricium Occident," &c, a *spaniel* (or a dog used for assisting the hawks). A still greater antiquity seems to be indicated by a statement in the "Notitia dignitatum Imperii Occidentalis," that a rank of soldiers, called *Sagittarii Venatores,* carried on their shield the representation of a hawk.

It may be asked, however, *who* some of these people were — the Riparii and the Frisians for instance — and *when* they lived. In a note of Gibbon to chapter xxxv. of his History, he says: "The Riparii, or Ripuarii, derived their name from their posts on the three rivers, the Rhine, the Meuse, and the Moselle;" and in chap, xxxviii. he seems to give the period between Clovis and Dagobert's reign over France, *i.e.* about 480 — 620, as the period in which the Ripuarian code was "transcribed and published." I do not know when it was *drawn up;* but we have seen enough of it to be sure that falconry was known on the Continent at a very early date, and probably before it was much practised in England. As for the Frisians, they dwelt along the coast of north-western Germany, from the Scheldt to the Elbe, in the fourth and fifth centuries, and their laws must have been written somewhere about this time. The "Notitia dignitatum Imperii Occidentalis" is a mere summary statement of the names of the different officers, magistrates, &c, in the Western Empire." Its date is somewhere about A.D. 400, but is not precisely known. I do not think, however, that any great weight can be given to Spelman's inference from the name and bearings of the soldiers whom the "Notitia" calls "Sagittarii Venatores."

We may gather from all this that falconry was tolerably well *established* as a leading sport in Europe, and possibly in these islands, at a very early period of our own history, — between the fourth and sixth centuries perhaps; England probably, however, being later than Germany in adopting it. I have now simply to point to its rapid increase among all civilised nations — a fact fortunately so well known, that the hard necessity no longer remains of bringing the reader to book, and insisting upon his close attention to various uncouth names and early dates, as proofs of the general correctness of my statements. It increased gradually from the Conquest, — established, as we have seen, long before it; but Edward III. is perhaps peculiarly conspicuous for having made stringent laws on the subject of falconry. The love of this sport had now become a perfect passion — nay, a mania. Europe was inflamed with it. Monarchs, nobles, and knights, disdaining the moderate draughts of its pleasures, drained them to intoxication, and lived for them, as for their fame. If a gallant were in prison he would carve falcons upon the walls; if in a court or in a church he would bear them on his glove; if in the grave, they would be figured on his tombstone; nay, his bride took a merlin to the altar on her wedding-day, and conversed with her lord in terms which became positively figurative, as she pointed every other sentiment, and hope, and (who knows?) command, with an allusion to some favourite twist of the head, or movement of the wing, or stretching out of the foot, proper to the birds which she had caressed twenty times daily since she was tall enough to reach their perches. Not to love hawking was a proof of the grossest vulgarity of disposition, and of many drops of churlish blood. Indeed, so exclusive were the well-born in this matter that, as is commonly known, particular hawks could be carried only by persons of particular ranks or conditions, or not below them, to which those birds were allotted — as, for example, the peregrine to an earl, &c. &c. These permissions and prohibitions passed away not very long before hawking itself was fast losing ground — though even as early as King John's time some modification was made in them. The sport was still in its palmy days after the Tudors' accession, Elizabeth herself patronising it. James Stuart, however, did not care for it, though his mother loved it dearly, and flew hawks while she was a prisoner. Towards the middle [1] of the seventeenth century the sport seems to have languished, probably abroad, but certainly in England. It could scarcely have flourished under the shadow of the "Protector." Towards the latter half of the eighteenth century there was a partial revival. It took more than a hundred years to raise into health even the *sport* of chivalry after the eleven years' infliction. Sixty years ago, or more, Lord Orford and Colonel Thornton did their best to revive falconry in England, and succeeded in a measure. They flew "passage hawks," after the Dutch fashion; but this part of their system does not seem to have reached Scotland, where "eyesses" have almost always been used. They used eyesses also. But when, more recently, fowling-pieces were brought nearly to perfection, and the art of shooting flying became thoroughly understood, falconry received another blow. Sportsmen, I suppose, persuaded themselves that the end or aim of field sports is. simply and only to kill game, and that no instrument is so much to be admired as that by which the greatest bag can be made in the shortest time. Hence the gun soon took the place of the hawk. Had they thought twice upon the matter, it would have occurred to them that fresh air, exercise, pleasurable and therefore healthy excitement, are of infinitely more importance than any amount of destruction; and falconry might, in that case, have gone hand in hand with the great and honoured sport of shooting. The present inclosed state of this country is, of course, inimical to the *general* spread of falconry; but I beg most courteously to inform the Rev. J. Gr. Wood, author of "My Feathered Friends," and other interesting works, that his assertion that "falconry in this country is just an *impossibility*," is being more strongly contradicted, and that practically, every day. There is a lingering vitality about the sport which, considering the many obstacles to its revival, appears to me wonderful. No dethroned queen — not Margaret of Anjou herself — ever, surely, strove with more determination to assert her rights, or to regain a lost inheritance. That falconry will always exist in the *world* — for its stronghold is still the east — I firmly believe; but I, hoping against hope perhaps, still look for the time when the sportsmen of these islands shall write, not with their pens but in their practice, another page of its history. At least, there is no violent improbability. We change the fashion of our sports almost as rapidly as that of our dress. I don't know whether we shall ever return to the long waistcoats and the powdered hair; but I am sure that a reaction of feeling has commenced, which is in favour of the leash and the hood.

[1] Considerably later than this, about 1730, lived William M'Arthur, gardener and falconer to the Duke of Perth. He, with his master, joined the standard of Prince Charles Edward, and fought at Preston Pans, Falkirk, and Culloden. In the last of these battles he was wounded in' the shoulder; but a disguise and the hills saved him, as they did many others. He ultimately became gardener at Danby in Wensleydale, and died there in 1808, at the great age of 92. This note is valuable, as it helps to supply the most doubtful link in our chain.

Chapter Three - Little Generally Known About Hawks

Very little is known about hawks by the generality of sportsmen; and not very much, I think, even by those among them who profess some passable knowledge of natural history. The thorough-going naturalist, of course, is a different man from these. He making it his business to inform himself of *all* animated nature's secrets, and probably placing the *Accipitres* at the head of his ornithological studies, arrives — after reading and personal observation — at sound and just conclusions respecting the history and habits of birds of prey. The falconer, too, if only from sheer necessity, possesses an intimate acquaintance with birds which he has examined in the nest, or observed close round it — which he has seen, as wild savage things, dashing after their dinner with even more than American haste and anxiety for that meal; whose nature he has made subservient — and whose singular alteration of plumage after the first moult (that stumbling-block to some ornithologists) he has noted, in its every stage, for hours, that would make up a sum of months or years, at the distance of his own eyes from his gloved hand.

Accomplished naturalists, and falconers of any kind, are, however, unfortunately few and far between. I think gamekeepers generally "know a hawk from a hernshaw;" but it is the exception, and not the rule, if they know a sparrow-hawk from a kestrel. Perhaps this is scarcely to be wondered at; for, with a few exceptions, they are plain hard-working men, well adapted to their station, and with too much on their *hands* to be able to spare a great deal for their minds. Still, however, a little more information and discrimination on the subject of "vermin" might be useful to them. As it is, I find that, in describing hawks, their favourite colour is *blue;* beyond this they commonly make no distinction, save perhaps that of size. "Oh yes, sir, I know which you mean. It is the *blue* hawk." How many gamekeepers have indulged me with this scientific definition, which seems indeed to be a pet and patent phrase with the fraternity, I forget — but they have not been few. As one might, without doing very great violence to the general idea of colour, consider as "blue" the adult males of the peregrine, merlin, hen-harrier, hobby and sparrow-hawk, &c., I have not always obtained any great amount of information in the conversations referred to.

Mr. Peter Bell, the potter, was not an amiable individual; neither was he intellectual; neither was he, as Wordsworth expressly informs us, a very close or enthusiastic observer of Nature, though she, for her part, seems to have taken some pains about him: —

"In vain through every changeful year
   Did Nature lead him as before;
A primrose by a river's brim
A *yellow* primrose was to him,
   And it was nothing more."

I have no doubt that, before the discovery of the donkey and her poor drowned master, he was a very stupid fellow indeed; but, respecting the matter of the "*yellow* primrose," I really do not see that he was much worse than his neighbours. However, we will try to make our ornithological information go a little further than his botanical, and prove, at any rate, that a "blue" hawk is known to us by something more certain and definite than its colour. In order that we may take the first step in the direction of this desirable end, I will just remind my readers that hawks are divided into two great classes — viz. the long-winged and short-winged hawks. The long-winged are called *falcons,* the short-winged simply *hawks* (but the female goshawk seems to be allowed by courtesy to assume the more noble title). Thus the hobby, for example, is really a true falcon, though she is not generally spoken of by that name. It belongs, in general parlance perhaps, *par excellence* to the peregrine — shared with her by the larger birds, shortly known as "Jer-*falcons,*" and also by the Barbary falcon. Indeed, we may paraphrase rather freely the old distinction drawn between the mare and horse by saying that, whilst every falcon is a hawk, every hawk is not a falcon.

The only short-winged hawks used by falconers (at any rate in Europe) are the goshawk, and the sparrow-hawk — both the male and female of the former — the female only in these islands, as a general rule, of the latter. These birds are termed " hawks of the *fist,*" because they fly from it at their quarry, not stooping from a height, as the falcons do, and as they are trained to expect food from the hand, to which they should come readily — an arrangement sometimes departed from, perhaps, in favour of an *extempore* lure, as occasion may serve, but of considerable use, as I shall hereafter point out. Long-winged hawks are called "hawks of the *lure,*" because they are taught to fly to it when necessary. It is a simple instrument, and will be explained in the proper place.

In temper and disposition, as well as in power of flight, the falcons have an immense advantage over their less noble kinsmen. I need scarcely say, therefore, that they are trained with much greater ease, and are flown with more pleasure, and generally with more effect, than the short-winged hawks. The following concise notice of the "three never-failing characteristics" by which falcons are distinguished from the true hawks is from "Falconry in the British Isles:" — "By the tooth on the upper mandible (this in some of the foreign species is doubled); by the second feather of the wing being either the longest or equal in length to the third; and by the nature of the stoop made in pursuit of their prey." [1] The peculiar size, colour, plumage, and disposition of each hawk will be given in the chapter or passage appropriated to it.

In olden times the terms used in falconry were very numerous, and there seems to have been a kind of freemasonry in the matter — a part, probably, of the exclusiveness which was claimed for the sport. Mystery is now, of course, entirely done away with, and the art open to all who think it worth their while to learn it. Indeed, we do not affect very many hard names; and I should be almost as likely to speak to a man about the *petty-single* of his falcon, as I should to ask him, supposing he had hurt his knee, how his *patella* was on any given morning. Nevertheless, there are some terms which it is desirable to learn, and which I will set down here. I may mention one or two not generally employed, but shall not omit any without the knowledge of which the young falconer would be considered ignorant. But, even in looking through these, he may remember that they can, in ordinary conversation, be occasionally exchanged for simple names. For instance, he may venture to call a hawk's tail its *tail,* and need not invariably task himself with the more craft-like expression *train,* when he wishes to signify a reference to that useful appendage. These are days, Sir Falconer, of very singular enlightenment; and a wise man will certainly be set down as a fool if he does not make his best bow to the nineteenth century. In this instance let him make it.

The following is a list of terms used in hawking, together with their explanations, which will, of course, be found in most books upon the subject, though I have taken chiefly as my guide in selecting them "Falconry in the British Isles:"

Arms. The legs of a hawk from the thigh to the foot.

Bate. To struggle from the fist, block, or perch, either through fright, or for liberty, &c.

Beam-feathers. The long feathers of the wings of hawks.

Bewits. Strips of leather by which the bells are fastened to the legs.

Bind. To cling to the quarry in the air.

Block. The conical piece of wood to which falcons are fastened when at rest, and on which they sit.

Brail. A thong of leather for securing the wings of hawks, to prevent them bating.

Brancher. A young hawk that has lately *left* the nest, thus distinguished from an eyess — one taken before it can fly.

Cadge. The frame on which several hawks are placed when they are carried to the field. In former days they were exposed for *sale* on the cadge. Hence, perhaps, the use of the slang term "cadger" for a person always asking favours.

Cadger, in hawking language, is the man who carries the cadge.

Calling off. Luring a hawk, from an assistant at a distance, for exercise.

Carry. A hawk is said to "carry" when it moves away with the captured quarry. This is done by some hawks on the near approach of the falconer, but is not always a proof of the bird being wild. A hawk that has no fear whatever of its master may yet dread the loss of its 'prize just taken. Such birds, generally speaking, have been badly trained, though some possess such a disposition for the fault that with them the best falconers have been unable entirely to prevent it. To *correct* it in any hawk is very difficult.

Cast, is a pair of hawks.

Castings. Fur, feathers, &c, given to the hawk with its food. They are afterwards ejected from the mouth, in somewhat of an egg-shape, and cleanse the gorge.

Cere. The *wax*-like skin above the beak.

Check. To fly at; to change the bird in pursuit.

Clutching. Taking the quarry in the feet, instead of striking it down;

Come-to. To begin obeying the falconer.

Coping. Shortening the bill and talons of a hawk.

Crabbing. Hawks fighting with one another.

Creance. A long string to which hawks (generally haggards) are fastened during their first lessons. A live pigeon is sometimes thrown up in a *creance* on occasions which will be mentioned.

Crines (or *crinets*). Hairs, or hair-like feathers, about the cere.

Deck-feathers. The two centre feathers of the tail.

Disclosed, is when the young just peep through the shell.

Endew, is when the hawk digests her food.

Enter. To fly the hawk at quarry (or a particular quarry) for the first time.

Enseame. An old term, signifying to purge a hawk.

Eyess. A nestling hawk.

Eyrie. The breeding place.

Feaking, is when the hawk wipes her beak after feeding — a custom scarcely ever omitted.

Flags. The feathers next the "principals" in a hawk's wing.

Frounce. A disease in the mouth and throat of a hawk.

Get in. To hasten to the hawk after it has killed.

Gorge. The crop, craw, or first stomach.

Hack. (I am not sure at present of the derivation of this word). Once used to describe "the place where the hawk's meat is laid." Hack is the state of liberty in which hawks taken from the nest are kept for some weeks after they can fly. Older birds are occasionally flown at hack, and sometimes weighted to prevent them preying for themselves. A term constantly in the mouths of falconers.

Haggard. A wild-caught mature hawk.

Hood. The cap used for blindfolding or "hoodwinking" hawks.

Imp. To mend a broken feather.

Inke. The neck, from the head to the body of the quarry.

Interviewed. A hawk moulted in confinement is so called.

Jack. The male merlin.

Jerkin. The male of jer-falcons.

Jesses. The leathern straps fastened to the legs of a hawk, and which are *not* removed when the bird flies.

Leash. The leather thong fastened by a swivel to the jesses, when the hawk is confined to block or fist, &c.

Mail, or *Mailes.* The breast-feathers of a hawk.

Make-Hawks. Old staunch hawks, sometimes employed in teaching young ones.

Manning a hawk. Making him endure the company of strangers.

Mew. To moult: also the place in which hawks are kept.

Musket. The male sparrow-hawk.

Mutes. The droppings of a hawk; and also (anciently) of a heron.

Naves. The nostrils of a hawk.

Pannel. The lower bowel of a hawk.

Passage. The flight of herons to and from the heronry during the breeding season.

Passage Hawks. Another term for haggards and red hawks, taken as they migrate.

Pelt. The dead body of the quarry.

Perch. The resting-place for short-winged hawks.

Petty-single. The small toe of a hawk.

Pitch. The extreme height to which a long-winged hawk rises before the game is sprung.

Plumage. Feathers given the hawk for a cast.

Point. The way in which a hawk rises (and thus "makes its point") over the exact spot where the quarry has taken refuge, i.e. been "put in."

Pounces. The claws of a hawk.

Principal feathers, or *Principals.* The two longest feathers in a hawk's wing.

Prunes, is when a hawk arranges its feathers, or plumes itself.

Pull through the hood. To eat through it.

Put over. A sort of squeezing the food from the gorge to the stomach, a process which hawks frequently go through after a full meal, moving their necks in a strange manner.

Put in, is when the quarry is driven into cover.

Quarry. The game flown at.

Rake. To fly too wide.

Raking. Striking the game in the air.

Ramage. Said of a wild hawk.

Rangle. Small stones formerly given to hawks. The custom is obsolete; but it is as well to have such stones within reach of peregrines, as it has been recently proved that they occasionally eat them.

Reclaim. To tame a hawk, and make him familiar.

Red hawk. A peregrine of the first year.

Ring. To rise spirally — said of either long-winged hawk or quarry.

Robin. The male hobby.

Rufter-hood. An easy fitting hood, through which the hawk can eat, capable, however, of being well secured, used in training haggards, &c.

Ruff. To strike the game without "trussing" or seizing it.

Sails. The wings of a hawk.

Seeling. Running a thread through the eyelids of a newly-caught hawk, to obscure the sight for a time — a cruel practice, now quite obsolete in this country.

Serving a hawk. Helping to *put* out the quarry from cover when it has been "put in," &c.

Sharp set. Very hungry.

Sniting, "is when a hawk, as it were, sneezeth." I insert this old term in joke rather than earnest, though it is perfectly orthodox. It may serve to show how the most trifling motion of a hawk was once noticed, and named. I am not quite sure, however, whether it is not used even now among the poor in some counties for the act of sneezing.

Soar Hawk. Any hawk of the first year.

Standing. Remaining in idleness at the block, &c.

Stoop, sometimes *swoop* ("At one fell swoop." — *Macbeth*). The rapid descent of a falcon from a height on the flying quarry.

Summed. Said of a hawk when the plumage is full grown.

Swivel. Used to prevent jesses and leash becoming twisted.

"Take the air." To soar aloft; said of the quarry. Much the same as to " ring."

Tiercel (Tassel. — *Romeo and Juliet,* &c). Male of the peregrine or goshawk; probably because these are a *third* smaller than the falcons.

Tiring. Any bony or tough bit (such as the leg of a fowl, with most of the flesh gone) at which hawks, when being trained, may pull, so that the meal is prolonged, &c.

Train. The tail of a hawk. Also, a live bird given to hawks for the purpose of "entering."

Truss. To clutch the quarry in the air.

Varvels. Little rings "of silver, at the ends of the jesses, on which the owner's name is engraved. Not in present use in this country.

Wait on. A hawk is said to "wait on "when it soars in circles above the head of the falconer, or over a dog which is pointing game. It is thus prepared to stoop at the quarry when sprung, or to descend on the lure, as the case may be.

Yarak. An eastern term, signifying the happy time when short-winged hawks are in a good humour, and ready to fly eagerly at a quarry.

I am specially thankful that this list is concluded; and if the reader has been bored with it, so have I — excessively. His revenge may be in that consideration.

A few more words, and this chapter must be sent after its two elder brothers, and room made for the peregrine.

This is perhaps the proper place to warn those who may intend to commence the practice of falconry next summer, that they should by no means begin with many hawks. If they choose to make their first essay with merlins, let them procure three at most, two of which may be hen birds. But if the peregrine be used by a novice, a cast is the utmost, and one is the best. I unhesitatingly recommend but one in the case of a man who feels sure that the bird is safe from powder and traps within a circle of from six to eight miles. And after all, if he do lose that one, he may be able to purchase another, and so not be utterly *hawkless.* Let this bird be a tiercel. It will soon take partridges beautifully, and may be flown even in a country that is moderately inclosed; though of course "the most open patches should be selected. An only hawk, unlike an only child, is seldom spoilt by notice. The master of such a bird will carry and fly him often; bring him, perhaps, frequently into the company of strangers; and, really with nothing that can be called trouble, make him as docile as a dog. I should like to see that man next year, supposing he take my advice — advice which, I may observe, is not mine only, but that of one of the greatest falconers of the day. I should like to see that man, I repeat, next year; he will have a cast and a half of peregrines, I warrant him; ay! and they will be good ones, and well-managed too. But I have not quite done with this *one* bird yet. Speak! Who has an only parrot, an only cockatoo, an only monkey, or what you will? My dear sir, *why* have you these? Why a parrot, for instance? Because you choose to have it. Truly. And because, besides, as the old women say, it talks like a Christian. Well put; though with respect to Christianity, if it spent much of its valuable time on deck in its passage to you, I rather fear it may not be quite so conspicuous a character in that way as report would seem to imply. Now, I wish to put it to you feelingly, whether you would not prefer to this parrot a right true honest British bird, handsomer, I think, than the gaudy foreigner (though tastes differ), and which will be your companion *out of doors.* He will astonish your friends, if that be any object, twenty times more than the parrot did when he asked the company in general to give him some more gravy. He will come through the air to you as you raise your voice or hand. He will delight you and others with the grace of his motion, the rapidity of his wing, and the wonderful courage which belongs, almost pre-eminently, to his species. And if you will forgive me, my dear reader, whom I am addressing all this time, for a terrible anti-climax, I will just hint that an excellent brace of partridges, though done to a turn by your unexceptionable cook, would have an additional zest in the recollection of the bright hour you and that tiercel spent together in the great field which is wheat-stubble this year.

I have often thought that two or three neighbours, each possessing a good tiercel, [2] might have capital sport at little "meets," which they might plan among themselves. Each hawk. would fly twice or three times; and six or eight flights would be a pretty morning's work. On a fine dry September day you may persuade ladies into stubble, even when they are not mounted, as I know by having tried the experiment. In short, this notion of hawking clubs, in a *small* way (which might develop into an extensive subscription affair or not, just as happened to be thought best), appears to me, though I say it, a very respectable one indeed. [3]

[1] Some further remarks on this head will be found in Chapter Fifteen.
[2] *A "good" tiercel.* — The price of a *good* (the best) trained peregrine ought not to be more than 5l. 5s. Dealers should remember the risk from powder and shot, &c. When the sport is well known, and trained hawks are consequently safer, perhaps a somewhat higher price might be asked for a first-rate bird.
[3] Since this was written a Hawking Club has actually been established, under the able management of C. E. Holford, Esq., Round House, Ware.

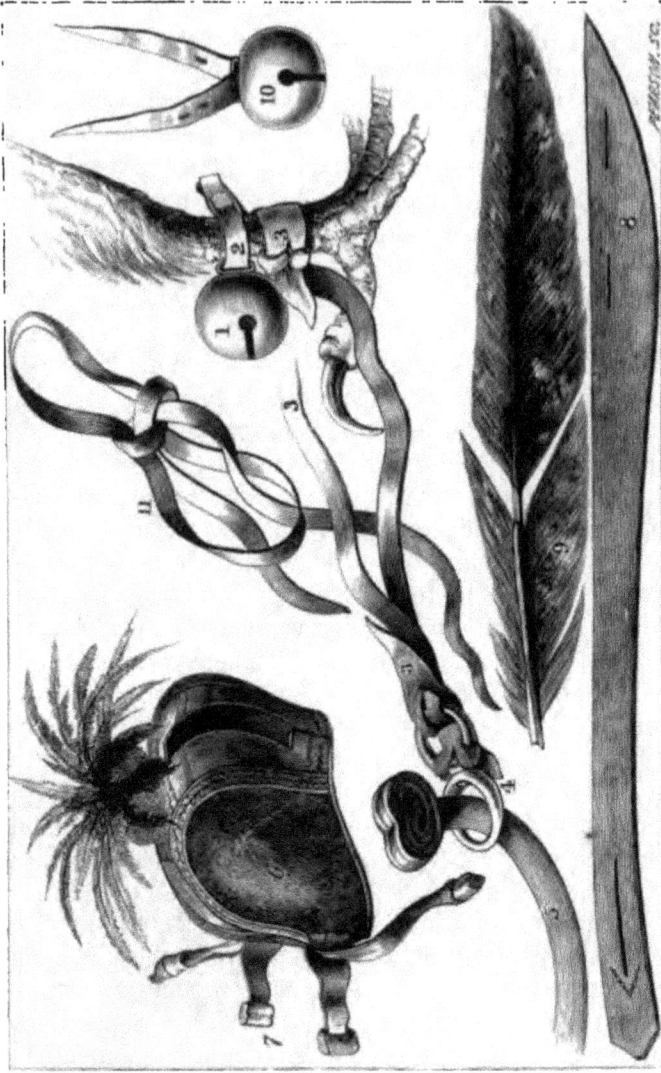

Explanation of the Plate.

1. The bell.
2. The bewit, by which it is attached to the leg.
3. 3, 3, The jesses, though the whole length of one only is given.
4. The swivel attached to the jesses.
5. The leash passing through the swivel.
6. A hood.
7. The hood's braces or ties.
8. A jess, the swivel-slit sewn at the end to prevent its tearing out.
9. A feather, with the imping needle inserted ready to push up.
10. A bell, showing the holes in the bewit through which the ends of the bewit pass.
11. The falconer's knot, which is always used for fastening hawks to the block or perch.

Chapter Four - The Peregrine Falcon (Falco Peregrinus)

Falco Peregrinus is the only name given by modern science to this bird, which seems at last to have escaped from a whole string of synonyms with which different men, and different languages, had overweighted it. *Haggard, falcon-genteel, pilgrim* or *peregrine falcon, red falcon,* &c, were names given to signify different species indeed, but such as existed only in the imagination of the nomenclators. The older naturalists called almost every bird of prey *"falco;"* it was enough for them that the word means "to cut with a bill or hook." I need scarcely say that the indiscriminate use of the term is now discontinued. Linnaeus includes twenty-six species under the generic appellation of "falcon." This was, of course, simply the carrying out of his system. But for my own part, I half suspect that the old falconers were not very clear in the natural history of the peregrine. [1] They lay themselves open to the suspicion, for instance, that they supposed a specific difference between the haggard and falcongentle (or genteel), whereas the former is simply the mature, wild-caught bird; the latter is the eyess. The young naturalist or young falconer may, no doubt, be easily led into error by the change of plumage at the first moult; but a peregrine, kept till he is a year and a half old, is the best and most practical instructor.

Out of this confusion, however, rises the peregrine; perhaps the handsomest and most courageous of all birds of prey, certainly the pet and favourite of falconers. No other bird in the world is more widely distributed. From North America to China and New Holland, that peculiar and brilliant stoop, known and loved by sportsmen for ages, is a terror not only to the weak, but often to the strong, among countless varieties of shape, size, and plumage. In our own country it is, alas! rarely seen. A strange and anomalous civilisation is fast blotting out the most complete type of speed, strength, and courage which belongs of right to these islands, and which the Mightiest Hand placed upon all their cliffs, as an index to the hearts and prowess that should protect them.

This glorious falcon almost invariably seizes his prey on the wing; or perhaps, to speak more correctly, *strikes* it on the wing. Individuals, however, differ as to their mode of taking quarry. The high, long, rapid stoop, with a passing cut [2] of the hind talons at the end of it, is the more brilliant, but perhaps the clutch is the more effective manner. To speak as a falconer, these birds differ in *quality*. I have seen a tiercel driven into the middle of a thick tree by a pair of kestrels; while, on the other hand, last year, an eyess tiercel repeatedly flew herons, though, of course, without the least chance of holding. The excess of courage, I am glad to say, is far more common than the excess of cowardice; and the peregrine is bold enough, as well as strong enough, for the game of this country.

On the coast the prey of this bird is usually waterfowl and wild pigeons, which inhabit the rocks; also jackdaws, where these are found. For his prey inland, reference can be made to the first chapter of this work. I think I need only add an occasional small rabbit or leveret.

The nest is made in the ridge or hollow of a rock; it is of rough construction and of coarse material. The eggs are three or four in number; colour, rufous brown, with darker patches.

The following is from "Falconry in the British Isles:" — "In colour the young peregrine differs considerably from the adult bird. During the first year the plumage is brown, the feathers of the back and wings being edged with a lighter tint; the breast and the thighs are more or less rufous, with dark brown longitudinal streaks. Whilst in the nest, and for some time after leaving it, the young birds have a blueish slate-coloured bloom over the darker parts of the body, which gives them some resemblance in colour to their parents; as soon, however, as they begin to bathe, this bloom disappears and they become quite brown. Like all other birds, they differ much in intensity of colour, being found both of light and dark varieties, with the intermediate shades. The colour of the cere and eyelids is at first blue, which generally changes by degrees to a yellow tint (we knew an instance of it changing to yellow in one night), and, by the end of the first year, becomes bright yellow, provided the bird be in health; the tarsi and feet from the first are light yellow, acquiring depth of colour by age. At the first moult the brown plumage is replaced by one of a blue slate-colour, approaching to black on the head, wings, and tail, while the longitudinal streaks on the breast and thighs give place to transverse bars."

The different sexes differ very materially in size and weight; a full-grown female weighing about two and a half pounds; a full-grown male one and three quarter pound.

If we would take the eyrie of the peregrine, we must leave trees behind, pass over all flat land, and search among something strong, bold, and dangerous, having a character like that for which we seek. High cliffs, and the rocky and perpendicular parts of inland mountains, hold the nest, and a hazardous thing it is sometimes to reach it. Plenty of men, however, and even boys, may be found willing to get themselves fastened to a rope, and so let down by their companions in search of nestlings, which ought to bring them a guinea a head. I believe the nests may be taken with perfect safety if *pains* be taken also. The strength and roundness of the cord should be well looked to; the person descending should have plenty of courage; and those who hold the rope must remember that a human life is hanging at the other end of it, which it is a sin to trifle with by any jest or inattention. The person descending should carefully dislodge any loose stones with his feet. If, when the nest is reached, it be found that the feathers of the young birds are only a little way through the down, the adventurer should signify this circumstance to his friends above, or at least let them understand that, for some good reason or other, he requires to be wound up. A day or two later the descent may be again made. If the young birds appear to be within a few days or a week of flying, let them be taken. They should be carefully placed on hay or straw in a *covered* basket, to which may be attached a string communicating with the top of the cliff, so that the young hawks may be drawn up before their captor reaches his friends. If they have to be sent to a distance, they must go, of course, by a passenger-train, having been previously well fed with fresh beefsteak, cut into small pieces, — each bird being allowed as much as he will take. Should the young birds be very forward, the hamper in which they are sent must not only be lined so as to present a soft surface to the young feathers, but so thoroughly as that light shall be all but excluded. Darkness keeps the birds quiet, and prevents much mischief. I have lined both hamper and lid with old *carpet* when I have sent hawks to a distance, and never found that the birds suffered in the least from want of air. Doubled matting or thin drugget is good.

I will now suppose the young hawks arrived at their destination. They have been expected, and some preparations made for their reception. These are not always precisely the same in every falconer's establishment; but I will mention first what I consider the best. Let a good-sized wine-hamper be fastened against a wall, [3] at about the height of a man's breast, in such manner that the opening shall be presented to your face, with the lid at the bottom, protruding like a platform, and fixed horizontally, with only this deviation, that there be the slightest inclination upwards. Into this hamper, which must be protected from rain and wind, put first plenty of clean straw, and then the young birds, with a bell and jesses [4] to each.

In these chapters I intend to take no knowledge, however slight, on the subject of falconry for *granted,* and to associate myself for the nonce with those who speak, .in their cant phrase, of "the mind being at first a blank sheet of paper, which requires to be written on," and so forth. Therefore I think it necessary in this place to say what hawk-bells and jesses are. Now, Messrs. Benhams and Froud, of Chandos Street, Charing Cross, have sent me capital bells; and, with regard to jesses, any one may make them for himself. They are made of leather; and perhaps the best kind for the purpose is dogskin, well tanned. Hounds' skin, generally to be procured in the neighbourhood of kennels, is strongly recommended. White, or whit, leather is also good; but it requires constant greasing, especially in wet weather; if this is not attended to it gets hard and stiff. I invariably soak the strips in cold water and stretch them before making them into shape. Each hawk requires two jesses, one on each leg. To make these, take a piece of the leather, of either kind mentioned above, and cut it into strips of seven or eight inches in length, and more than half an inch in width; now, with a sharp knife laid on a corner of one of the ends of a strip, which itself is placed flat on a board, boldly take off the other corner with a long oblique stroke, which should not reach the side of your strip till it has, lengthways, cleanly cut at least an inch. As it touches the side at this point, or almost before it touches it, incline the knife inwards, and, with another long oblique stroke, cut till the leather is narrowed to less than the third of an inch. Continue that breadth, as you still cut on towards the opposite end of the strip, until the knife is within an inch and a half of the end; then turn the blade a little outwards, so as to make a *bulge* here, tapering off, however, to a point. Half an inch from this point stamp a small hole, and cut a slit from it, two-thirds or more of an inch in length, in the direction of the end at which you commenced your operations. This is for the swivel. Make a smaller slit at *that* end, about half an inch or moore from *its* point; also another, — about an inch and a quarter further down the strip. There are now three slits, — two at the broader end, where you commenced cutting, and one at the narrower or swivel end, where you left off. Having made two such jesses, write your name on one and your address on the other; the ink will last a few weeks at any rate. Now get some one to hold one of the young birds, — a hood being on the head of the hawk if you like — gloves certainly on the hands of your friend. Take one of the jesses, holding it at the end where there are two slits. I will call the slit nearest the point or end, No.1; the slit "an inch and a quarter further down the strip," No.2. Take the point of the jesse and pass it through No.2 till No.1 appears through the opening, inclosing the bird's leg as you do so; now take the swivel end of the jesse, draw it through No.1, the whole jesse, excepting the portion already disposed of, following. This makes all secure. When both jesses are on, they are fastened to the ring or ordinary swivel as follows: — Pass the swivel end of the jesse through one of the rings; pass the second ring through the loop of the jesse; press the loop onwards (opening it) to the extremity of the first ring. This, I hope, will not seem very complicated when the jesse and swivel are in your hand: the process is very simple in reality, though on paper it does not appear so. The manner of using the *spring* swivel is evident, and requires no explanation.

The bell is attached above one of the jesses by a *bewit*, having the same kind of fastening as the jesses themselves.

Let us now return to the hamper in which are snugly deposited two or three young peregrines (a nest holds from one to three, seldom four), properly equipped. They have come perhaps from a distance, and it is necessary that they should be well fed at once, Take therefore a fresh juicy steak, raw of course, and, having cut it into small oblong pieces, present a morsel on your finger, or on a short stick which has no sharp point, to the boldest bird. From him proceed to another, and continue your rounds, occasionally pausing, but often (especially as you administer a dainty piece) shrieking on the whistle you intend to use afterwards in the field. A guard's railway-whistle is not bad for this purpose. Feed in this manner as long as the birds can be induced to eat, three times a day, and this at stated hours, say, six or seven — one at noon — six or seven; but whatever the hours may be, keep to them. It will not be amiss if the midday meal consist of the chopped flesh of rabbits, pigeons, or rooks. Beef is somewhat heating and feverish food, if not relieved by a less stimulating diet.

In a day or two you will find the birds on the ridge of the hamper's lid, expecting your approach. It is not absolutely necessary at this period to show them the *lure,* but I would advise you to do so. And here I must make a slight digression in order to describe this instrument. [5]

The *lure* may be made in several ways, any of which will answer the purpose. For instance, take a heavy piece of wood, and cut it into somewhat the form of a horseshoe, which may weigh about 1 ½ lb. At the two ends fasten the wings of a pigeon, as that will probably be the bird to which you will first "enter" your young hawks. Through the sides bore holes, and pass strings through them, by which, when the lure is in use, food can be attached. Red cloth may or may not, as you please, be nailed on a portion of the sides. In the centre of the curve, at the outside, fix a ring; and to this ring fasten the strap of a shot-belt by its swivel. Here is a lure. It is sufficient for your present purpose, though hereafter you will probably use both live and dead pigeons, &c.

The nestlings standing on the lid, eagerly attentive to your whistle (which I recommend you now to sound for a minute or two before you present yourself to them)', gently place the lure, well covered with beef, in the midst of the hungry creatures. Encourage them to peck at it — constantly, however, supplying them with the choicest pieces from the hand. On the next occasion swing the lure round your head as you approach, taking care, however, not to alarm them; they will soon place this movement in their list of signs which denote a full meal. In a day or two the hawks will have left the hamper, or be found perched on the top of it. It is now that the falconer may add a peculiar shout or cry to the whistle and swung lure. This sound is designed to induce the birds to approach him, and therefore must be distinct from that which he intends to employ when he would cheer them on the flying quarry. It may be "Yoho-hup, yohup, yohup;" or "Hi-away! (boy or lass) hi-away!" a call which I use, and learnt I know not where. If the birds understood English, I confess there would be perfect insanity in employing that which bids departure while it requires approach.

I may as well mention here, in a sort of parenthesis, that "Hooha, ha, ha, ha!" is a good cry for inciting hawks to make every effort when the quarry is viewed, and also for calling their attention to it. These syllables, when shrieked out on a high note, have a wild, dashing, blood-stirring spirit in them that suits the occasion well. "Who-whoop" is the death-cry; and "à la volée!"or "au vol!" is common as a warning cry in heron-hawking when the quarry passes sufficiently near to justify the falconers in unhooding and dismissing their winged warriors to the encounter.

However, you and I, reader, are concerned at present only with the first sound, which signifies to the hawk that he must *approach* you; and your great care of course will be to associate this invitation with something exceedingly agreeable. Now, we all differ in tastes; but I imagine that you can offer nothing to a nestling peregrine which he will esteem a greater or more exquisite delicacy than raw beefsteak. Offer it, therefore, when you make this cry, having now (as the hawks begin to take wing a little and leave the hamper) a lure for each bird, on which the meat is carefully fastened. During the first few times that these lures are thrown down before the birds, let the meat upon them be juicy and tender; but as soon as the hawks fly to them eagerly, change your policy, and garnish the lures with tough though fresh pieces. As the birds are tugging and straining to get their meal, quietly lie down on the grass amongst them, and as you turn yourself from one side to the other, place, with a shrill sound on the whistle to give a point to the circumstance, a peculiarly juicy mouthful into each beak. Allow the hungry hawks to pull again, and still continue to produce your choice bits; now coaxing the birds with words, and now whistling softly. Prolong the meals as much as possible, always showing that your hand contains something better than is to be found on the lures. The object of all this is to nip in the bud that dreadful fault of "carrying," the seeds of which are in all hawks, and which, if encouraged, through your own carelessness, or, indeed, if not checked by your forethought, will grow into a habit so distressing to the falconer, that I know of no other equally villainous. It is evident that a bird taught to understand that *you* feed him easily, and with more palatable food than any which he himself can procure by the greatest amount of pulling, will not, in the first few instances at any rate, be anxious to move away at your approach, on his capture of a pigeon or partridge. It is only honest, however, to say that a very little mismanagement, when the time arrives, may induce him to move with the third or fourth quarry which he may take; but I will anticipate no directions when I can avoid doing so, and full advice and warnings will be given in their places.

Day after day the hawks will fly further and further from home, but will return at feeding times (which may now be twice a day), and that quickly when they hear the shout or whistle, and see the swinging lure. They are now "flying at hack."

They will become, however, I am sorry to say, somewhat wilder as they gain strength; but if the lures are so heavy that they cannot easily be moved by the birds, and if the meals are carefully prolonged, in the manner before described, you may continue to feed the hawks from the hand for two or three weeks. Probably one will be wilder than the rest, and you may possibly have ultimately to take him up in the bow-net, an instrument which I shall presently describe. If you prefer it, however, take him up by hand as soon as it becomes difficulty and before it becomes impossible, to touch the jesses; it is by these that you must secure him, not of course attempting to lay your grasp on the bird himself. It used to be considered absolutely necessary to fly hawks at hack if they were to turn out swift and good birds; but recent experience has shown that it is possible to have first-rate high-flying eyesses which have never been flown at hack *at all*. Hack, however, must be very desirable, as it tends to stretch and strengthen the growing muscles of the wings, and also as it affords a fine opportunity for making birds to the lure; teaching them, moreover, at little cost of time and trouble, to return to the spot from which they started. Still, for my own part, I should take up a bird that had been at liberty for a fortnight, if his conduct seemed to threaten the use of the bow-net. But this is a matter of choice, and I am far from insisting upon it. The usual period for hack is about a month or five weeks; sometimes longer. If it be protracted after birds are forward enough to prey for themselves, leaden weights, covered with soft leather, must be fastened to their

34

legs to prevent them doing so.

There is another method, adopted by some falconers, of rearing nestlings at hack; but it has this very grave objection, that it forbids, in a great measure at any rate, making hawks to the lure as long as it lasts. The young birds are placed in a large outhouse, on clean straw; and, as soon as they can move about easily, and tear the food, it is fastened on blocks at stated feeding-times, when they are called to it by the whistle, &c. The door of the outhouse is left open, so that they may fly out when strong enough to do so. It is said that for weeks they will come to the blocks; and when it is required to take them up, they may be captured by a long string attached to the door, and pulled from a distance to close it at feeding-time.

Let us suppose, however, that the former plan of hamper and lure has been adopted, and, after a few weeks' hack, one of the hawks "taken up;" the details of which process will appear in the next chapter. It will be necessary now to look well to the jesses, changing them if they are injured; a *hood* also must be provided that will fit the bird comfortably. You will require, too, glove, swivel, leash, and block. I must content myself now with a short notice of these implements, and leave to another chapter the particulars which belong to their use.

A falconer's glove should be made of the thickest and best buckskin: a good saddler can make it. To colour it, use a mixture of yellow ochre, burnt umber powdered, and water; the whole to be the thickness of cream. It is to be laid on with a brush, and beaten out when dry. If the glove is very dirty, it should be first washed with a brush with soda and warm water.

With regard to the *making* of hoods, I feel it to be in vain, without a considerable assistance from woodcuts, to offer any directions which would be useful or even intelligible to my readers, and satisfactory to myself. I may mention, however, that hoods are made of calf-leather for a peregrine, which, when wet, is stretched on a wooden block (not to be confused with the "block" on which hawks sit), cut somewhat into the shape and size of a hawk's head, without the beak; great care being taken that the wood bulges out in the region of the eyes. Three pieces of leather are used in making a Dutch hood, though it may be fashioned out of one piece. In the Persian or Syrian pattern we have the addition of a buckskin curtain behind, or more properly speaking, perhaps, this curtain supplies the place of a portion of the back of the hood, which is cut away to make room for it. The side pieces are ornamented with velvet or bright cloth; the fastenings are behind; and there is a plume at the top, by which the hood is generally held when it is placed on the bird's head or removed from it. Imperfect as this description necessarily is, the imperfection is of little consequence, as excellent coloured illustrations are to be found in "Falconry in the British Isles," and Mr. W. Pape, gunmaker, West Gate, Newcastle-on-Tyne, supplies hoods ready made at a moderate price. [6]

Swivels are supplied by Messrs. Benham and Froud, Chandos Street, Charing Cross. The spring swivels answer for use in the field; for the block they are not so safe as the ordinary ring-swivel. However, should their simplicity tempt their use on *all* occasions, at least guard them by a piece of leather stitched in such a manner that it can be moved over the opening.

The leash is simply a strong strip of leather, full two feet in length, one end of which is either fastened to the block, or wrapped round the hand of the falconer, as the case may be; the other end is attached to the swivel, and the swivel to the jesses. Strong calf-leather, called by shoemakers "kip," is the best for leashes.

I can give no better description of a peregrine's block than the following, taken from "Falconry in the British Isles:" — "For a peregrine this block should be about a foot in height, six inches in diameter at the top, and nine at the base, to prevent it being overturned. An iron spike may be driven into the centre of the bottom of the block, which, running into the ground, keeps it firm. For facility in moving, a ring may be counter-sunk into the top of the block. If a hole is bored quite through the wood of the block it will be less liable to split. The blocks that are placed under cover should be padded on the top, to prevent the hawk's feet from becoming swollen, — a disease they are apt to acquire if kept at all times on a hard surface."

In the next chapter we will take up the hawks from hack, break them to the hood, and do various other things.

[1] The old falconers certainly *seem* to be guilty of blunder in this particular; and yet, as they moulted their hawks, it is difficult to believe that they were puzzled by a change of plumage.

[2] If you bold out a piece of meat to hawks at back you will see the nature of the stoop. They seem to fly downwards for a short distance to get impetus; they then close their wings and, coming wedge-like through the air, appear to rake their hind talons through the object stooped at, their *legs being kept quite stiff and still.*

[3] A small, unused outhouse, having a large doorway, is an excellent place for the hamper. The young birds have in this way no rain, little wind, and get plenty of air. They must not, however, be out of the reach of the morning sun.

[4] Some excellent falconers omit the jesses till the hawks are taken up, fearing that the young birds should be entangled by them. When used during hack they should be short and of stiff leather, with a very small slit at the swivel end. I have never had an accident with these,— nor indeed with any.

[5] The Indian lure consists of four jackdaw's wings made (so to speak) into *two*, by fastening each couple face to face, and tying the pair so formed at the joints. This lure is tossed to the approaching falcon, who catches it in the air. A long string prevents "carrying:" there is no meat attached to it, the falconer taking the hawk from it with food in his hand. In *breaking* hawks to this, however, meat may be added.

[6] In fact *all* hawk-furniture may be had from Mr. Pape; also from Mr. Fells, Feltwell, Brandon, Norfolk.

36

Chapter Five - The Peregrine (Continued).

Our young hawks [1] have been flying at hack a few weeks, and have assumed a very different appearance from that which they presented when we were first introduced to them in the hamper. The white down has entirely left them, and they have become fine sleek birds.

I hope that, even before they quite left the edge of the hamper, they were accustomed to the presence of dogs and horses — at any rate of dogs, which, perhaps, were fed near them. I hope also that they saw somewhat more of human society than that afforded by the visits of their trainer; nay, the presence of children, if they had it, was far from objectionable. When the birds became tolerably strong on the wing, it was no doubt found that a shyness, which at first was only just perceptible, slightly increased day by day. Notwithstanding this, it is to be desired that the presence of dogs and strangers was persevered in; carefully, of course, as the hawks were found to bear it: pains also, I will suppose, were taken to prevent any sudden fright, such as that arising, for instance, from the playfulness of a young dog, or the snappishness of an old one.

Assuming that all this, or something like it, was done, taking up the hawks, breaking them to the hood, and entering them to quarry, will not be found difficult tasks; and the truth is, that the foundation of their training has been laid, and its rudiments acquired already. For, observe what *has been done!* Birds, which, had they been reared by their parents on their own wild crags, would, at this period of their existence, scarcely have permitted you to come within shot of them, are not only so domesticated, but so dependent upon yourself (as they imagine at least) for their daily food, that, instead of dreading your approach, they positively look for it with anxiety, and welcome it with pleasure. More than this, they have been taught to comprehend the meaning of sounds and signals. They know that a certain tone of your voice, and a particular motion of your hand, are intended to inform them that their immediate presence is required, and that their obedience will be rewarded. Settled round you on the grass, they look for your assistance in enabling them to procure the choicest morsels, and even exhibit a kind of jealousy when they perceive that you indulge one of the party more than the rest. You have, in short, in the space of two or three weeks, established in the hearts of those of the fowls of the air which are proverbially the most wild, a confidence in your honesty and a dependence upon your power and kindness which, I will make bold to say, no sportsman, and certainly no naturalist, can look upon with feelings short of wonder and respect. This is what you have done, or rather what you will have done when you have in practice followed these directions up to the conclusion of the last chapter. It must now be my business to inform you what you *shall* do.

Hack being over, the hawks must be taken up as quietly and gently as circumstances will permit. If they have been flown with jesses, and have remained tolerably tame, it will not be difficult to secure them after a simple fashion. Approach them as usual whilst they feed, and insert the hook of the spring-swivel into the loops of the jesses; the swivel being of course attached to the leash, and the leash to your gloved hand. Lift the bird which you are taking up (and I would not take up more than one a day) by the lure on which he is feeding — your hold on the leash, somewhere near the swivel, being firm; carry him, if he will permit you to do so, slowly to the door of a partly darkened outhouse. As he is finishing the last few mouthfuls, walk into the room. Try, as the last large piece is going down, to slip on a hood which has been well cut away about the beak, and which, whilst fitting most easily and having no unfair pressure upon any one part of the head, is yet capable of being well and securely fastened. The meal which the bird was discussing when you captured him ought to have been a small one — the leg of a rook, or part of a leg, for instance; because it is a maxim amongst falconers that "bating on a full crop" is bad, and sometimes even dangerous. Remember that you may not be skilful enough to put on the hood at the first, second, or third attempt, and that the hawk may make some violent struggles before you succeed — he may even continue them afterwards. You have succeeded, however, let us suppose. The bird, perhaps, is still rather sharp-set; give him a chance then to "pull through the hood" at a small and delicate piece of beef, or a pigeon's leg: he will most likely decline. It is of little consequence: you need not be disappointed. I will suppose that you took up this bird a couple of hours before dark: carry him *till* dark. You would like to take the hood off to-night, in order to see how he bears the replacing it. If you dare make the venture and the hawk show the least disposition to "pull through the hood," take it off by candle-light. There is certainly something in lamp and candle-light peculiarly adapted for breaking hawks to the hood; it is better than twilight. There must be, I suppose, a sort of dazzle and indistinctness about it to eyes opening on it for the first time. Hood and unhood two or three times, letting the bird "pull through," if he will. When this is over, take him to the outhouse which you have set apart for hawks — the "mews," if you like to call it so; fasten the leash to, and place the hawk upon, the block. Now draw a thick curtain over the window, or close the shutter; quietly unhood your pupil, and say "Good night" to him. (Or you may, if you please, keep him hooded for a night or two — this is Captain Salvin's practice; in this case *absolute* darkness is not necessary.) The floor of the mews must be covered with sand several inches deep. A ventilator may be placed in one of the walls; and the window made of glass guarded inside by perpendicular, not horizontal, wooden bars.

I have described the "taking up" and hooding of a tame and good-tempered bird; but I by no means answer for it that the majority of peregrines will be found like him. On the contrary, it is probable that you will not be able to take the first step with comfort; I mean, you will hardly perhaps carry him on the lure to the darkened outhouse. Suppose, then, he should bate off on the way, and hang by the jesses, perhaps, screaming and biting; or suppose you found it necessary to take him up with the bow-net — in these cases a hood must be put on as quickly as possible, and in the most gentle manner that circumstances will permit; the bird must be carried and put in the mew, as before described. In the morning you will take the bird (be he wild or tame) from the block, not by touching a single feather belonging to him, but by carefully placing your hand under his feet, and so getting him upon it — a little light having been let into the room. By this light you will (if he were left unhooded) hood him — the leash, of course, having been disengaged from the block, and wound round your gloved hand. Perhaps it need scarcely be mentioned that the *left* hand is invariably employed by falconers as a seat for the hawk when carried.

The hood which you are using, it has been said, has rather a large opening at the beak; the bird can therefore just get a glimpse of something red on your glove: draw the beef over his feet and he is almost certain to seize it with his bill, and nearly as certain, having once tasted it, to continue his meal. Move now (a small bit of meat having been demolished) towards the half-darkened outhouse; open the strings of the hood with your teeth and with your right hand; slip it off, and on again, speedily; take a step out into the broad daylight, and offer a morsel instantly,, Continue this hooding and un-hooding, invariably rewarding the hawk, if he will eat, the moment the hood is *on*. In all probability it will be necessary to wet the bird thoroughly with cold water from a sponge, during the first few lessons; you will find him not nearly so inclined to. bate while the feathers are soaked and heavy; and if the water is made to come from a distance, it gives a *shock* which is of service. In a few days he will begin to look for the hood, as an introduction to a feast — that is, if you have avoided anything approaching to a "fray" whilst teaching him to wear it. Hawks are not like dogs in disposition; they distrust you, even if you tease them in the purest fun; and they remember for weeks any exhibition of bad temper on the part of their trainer.

The eyess, I will now suppose, is thoroughly broken to the hood; sits, bareheaded, without showing signs of fear in the presence of strangers, and dogs; and when tolerably sharp set, flies well to the lure. [2]

As it is absolutely necessary that a peregrine intended for game or magpie hawking should "wait on" properly, a few lessons may be given in the following manner before the hawk is introduced to quarry: — Let him be taken out, hooded and sharp-set, by an assistant, who should stand about 100 yards from the falconer. The latter is now to swing the lure, whistling or shouting for the hawk a moment after the former has freed the jesses from the swivel and unhooded. On the bird's near approach the falconer must conceal the lure for a few seconds; this will cause the peregrine to mount, in short circles, the better to look for his suddenly vanished meal, which he must then be allowed to enjoy, the lure being thrown on the grass. After a good meal, he is of course hooded and taken home, the last two or three pieces having been given through the hood.

During the third or fourth lesson the hawk may be kept rather longer on the wing; but great care must be taken not to go into extremes in this matter, or the "pitch" may be lowered — a great misfortune indeed, as it cannot be too high.

These lessons over, and the hawk being more than commonly sharp-set, and confined to the block, give him a live pigeon from the hand. [3] If a large one, its wing might be brailed before offering it to a tierce; but the precaution is seldom necessary. Let the hawk kill and "take his pleasure" on the quarry, *i.e.* eat as much as he likes. On the following day, give a *very* slight meal in the morning only; and on the third day, an hour after feeding-time, give a live pigeon on a long string, or "creance," as you will remember such a string is called. After another interval of a day, take the hawk into a tolerably open place, and fly him at a pigeon that has a couple of long feathers taken out of one wing. The peregrine is now "entered" to pigeons, being ready to fly strong untouched ones; and I have to make only two leading observations before I dismiss your bird to fly at this quarry three times a week for a fortnight or more.

In the first place, it is to be most carefully observed that the great pains taken when the hawks were at hack to prevent them from contracting the habit of "carrying," must not be rendered useless by carelessness now. Gro up therefore quietly, but yet with confidence, to your eyess when he has killed; whistle gently, as you always do at feeding-times, and, if he be on the first pigeon he ever caught in a fair flight, put the hook-swivel through the loops in the jesses, peg him down, and suffer him to take his pleasure on his prize. On a subsequent occasion, allow the hawk to commence eating before you lift him on the fist. He is raised on it simply by your seizing the quarry, which he will not loose; secure him to the swivel, and feed him up from the quarry or from a piece of beef placed under the quarry's wing, if you have done with him for the day. If, however, you expect him to afford another flight, hold the neck or "inke" of the pigeon between the fingers of your left hand, the body being suspended under it: now cut away at the very root of the neck till the body or "pelt" drops, or is left in your hand. Hide this in your pouch or pocket at once. When the head is finished, hood the hawk, giving one small mouthful through the hood. The object of all this (and the great secret in preventing hawks carrying) is to make them believe, as far as possible, that you *take nothing from them,* while, in point of fact, you deprive them of nearly all the wild quarry (in game-hawking at any rate, and always when you desire a second flight) which they kill. If these minute details seem troublesome, pray remember that your hawks are scarcely formed yet, and that no trouble is thrown away which will tend to insure you good birds for the season, and may be for years. I am certain that the taking a hawk roughly, or even suddenly, from his prey, is sure, in a very short time, and at any period of his life, to induce the tiresome habit against which I am so anxious to guard.

The second special matter I wished to mention is, that "waiting on," which has been taught to a certain extent with the lure, must be still taught with pigeons. You will not long be without an instance of a chased pigeon dashing into low cover just in time to save himself from a stoop. The peregrine, partly from his nature and partly from practice at the lure, will "wait on" in circles above the place where the quarry "put in." Now, either get this quarry out in a very few minutes, or — after sending in the spaniel and making a show of beating the hedge — take a live pigeon from your pouch or basket, shorten its flight considerably, and release it with head away from the cover, making it appear that you have just driven the real quarry out, and shouting "hooha, ha, ha!" with all your might, running also in the direction of the pigeon. The hawk will kill at the first stoop, and consequently will be strongly impressed with the opinion that "waiting on," when beaters are underneath, is a most interesting and profitable proceeding.

Here, then, is a **trained peregrine:** he is entered to one quarry, viz. pigeons, and is ready to be entered to others. If a falcon, she may be flown at anything, from a snipe to a wild duck, — nay, even perhaps at a heron, though passage-hawks are commonly used for so large a bird. Rooks and grouse she may, as a general rule, be made to take beautifully; but the more she is kept to any one quarry the better she will fly it. The *best* tiercels will take grouse and rooks; those of not the highest courage will certainly take partridges, and very likely take them well. I only glance at these matters now in order that the tyro may have an idea of what he may expect from his birds: every kind of hawking will presently be treated in detail.

I was exceedingly anxious to bring my readers to the point whither I have, in fact, conducted them, before this chapter should be closed. But, in employing space for this purpose, I have been compelled to omit directions for the daily management of hawks. These, however, I purpose to supply in the next chapter; for in truth, my good pupils, though I have been with you in the field, I have left you very much to your own devices with regard to feeding, bathing, my promise redeemed with regard to "imping;" neither shall the "bow-net" be forgotten, though perhaps that may not be explained till we reach Chapter Seven, on the catching and training of passage-hawks, &c.

We are now in the midst of rudiments. I know that they are dry, and I can conceive them to be difficult But wait with a little patience till we are out of the wood; — we will shout then. Yes, I really hope to make some of these chapters interesting, when I shall show you the heron taken on his passage; the grouse struck down amongst the purple heather, as he flies like a black ball over it; the cunning magpie falling to "Highland Laddie's" [4] stoop; an eight-pound hare to "Bushman's" clutch; and the rapid lark driven at last out of the white cloud, after a ringing, panting flight, by a bird who is quiet enough now, with head under wing, about thirty yards from the room in which I am writing.

[1] Peregrines are commonly strong on the wing early in July, and may, as a role, be taken from the nest in the first week of June.
[2] Some falconers fly a hawk of uncertain temper once or twice with a creance at this period, lest it should rake away. If the bird has not been flown at hack it is quite necessary to do so.
[3] When a pigeon is killed at the block, put an iron-eyed pin in the ground near the block: by a string, which passes through the eye of the pin, the pigeon can be drawn within the hawk's reach.
[4] "Highland Laddie." Since the above was written, this excellent tiercel, the property of Captain Salvin, lost an eye, daring its absence from its master for a day or two.

Chapter Six - Daily Management of Trained Peregrine

"The merciful man is merciful to his beast," truly; and so is the practical man. He who can eat his dinner, and warm himself by his fire, and criticise the flavour of his wine, while he knows that his dumb servant is shivering, hungry, and miserable outside, is simply himself a brute; but the man who supposes that the faithful creature he has so shamefully treated will, however willing, be capable of rendering him in future the service he may require, is *definitely* brutish — he is an ass.

In this chapter we shall consider the daily management and treatment of trained peregrines when they are not in the field; how we may best make them comfortable when they rest, and therefore useful when they work. And I have only to premise that, in writing and in reading this, the wild parentage of our hawks must not be forgotten. Domesticated themselves, or semi-domesticated, they yet come of a family which never felt a chain; for the imprisoned hawk, like "the imprisoned eagle, will not pair;" and therefore, when it would be cruel to refuse a horse a warm stable, or a dog his snug kennel, it might be still more unkind to shut up the peregrine falcon in her mew.

Falconers differ among themselves somewhat in the daily management of their birds. Some take peregrines into a room or outhouse at night in all seasons, and in all weather, while others allow them to remain out of doors almost from one year's end to another. In India, hawks are kept hooded all day when they are at rest; and in England, especially in the hands of our best falconers, they scarcely ever wear the hood (though of course thoroughly "made" to it): it is only worn, as a rule, when they are carried to the field. Blocks are solely used by some falconers; others adopt almost entirely the screen, or perch, at any rate in-doors: in most establishments you will see both. The truth is, that hawks may be kept in tolerable health under any of these systems; but I believe that, by cutting away the ugly and awkward portions of each, the remainders will dovetail into one another, and form a tolerably perfect whole. Let us see then whether the result is not strong and shapely.

You have a south wall. Do you object to have a long sloping roof — perhaps a thatched one is best — projecting about seven or eight feet, at the height of seven at the *highest* part, run along this wall for some yards? You may have the thing made to look very rustic and sightly, and any one who can knock up a rough summer-house can knock up this. Let him close in the sides thoroughly, but leave the front open. He must be careful too about the position of any props which he may place to support the roof: if they are used, they must be at equal and proper distances; but I decidedly recommend that the shed be cu4 into compartments, and the dividing walls will secure the roof. These compartments may be eight or even nine feet in length; and their sides, and also the wall, should be hung, or rather perhaps covered, with matting. In the centre of each, by driving its spike firmly in the ground, fix a peregrine's block. That ground may be *turf;* but the block should be just surrounded by a small but deep bed of sand, and this sand is to be changed frequently. This year I shall try *all* sand behind the blocks, and all turf in front. If it happen that some low evergreens are not far from the front of the shed, so much the better; at any rate, it must be protected as much as possible from the wind. Canvass, a yard high, pegged in the shape of a triangle, is useful as a guard against wind; the apex being the point farthest from the shed, and opposite its middle, while the base of the triangle is represented by the front of the shed. Here is a dormitory for the warm months, and a place of shelter in bad weather during the day, as nearly as may be, all through the year. On fine calm days, blocks and birds should be placed on the open lawn, under the shade of a tree when the sun is very powerful, and as night approaches conveyed to the shed. It is better, perhaps, to have two sets of blocks, one set for the shed and the other for the open. But in moving the birds from one position to another, the falconer has only to call the hawk to his fist by a "tiring," or well-picked leg or wing of a rook, &c, and then to hold the jesses between his fingers — all this with the left hand; with the right hand he will either carry the block, or untie the leash from it (to be fastened to another block), just as his set be single or double. In very windy, perhaps in very wet, weather, but certainly in drifting snow from the south, it will be necessary to take the hawks into an outhouse, such as this, viz. a dry room having several inches of dry sand on its floor, and the window of which can be completely darkened by a shutter. Here they may rest on blocks, or on the perch or screen, day or night, or both, till the storm is over. [1] Care must be taken to make the darkness complete; hawks do not dislike its sedative influence; and it keeps them *perfectly quiet.*

The perch or screen is a simple contrivance. It consists of a broad horizontal bar, placed breast high, and resting at each end upon perpendicular shafts, the bottoms of which are either heavily weighted, or secured to the floor, or. attached to a long wooden tray, full of sand or sawdust. The last method is the best. The bar, as I have called it, the perch itself in fact, is covered with green baize, which must be continued downwards, after the manner of a tight curtain, for two or three feet. Attached to the perch, at intervals of three feet, are spring swivels, [2] secured by little leashes of only a few inches long. The hawks should be hooded whilst their jesses are hooked on the swivels; but, when all is safe, the hoods may be removed one after the other, the falconer immediately retiring and rapidly closing the shutter. If utter darkness can be insured, the birds won't bate off; but, should they do so by any chance, they will climb up again by the curtain, provided the leashes are short ones. I confess, however, that I knew a case of a tiercel failing to regain his perch, and so dying. Still that happened, I believe, by daylight; and I do not know the length of the leash. Certainly when hawks are first placed on the screen they should be frequently visited;. but, in a short time, all anxiety may cease. Should any one feel nervous about the perches, he can use blocks, which are nearly as good, and perfectly safe. The screen, [3] in fact, has generally been considered as the resting-place for *short*-winged hawks — though the bow-perch is better — and I only recommend it, I repeat, for falcons, on the understanding that it is placed in perfect darkness.

It will, perhaps, be thought a simple and unobjectionable plan merely to take the hawks and blocks into the sanded room in boisterous weather, without troubling oneself about screen or shutter. If the room is well littered this may be done, as I have said; but they are disposed to be restless, and to bate very much. Like the famous starling, they "can't get out," and they want to get out *because it is light.*

We have neither hooded our birds in the mew, the rustic shed, nor the open lawn; but there is a time when it is absolutely necessary that they should be hooded. I will mention it in a moment: let me describe feeding first. It is Saturday evening; give each hawk, at his block, as much rook or pigeon as he will eat, or else carry him, and while he is tugging at a bone feed him up to a, *full* crop with very small pieces of fresh beef. In fact, Saturday night is "gorge night," and it is selected for a feast because a day must intervene between it and flying; and by giving a slight meal on Sunday morning, the birds are ready for the field on Monday. I do not mean to say that a hawk ought to be flown on all the six days; on the contrary, three or four days a week are quite enough. However, as a general rule, weather will confine your sport sufficiently, and therefore advantage ought to be taken of Saturday night. On Sunday morning, then, give a slight meal about eleven o'clock; and on Monday, at twelve, "hood up" for the field. It is *now* that the hood is necessary. If you do not intend to fly till three or four o'clock, give just two or three small mouthfuls of lean beef or bird, without the least particle of feather, at ten;

this must be only a taste of breakfast One meal a day is sufficient for pere-grines, and it should be given in the morning; but, when you have made up your mind not to fly a particular bird on the morrow, he may be indulged with a few pieces on the evening of to-day. Castings are also necessary: these are feathers or fur given with the skin, which, in order to make the hawk swallow them, may either be dipped in blood or offered with a small piece of flesh attached. Mice make excellent castings; but the stomach may as well be taken out: some falconers consider it dangerous to give them without this precaution. The birds, if allowed to pick and eat part of a pigeon, &c, will get some castings in the natural way; but these must not be altogether depended on, as half your hawks' food is probably beef. The use of castings is to cleanse the crop or gorge; they should be looked for on the sand, and, if nicely rolled, and free from smell and undigested meat — and if the mutes are white, hav-ing a slight dark mark in the middle, but no red, yellow, or green — the bird is healthy. Do not fly the birds till they have cast.

Hawks must not have as much as they can eat, except on "gorge nights;" their condition may be known by feeling the breast. There are many ways of feeding them; but they should be often fed on the hand; this, in fact, is done almost of necessity, after the capture of any bird which is not game, by letting the hawk eat it on the way home — and a warm meal of this sort is a good thing occasionally. In game hawking it is an excellent plan to take beef, ready cut, and cut small, into the field, and, when the head of the quarry is demol-ished, the feeding may be finished with the meat, which can be carried in a clean tin box, or in a pouch strapped round the waist, and having a division for hoods. (By the way, a spare hood or two must not be forgotten.) The daily meal, however, when it is a bird, may sometimes be given at the block; not so when beef — for a hungry hawk, left to himself, will be apt to *bolt* that which he can tear so easily. Remove also, for fear of this same bolting, all intestines: wild hawks do this for themselves; but then they commonly feed more delib-erately than tame ones.

Some falconers take the trouble to dress the meat in the following manner; and the plan is a good one: — A rook or pigeon is divested of all its feathers; if a pigeon, it is plucked; if a rook, or any bird that will skin, it is skinned. The breast bone is taken out, the beak and feet are thrown away. The remainder is placed on a board and chopped, bones and all, with a strong chopper; a few drops of water are added, and the whole becomes a fine mass. If beef be used, a raw egg may be mixed with it, when it has been well chopped. Of course such food as this is invariably given while the bird is carried, i. e. from the hand. Hawks not at work will do better with a whole pigeon or rook, or part of one, at the block, as the pulling is exercise. If beef is not quite fresh (though this is a misfortune), it can be dipped in cold water and squeezed dry; and the same thing may be done with fresh meat when it is desirable to reduce the hawk's condition.

A *bath* must be offered to eyesses in the early part of almost every day in hot weather, and two or three times a week in winter. Messrs. Benham and Froud sell baths: but you may make one out of the bottom of an old tub. It should be six or eight inches deep, and, for a falcon, nearly a yard in diameter. I would not place it before the compartments of the shed, as it would be very much in the way there. Let it be sunk in the ground nearly its own depth (a stationary block being close to it) in some retired place on the lawn, out of sight of the other birds; for hawks often bate a good deal if they observe one of their companions bathing when they have no bath themselves. As a sort of converse of this, you will take pains that a bad bather *does* see his fellows in the water. You may do a good deal by calling to your aid the two powerful genii, imitation and jealousy. However, you may have several baths.

Grease the jesses every week or ten days. And now a word or two about *imping* (mending a broken feather). Though a simple, it is a very important operation, and deserves the attention of every falconer. It is clear that a broken feather in the tail or wing, especially in the wing, is not only unsightly, but likely to interfere with the bird's speed. There is no particular reason, however, why its loss should be regretted; for if the stump remain, it can be mended. The falconer should collect all the feathers he can of the species of hawk he uses. If any stupid fellow has shot a peregrine, perhaps he may be prevailed upon to part with the "vermin's" skin; and when a hawk moults the falconer must save the tail and larger wing feathers. It is well, when it can be done, to keep the tail and wings entire — for instance, in the "vermin case," and when a hawk dies. The best way of keeping feathers from the moth is to inclose them in *brown* paper bags.

Imping is necessary, or at least desirable, even with a hawk just about to be put up to moult, which has an important feather broken off some distance from its point. In this case almost any feather will answer the purpose — which is only to afford support to the new and tender feathers whilst they are coming down. But when it is intended to fly the bird, great pains and neatness are necessary. Then any feather will not do; but one must be selected with regard to the sex of the bird requiring it, and to the number (first, second, or third, &c.) of that which is lost. The operation itself is performed in this manner: — hood the hawk, and get an assistant to hold him in such a manner that you can easily handle the broken feather. Take a sharp penknife (an unusually sharp one) and, having selected a firm pithy part at a reasonable distance from the quill, if the point of fracture will admit of your so doing, let the blade feel its way between the web to the shaft of the feather; now turn the edge towards you and cut cleanly and obliquely from quill to point, great care being taken not to injure the web on the side at which the knife comes out. The false feather — that which is to supply the place of the broken part — must be cut at an angle, through a thickness, and at a length, which exactly match the stump in the live bird. An *imping-needle* is now taken. It is made thus: — Take a piece of iron wire rather more than an inch long, file it in a triangular shape and to a thickness which will suit the feather you are mending, produce it to a point at each end, dip it in strong brine or in liquid glue, insert half into the false feather and the other half into the true feather, pressing firmly at the point of contact. The needle, of course, remains in the pith, and the feather is imped. If, as often happens, the original feather is broken without the end being *lost,* no false feather *may* be necessary. Imp the bird with a piece of his own feather in this case. Frequently, however, the end of the feather is broken so near the point that the shaft is too thin for the needle. Then cut further down, and use the false feather. Should the fracture be so near the open quill that the imping-needle will not hold, recourse must be had to *plugging.* This is done by taking off the web from the shaft of any feather of the proper size, and inserting this shaft (perhaps for an inch) into the natural hollow quill, both plug and natural quill having been cut straight across, and the plug having been dipped in liquid glue. A turn or two of waxed thread makes matters still more secure. Then the artificial feather is imped on the plug with the needle in the usual way. Sometimes the artificial feather is cut straight across its hollow quill, instead of obliquely through the pith; in this case the plug, well smeared with liquid glue, must be passed up *it,* as well as up the natural quill on the bird's body. It is sometimes advisable to pass a common needle, with double thread, waxed, once through the plug and feathers — natural and artificial — tying the thread firmly on both sides. On no account must a feather be pulled out; if it be, ten to one it grows a weak and deformed thing, and sometimes bleeds. I had a merlin, however, last year, which lost a tail feather through the weakness of starvation, brought on before she came to me, and this feather grew perfectly. The original one *dropped* out. Goshawks, too, seem sometimes, but I think rarely, to get feathers replaced healthily.

Be careful how you fly hawks near light and almost imperceptible wire fences. The prince Dhuleep Singh had a tiercel severely injured in the head and neck, not long ago, just as the hawk was making his last dash at a magpie, through a wire fence. The quarry's life was saved, who chuckled in a most cunning and triumphant manner; that of the hawk nearly lost.

There are a few men in this country, calling themselves sportsmen, who would shoot a trained hawk, knowing it to be trained. I shall not designate them by any epithet. It could not, indeed, be too coarse for them to receive, but it might be unworthy of "Peregrine" to write. There is a vulgarity too despicable for censure; and I am unwilling to disturb these gentlemen in their natural and unalienable possessions.

A kind and honest man, however, may shoot your hawk innocently; and much may be done to guard against this accident. An advertisement put in a country paper; a notice on the blacksmiths' shops in the neighbourhood and other public places; an occasional public "meet" to fly pigeons, if your hawking establishment be a large one — all these will protect you with honest men: against rogues I fear you have no protection. You must wait with patience, my brother, till the sport is better known. That it may be better known, or at least better appreciated, propagate the undoubted truth, that a good shot and game preserver, a good rider to hounds, a man who has the best greyhounds, or who shoots the most deer, who throws a fly to perfection, or who flies the best hawks, is not *necessarily* a sportsman. Your true sportsman is greater than any of these. He is a generous, liberal-hearted man, who loves *sport* not only for the bulk of its bag, but for itself; who loves it so well that he likes to see others enjoy it; who, while he abhors the slander which would dignify some spurious pastimes with its name, rejoices to find it in a new or a revived garb, legitimate in birth; and is ready to welcome the lost stranger to all the rites of his hospitality.

One more hint, and this chapter is done. A stray or lost hawk must be sought for immediately, and by two people at the least. In order that the assistance of a second person may be efficient, the birds must have been made thoroughly acquainted with him. If you have no regular falconer or gamekeeper, a friend, groom, or gardener, should now and then fly the hawks to the lure, in your presence, and take them up, feeding them *well;* he had better not hood them perhaps, unless he is naturally expert at such matters; though it is most desirable that he should, if possible, be taught to do so nicely, While you seek in one direction for the stray bird, this assistant will seek in another, both of you having a live pigeon in pocket, fastened to a short creance, as well as the usual dead lure. A third person should ride to the farm and public houses at the distance of several miles, to engage the earliest notice, to he sent at once to you, should the hawk be seen. If the truant should be found after the absence of a week or two, he may be a little shy; for nature soon asserts herself when she has a chance. In this case it may be necessary either to peg a live pigeon under the bow-net (an instrument to be described in the next chapter), or to peg down the dead lure, should the bird settle within sight of it when thrown up (a practice more common with merlins than with peregrines), placing a noose of soft string over the meat, which you may pull over the bird's feet and *bell,* if possible, at the distance of a dozen yards. If however the peregrine be seriously wild, a live pigeon should be thrown up, fastened to a long string which is pegged. Permit the hawk to seize and *kill* the pigeon; then gently walk up, till he flies off. Now peg the dead pigeon firmly to the ground by both wings, its breast being exposed; draw out the long quill feathers, and stick them in the turf round their late owner, their ends pointing inwards. This arrangement will cause the noose, which you are about to place round them, to run up high and close to the legs of the hawk. Set it quickly and with care, retiring to some distance, taking the end of the long string to which it is attached in your hand; the hawk will return; on his return, jerk the string, and you will have him. Should you use the bow-net, you can hardly be expected to rush frantically over miles of country with it in your hand; and it is a good plan, if the hawk has been watched to his roost, to go straight to that spot before dawn, taking the net, and so present him with a pigeon the moment he is disposed for breakfast. The father of one of our professional falconers, having lost a hawk, sought it for hours in vain. At last the poor man, overcome with heat and fatigue, flung himself on the ground and fell asleep. The first object that met his eyes on opening them, was the falcon; she had found *him*. faithful and devoted "vermin," I would that some men knew thy nature, and then their good hearts would prompt them to call thee by a better name!

Wild rocky ground, though some miles from home, is a likely place to hold a lost peregrine. But if there is a ruined castle in the neighbourhood, go there at once. It is strange how fond our birds are of these relics of the olden time. The *truth,* I suppose, is that piles of stones, which resemble crags, attract them. But it is a stern and exacting truth. For my own part I will try to believe that the voices of other days, as they rustle in the ivy, and pass through the broken oriel, and go forth with the wind by the bastion-wall, still find ears that heed them. They call for the children of buried years; and the children hear the old music, even through the din of cities and the hum of wheels; — and the children come.

[1] Darkness may be dispensed with, if the floor is well littered with straw over the sand. Indeed there should be straw in any case.
[2] Spring swivels are safe in darkness, for there is little or no bating.
[3] The advantage of the screen is that it can be placed in a small room, whilst blocks require a large one.

Chapter Seven - The Haggard Peregrine

The peregrine falcon is termed a "haggard" when it is taken wild in the adult plumage. During its first year the wild peregrine is called a "soar hawk" or a "red hawk;" and, when caught during the migration, it is called a passage hawk." All this will be found in the Chapter of Definitions; but I mention it again for the sake of convenience.

I am quite ashamed to allude to Mrs. Glasse, even in the most distant manner. She and that unhappy hare are so continually pushing themselves into notice — they so struggle into the *Times,* so parade themselves in the reviews, turn up so unexpectedly in heavy and light literature altogether — that one really begins to think the moral and illustration (if they have such things to offer) no compensation for the perpetual plague of their presence. And yet "here we are again" — the old clown in the old pantomime! Name "silence," and you break it. Revile Mrs. Glasse, and lo! she is on the page before you: with one outstretched arm she directs you to the flying hare; with the other she pathetically points to the currant jelly in the background. She conjures you to snatch the day — the moment; by all your hopes of happiness and of dinner, to take the initiatory step with a decision and enthusiasm worthy of the cause. Well, Mrs. Glasse, I don't remember to have sought your society before to-day, so please do me a good turn: tell these kind people for me that a haggard peregrine must be caught before it can be trained; and, when you have made that sage remark, we will consider both *how* to catch and *how* to train.

First, how to catch, and also where to catch. The wild peregrine may be taken in the British Islands, and often is taken here, though not frequently for the purposes of falconry. A haggard tiercel was captured the year before last in the south of England, and came into the possession of a friend of mine: several others were also taken. This bird was caught in a trap, and, strange to say, was entirely uninjured. A pole-trap is commonly used by gamekeepers for all hawks: it is circular in shape, and has no teeth. I shall say nothing more about it.

If any of my readers wish for a haggard they may perhaps be able to procure one, either trained or untrained, from some one of our professional falconers. The great heaths of Valkenswaard are resorted to by men — often cobblers, I believe — who pick up a good deal of money by taking peregrines on the passage, during the months of October and November. I should enjoy a *day* of this work, or sport it may be called, but should wish to be spared a very long apprenticeship, for you have to sit in a *hole* all day, to be nearly buried alive, while you pass the time, if you happen to be a cobbler, in alternately mending your neighbours' shoes and looking through a little aperture in a very low wall which surrounds your dwelling, with the object of discovering wild peregrines. That wall consists of pieces of turf, which you cut away before you begin to dig; you are roofed in, too, with more turf, laid on a rude frame. There is, of course, an *exit.* I hope you admire your quarters, and that the "event may justify the means," &c. You are looking through your aperture on a "bow-net," which is placed at some little distance from your new home. But what *is* a bow-net? Refer to "Falconry in the British Isles;" but here is the passage. It "is a circular net of fine twine, and is made to bag sufficiently in the centre so as not to press upon the captured hawk. It is fastened to a round frame, made by binding two iron bars (five-sixteenths in size) into semicircles, and joining them by loops at their ends, which act as hinges. When put together and laid out flat, this framework should measure 3 feet 4 inches from hinge to hinge, and 4 feet 10 inches across the other way. When set, only half the net is allowed to move, viz. that half to which the pull-line is to be attached; the other half is firmly pegged to the ground by means of three square-headed pegs, which hold better than the round-headed. The net is set by turning back the movable bow and pull-line, and after adjusting the net and covering the whole with either soil or pulled grass, or moss, it is baited with a pigeon."

You are supposed then to be looking in the direction of such a net as this, which is spread out on one of the heaths of Valkenswaard. A pull-cord passes from it to your hand; but there are two other cords, or rather strings. They are thin, and one of them runs through a ring-peg placed in the ground in the centre of the bow-net. To the end of that string is attached a live pigeon, which is put into a small box that has a door through which the pigeon can be easily pulled to the net's centre. The box is about eight yards from the net. (Hawks may be caught with this *one* live lure — no box being used.) But to make the affair even more attractive, another pigeon is fastened to a pole — to a *pole,* I fancy, for the convenience of a hawk that wishes to perch in order to reconnoitre and see how matters stand. This pigeon, however, has a piece of turf so placed for it as to afford a refuge on the approach of the passage-hawk. The second string of which I spoke is fastened to this lure, which can be stirred up when the falcon is seen. The hawk approaches: she makes for the pole-pigeon; the pole-pigeon vanishes under the turf. The disappointed and angry hawk rises in a short circle, the better to see where the little wretch has crept. But you, my friend, inside the hut — you have another notion; you pull the string, and out comes the other pigeon from the box. The hawk probably takes him between the box and the net as he is fluttering. Draw the struggling birds gently to the net's centre, and with a jerk of the pull-line secure your prize.

There are two little adjuncts to this. One is a butcher-bird. This fellow has done a good deal of private murder, on his own account, on the persons of little birds in thorn bushes; he has impaled them, or he has been slandered. But the best of him is — at least for practical purposes — that he has a conscience. He sees the ghosts of his victims; they seem now to have great wings, immense talons, and crooked beaks. They pass, or would pass, but he shrieks in terror, and runs behind *his* turf. Down goes the half-mended shoe in the cellar hut; glimmers the eye of the cobbler through the aperture; snatch goes the string which rouses up the polepigeon, and so on to the end. In fact, the butcherbird tells the hawk-catcher when a peregrine is within sight. The *second* help to the individual in the cellar is not always used; but it happens sometimes that he has caught a hawk which is weakly, or at least not all he could wish it to be. To the feet of this bird he ties a bundle of feathers, and fastens him to a string near the net. The hawk of course tries to escape, but presents to his fellows the appearance, not of being in difficulties, but of being in (literally) very "high feather." He seems to be struggling with some prey; and a chance passer-by through the air comes to see whether a spot which afforded a feast for one may not afford a feast for two. So the passer-by is caught. I don't want to be sentimental; but are not men sometimes a little like birds? Of course I remember all about the plucked fowl of the philosopher; but they are like, notwithstanding.

Now, Mrs. Glasse, we have caught our hare; let us cook her!

The peregrine, on being captured, is hooded with the rufter-hood (explained in the Chapter of Definitions), and sometimes put into the *sock* — a piece of a cotton stocking drawn over the hawk's head, (which is left exposed, except as far as the hood is concerned,) and fastened round his neck, the joints of the wings being allowed to project through slits. He is fastened round the body; and his feet, which pass through another slit, are wrapped up in cloth. It is not well, however, to leave him much more than half an hour in this state. Get him on a sort of turf block, fastened by his jesses to it, as soon as possible; but perhaps you may catch another hawk or two before you make him quite comfortable.

The passage-hawk is now at home. He has jesses, but scarcely any leash to the swivel, and is secured — the rufter-hood never having been taken off — to the block of turf; there are no angles, nothing by which he can injure his feathers. It is not necessary to commence at once a regular and systematic training. In fact, the first steps taken with a wild caught hawk are more in the direction of *taming* than training. For the first ten days or so he is removed from the block to the fist, only to be fed and carried, the hood remaining on the whole time. So far from there being any cruelty in keeping the bird hooded so long, you are kind in doing so; for, at this stage, he would do all in his power to dash himself to pieces were he to see broad daylight. Neither is he in perfect darkness, the rufter-hood being cut away rather more than is usual with the hood-proper, at the beak opening. It is not amiss, by the way, to change the hood (in a dark room) for one with a somewhat larger opening (on the same principle as cutting the "seeling" — see Definitions) when the haggard has become a little reconciled to captivity. But this is anticipating. Lift the haggard, then, on your fist, draw a piece of raw beef over his feet till he is provoked to peck at it; let it be very tender, so that he may take a small piece up. He will probably shake his head and flip it away. Try again; should he swallow one bit, he is almost certain to swallow more. But it *may* be necessary to cram, for the power of digestion is lost by a too long abstinence. You can, however, pass a good twenty-four hours, even allowing for a fast before the hawk was captured, in perfect safety; longer, I think.

The dispositions of hawks vary; but we will say that at the end of ten days or a fortnight the haggard feeds eagerly through the hood; he, also, perhaps, just begins to recognise the whistle which you sound as you approach him. Now begin in earnest. Though in health, he has not been kept in high condition, and soon becomes "sharp-set." After a slight feed early in the morning, the bird must be carried. About two o'clock brail one wing, thus: take a strip of soft leather, about a foot long, as broad as a shoestring, but three times the breadth in the middle; let it taper to points. Cut a slit down the middle, two or three inches in length. Place the joint of the hawk's wing through this slit; bring one end of the brail under the wing, let it meet (outside) the one above; tie the ends; the joint is immoveable; and the wing brailed. The picture in "Blaine's Encyclopaedia" makes it appear that the brail goes round the body of the hawk; this is a mistake, and has led to mistakes. The brailing being completed, wet the bird thoroughly by squeezing a sponge full of water over him, it being held some height above him, so as to add a shock to the wetting. Go to a perfectly retired place, an out-house perhaps, remove the rufter-hood, immediately replacing it by the hood proper, and continue the lesson of "making to the hood," as explained in a previous chapter on eyesses.

It is recommended that haggards and passagehawks should be kept, while they are in training at any rate, upon the perch, in a dark room, the shutter of which is thrown open only at feeding times. They seem to fly to the hand for food better from the perch than from the block, and the reason, no doubt, is that you do not stand over them when they are called from the former resting-place. These birds are first taught to come to the fist in a house — *i.e.* under a roof of some sort, where it is impossible that any passing object can steal that attention which ought to be devoted seriously to dinner. The truth is, that *all* hawks come to the hand better in a room than out of doors; and I should not be quite satisfied that a hawk, say a sparrow-hawk, was perfectly broken to hand simply because I had seen her fly to it in a room; out-of-door practice is necessary, and is the second step; take care, however, not to make it the first, or you may lose time by frightening the bird at the outset.

Haggards, when seriously taken in hand soon after their capture, are often rapidly *tamed* by being constantly kept awake for some days and nights. This can, of course, only be done by a relay of assistants to the falconer, as the bird must not be allowed to sleep for a minute. Such treatment, with a spare diet, soon conquers a rebellious, and even an obstinate spirit, and is, I think, to be recommended. It is not, however, absolutely necessary. Mr. Newcome saw some haggards trained in Holland which were only carried from two to nine p.m.

When the haggard, or wild-caught hawk of any age, comes readily to the hand out of doors, it is time to offer him a live pigeon *in the house.* Strange to say, he *may* refuse it. This bird, which when wild perhaps struck down the heron, may be now absolutely cowed at a quarry he could kill in a few seconds. All will be right in the end: offer a live sparrow; let him kill several sparrows; then, having kept him sharp-set for a day or two, give another pigeon with its wing brailed. When a live pigeon is given, the hawk must be on the block, fastened by a long leash, and the string attached to the pigeon must go through a ring-peg, in order that the quarry may be brought up to a particular spot within the hawk's reach. This is certainly the least agreeable part of training; but once done, it is done with. The next step is to fly the hawk, in a creance, at a brailed pigeon; then he may be trusted at large, when very sharp-set, at a pigeon, to which is fastened a long string, to be shortened as the hawk improves. And I am sorry to say that as far as pigeons are concerned for a *flight,* we must go no further, at least not for many months. A wild-caught hawk, however well broken, is sure to carry light quarry; hence the necessity of the string to the pigeon, the end of which is taken up by the falconer as he approaches the hawk. All that, however, is only preparation. Your haggard falcon is now prepared for being entered at heavy birds, such as the heron or herring-gull; though she will be a wonderfully good hawk if she fly the latter quarry well. She can't carry these. The tiercel may be at once entered to rooks, crows, and Norfolk plover. But time accomplishes much that skill alone is insufficient for; and, when a year or so has passed, the haggards will perhaps "wait on," and show no disposition to carry. When this happens they can be flown at game. Until it happen, they must be ridden up to after an unsuccessful flight, and taken down to a live pigeon in a string; for they have no notion at first of returning to the falconer as eyesses do, and are sure, if sharp-set, to dash after the first bird they may see in the distance. As for the dead lure, to which nestlings are trained, it can only be engrafted on the affections of haggards by very slow degrees, and the consequence is that wild-caught hawks are nearly always taken down with a live bird in a creance. Yet the passage-hawk is a noble bird, and, in experienced hands, more powerful than the eyess. I shall have something to show on that head when we come to "heron hawking."

I have now entirely concluded the *training,* properly so called, of the peregrine. The grammar is done with: let us try to enjoy the language. It has many beautiful passages, and perhaps a few that are instructive. *Au revoir.* We shall look for grouse and partridges with the eyess and pointer in the next chapter.

Chapter Eight - The First of September

It is the first of September! I know it is without an almanac. The morning air carries something peculiar with it; not exactly a scent — nothing so gross as that — but a sweet, charming, invigorating freshness. Summer has just gone away, with her red flowers and her hot face, with her jewels and her glitter: and Autumn has grown tall enough and strong enough to put the sickle into the corn, bind up the sheaves, and carry home all the harvest.

I can sleep now on the night of the 31st of August. There was a time when I lay awake then: had they been erecting a scaffold for my accommodation in the early morning, I could not have slept less. A few grey hairs have a wondrously somniferous effect, at any rate when the exciting cause is only amusement.

It is the first of September, I repeat; or, what amounts to the same thing for our present purpose, I insist upon your allowing that it is. My friend Brown is sitting opposite to me at my own table. He has just finished breakfast; so have I. Now, Brown does nothing by halves, and he does not make half a breakfast. It would be inhospitable to him, however, were I to tell you, even if I knew, how many sardines he has swallowed, how many applications he has made for ham, and how frequently he has referred to the marmalade. Enough that it is over: enough that rest follows labour.

People differ as to what sort, and what amount, of breakfast a man ought to eat before a hard day's work out of doors. I have known people refuse meat, and even eggs, altogether, on the ground that such things are too heavy, and also induce a fevered state of the blood. Some men dare not drink tea, others refuse coffee; the majority, I think, allow that chocolate is innocent. Well, I know nothing of medicine, but I know this, that a man in *good health* is better, and better able to work, after a moderately substantial breakfast than after one composed only of toast and tea. You will be careful, however, if you take my advice, to avoid anything *salt,* for thirst will come without being coaxed to the moor side — yes even to the stubble. However, the most difficult thing to determine is, what one ought to drink. It is the fashion of the day to take into the field huge bottles of cold tea, and indeed to refrain altogether from any more stimulating fluid. I don't like the fashion of the day; but I like it better than the fashion of yesterday, *i.e.* in other words, I would rather not have all tea, as we do now, nor all brandy and water, as they did then; but would rather have all the tea than all the brandy.

On the white cloth before me — I won't tell you what is before Brown — is a large flask of tea and a small flask of brandy-and-water. I intend to shoot till luncheon; and I know full well that if I should get very hot, or tumble over a hedge, or struggle for long through very high turnips, I should miss two or three shots unless I applied to that brandy. Still I shall not touch it wantonly; I shall not attack it without provocation; I don't want to make an enemy of it.

* * * * * *

Brown and I have had a nice four hours: we have bagged three and a half brace of grouse from points and fifteen brace of partridges between us. We first took the edge of the moor, and then beat stubble, grass, and some patches of potatoes, all which lie not very far from the heather, on open table-land. We have taken pretty good notes too of the whereabouts of the birds we left behind us, and, if they don't move, shall be able to go almost straight to them after luncheon. We must be quick, by the way, for the hawks are hooded up, Jones and Robinson have arrived, and the ladies who join our meet will be in the field before an hour is gone.

Robinson is a pupil of mine, and he suggests with deference that we should have had a better chance of good flights had we "unhooded" immediately at some partridges which I told him Brown and I left scattered in a little field of turnips. It was a pity, he thought, to have to go home for the hawks, and so let the birds get together again. "Not so, my dear Robinson," said I, "and for these reasons: in the first place, as Dr. Johnson was not ashamed to say, 'Sir, I *like* to dine,' I may perhaps venture to remark, 'Sir, I *like* to lunch.' Again, although the partridges might have been found separately, kicked up one by one and shot, yet they were in a small field, surrounded by thick and tall hedges, and would not have afforded the sort of flight I intend to show to-day. There are plenty in the open," I added; "we will go to them." Robinson looked submissive, and offered me a cigar out of an immense case, somewhat after the manner of a penitent chief conciliating Dr. Livingstone with ivory and cattle: he evidently considered that he owed me all the reparation in his power.

We must make haste: the hawks are 100 yards on their way already, — I see the cadge by the gate. Look at that little idiot "Erin," how he tries to bate off! — I would not be the partridge before him in an open country, even if I had 300 yards' start, for all that. Whilst the cadge is preceding us on our way to the field, let me describe it. It is a wooden frame, about four and a half feet long by two or three feet wide; it may be set down on its four short legs, or carried by a man, who stands in the middle of it, by straps which pass across his shoulders. In fact, it is generally an affair of four light poles fastened so as to form an oblong, with straps and legs, — the poles serving as perches for the hooded hawks, and being padded. At each end two or three bars of wood are fastened, to prevent the birds bating off inside, and the only objection to which is that they sometimes interfere with the tails; but canvass would interfere more, to say nothing of its catching the mutes (of which, however, there are not many when birds are in flying order), and netting would be worse than bars. An excellent falconer has suggested the addition of a piece of carpet fastened screen fashion, and has used such a cadge for *unhooded* merlins; peregrines, however, must be hooded on any cadge.

We are now in the field, with three eyess peregrines of the year on our "cadge," viz. two tiercels and a falcon: added to this I have one old favourite tiercel on my glove. "Major," the pointer, keeps to heel; but he is young, and it will be necessary to use the check-cord when we begin work. Let us try for grouse in this stubble: they come from the moor to it at all hours, and we were not near it this morning. We will fly against the wind, which is blowing gently from the heather: be quiet, and let "Major" hold up. The young dog quarters the ground *like* a young dog — there is a little too much gallop and romp, but the check-cord is a slight drag on him, and he will soon settle down to his work in style. Suddenly he pitches nearly head-over-heels. Toho! "By Jove!" says Jones, "he's got them." "He has," I answer, "at least I think so, but I wont hood-off to a false point if I can help it; however, I've so often put them up from that very spot that I'll cast off the 'Earl.' As for you, Jones, instead of swearing by your heathen gods, do me the favour to canter after 'Major,' on that little pony of yours, the moment the flight begins, and if the 'Earl' kills, stop the dog, and peg him down near the birds; here's a peg, and the cord is on him." Whilst giving these directions, I unhook the swivel from the jesses of the old tiercel, take off the hood, and, as I raise my hand to hold the bird aloft, he starts from it. In a moment he recognises the dog, and knows well what that statue-like position means: nay, perhaps, he can detect the very movement of the jaw (as though the pointer were *eating* the scent), and see the saliva running from it. I, however, at 200 yards, can only see the dead staunch point. Walk up gently, my friends; let the hawk get his pitch. Pray do not hurry him; the grouse know what kind of fellow has got above them, and won't rise till we make them. Well, *that's* high enough, at any rate, and now his head is turned in towards the birds and towards the moor — so, here goes. "Hi, in! 'Major,' lad! Into 'em, old boy!"

And I set the example myself. Up get a brace of full grown young birds, as the dog plunges forward. "Hoo-ha-ha-ha!" The practised hawk answers the shout by flying forwards, rising (if anything) as he does so, and then, in one terrible stoop, passing downwards through the air almost with the speed and the hum of a rifle-ball. It was a glorious stoop, but there must have been a clever shift too, for though he appeared to brush by, he has not killed, and not badly wounded, the quarry. Bounding, at the distance of a few feet from the ground, which he almost seemed to touch, the good hawk rises again, not in rings, but in an oblique line, after the still flying grouse.

Another stoop, from a pitch not so high as the last, at the same quarry again, which (evidently owing to its hurt) lags behind its neighbour; and down it goes, with a wing broken, and the skull nearly laid open (as we afterwards discovered) by that single blow. Look at Brown and Robinson! they "Wowhoop" like wild Indians, and dance on English stubble the dance of Africa — a polka worthy Makololo. Hasten, redoubted Jones, on thy mission, and leave these, thy brother chiefs, in their ridiculous ecstasy! Jones did well: he caught hold of the check-cord and stopped the young dog, who, though too well broke "to run in" on the struggling birds, conducted himself in so excited a manner, at the distance of fifteen paces from them, that a less experienced hawk than the "Earl" might have been frightened from its quarry. All was right, however, when I got up. The old tiercel was fed from the head and neck of its victim, hooded and placed on the cadge. (He might have been "fed up," for we did not fly him again that day.)

Take the falcon next; see what she will do — she has killed one bagged-grouse and three wild ones, since she was entered to them, and I know she is "sharp-set." Look, another dead point! off with the young falcon! She's well up now; flush the birds. "Body of Bacchus!" said the enthusiastic but unclassical Jones, who, had he sworn at all, ought to have invoked Diana; "Corpo di Bacco!" (as if the accusing angel did not understand Italian) repeated he, "it's a hare!"

It was indeed a hare. "Major" looked foolish and slunk back: I expect he had felt the check-collar for chasing not many weeks ago. The falcon wheeled off in disgust; and just as the whistle shrieked, and the lure took its first whirl, a wood-pigeon passed in the distance. "Au vol!" shouted Robinson, who had heard me lecture on heron-hawking. The hawk never thought of Robinson, but she saw the pigeon, and off she went, like the wind, over some rising ground. "What a nuisance!" exclaimed I, in humble vernacular; "but ride, Jones — ride!" Well, we were an hour finding that hawk; she had killed the pigeon a mile or a mile and a half away, and, had it not been that some rooks stopped to caw and circle about, we might have searched another hour. She had left the quarry, and was pretty well gorged when we found her, and had to be taken up with a live pigeon in a creance.

Time gets on; we shall dine at half-past six, and little has been done. We must go lower down, and get a brace of partridges at any rate. There! somebody or something has put up that covey, or else they are passing out of the grass to feed on the stubbles. Mark them down! We shall have to fly down wind I fear, but, as there's scarcely any to fly down, it won't matter. There's time or rather distance for one stoop, and I should think two stoops, before they can "put in" at all. Speak quietly to the dog. "Have a care! steady, 'Major!'" There he is again! Now for "Erin" and "Comet," the two young tiercels; I'll cast off both at once, and chance their taking separate birds, which they are nearly sure to do." "That's right, Potterer," said I, speaking to a stupid gamekeeper who came with one of my friends, and carried the cadge — "that's right, and done without a blunder. Now you have given me ' Comet,' give 'Erin' to Mr. Robinson." So Robinson and I cast off our birds. They knew a little what the pointer meant, and seemed to regulate the position they took at their pitch with *some* reference to him — at least, I thought this was all, until, when the dog did not move, and we came up but slowly, little "Erin" proved to demonstration that he knew the dog's business as well as his own, for he fell almost as if he had been a stone, on "Major" 's back, or within a few yards of it, as much as to say, "Get in, sir, get in," and then regained his pitch before the dog— who seemed to be equally well up in the matter — flushed the partridges. [1] Down they came, "Comet" and " Erin," almost side by side; but I was a little wrong in my calculations as to the number of stoops possible before the birds could reach cover. Whether the bird which "Comet" struck at the first stoop intended to "put in" the hedge or to pass over it, I could not see, though I suppose the former; however, he never reached the hedge alive, though he did reach it. The rush — not so much of wings as of the feathers of an arrow when it leaves a 70 lb. bow— the falling of a dark object from somewhere between us and the sky — something almost like the "thud" of a striking ball in the target — and the partridge falls dead on the hedgetop, his head cut away clean from the body. [1] That Brown and Robinson, nay Jones to boot, would have relieved their excited feelings by some such exhibition as that with which two of them had already favoured us is more than probable, had it not been for the circumstance that the partridge pursued by "Erin" "put in" not far from the spot where his companion fell, and so made it necessary that those gentlemen should exert their talents and energies to get him out again as quickly as possible. To this end they called a small but courageous spaniel to their aid — a little fellow who did not recognise thorns as thorns; and as the bird again took flight, it was brought down, at the first stoop, by the hawk, who, knowing what to expect, had a "waited on" above for that express purpose.

And what has become of our fair friends all this time? Have we ungallantly forgotten them? If so, we have forgotten ourselves too. But no: they rode well — nay, they cheered well. "Comet" heard one clear silver sound when he gathered himself for the stoop, which proved to be the most brilliant of the season. Sir Edwin Landseer, look at that flight! dip your brush again in those undying colours, and give a picture to all time which it shall be as impossible for pen to rival as fully and sufficiently to praise!

Well, our bag was not large. It consisted of but one grouse, one wood-pigeon, the brace of partridges killed by the young tiercels near the hedge, and one other old cock-bird cut down afterwards by "Erin." "Comet" put in a single bird, but it was lost simply because neither dog nor man could put it out again. However, five kills out of six flights was not so bad, — at least we thought not.

I was solicited to beguile the mile and a half that lay between us and home by a lecture on game hawking; but I had enough to do to answer all the questions which were put to me. "Did you not once say," asked Robinson, "that a beginner should attempt to train but *one* peregrine, and that the bird should be a tiercel? Now, I have heard that when a hawk is lost the best plan to recover him is to fly another hawk of the same species (as a sort of call-bird), — the companion of the lost one, if possible." "True," said I, "the plan you mention is excellent; it is patent to all falconers; but you will remember that I recommended an 'only tiercel' to none others than to those who had never taken a hawk in hand, and who knew nothing practically about the matter. For such I know my advice is good; and any one who really desires the spread of falconry should repeat it, and for this reason, that many would-be falconers have already been discouraged *in limine,* disappointed and disgusted altogether, simply because they have commenced with too many birds. They have been 'too *greedy,*' as a great falconer expressed it to me. Besides, a hawk, which is the constant companion of its master, is not very likely to be lost; and, if it *be* lost, can probably be recovered by the lure and shout." "What is the best way of restoring feathers on a living bird, which have become bent, but which are not broken?" "Hood the hawk, and dip the tail or wing (as the case may be) in hot water," said I. "Do you think we could have good sport with the gun if, at the end of September with grouse, and later on in the season with partridges, — in short, when the birds became wild, — we were to fly a peregrine to the lure, allowing him to rake away pretty well, and the moment he was taken down and hooded beat for the game?" "You would have excellent sport for a short time after the hawk was taken down, being able to walk perhaps even into the midst of grouse; but it would be prettier sport to put the bird on the wing again to the first point, and to kill right and left while he struck down a third." [2]

"Can you tell us an anecdote *apropos* of gamehawking?" "Here's a fine stoop for you, at any rate," said I. "Col. the Hon. E. Gr. Monkton saw a favourite falcon of the late Col. Bonham do *this*: the falcon was 'waiting on' rather wide, there being a strong breeze at the time, when up sprang an old cock grouse, uttering his wild cry as he skimmed rapidly down wind. In an instant the falcon (which seemed, from its great pitch, hardly larger than a pin's head) made a straightforward flight for a short distance, and then, with a pause as if to take aim, but which was almost imperceptible, came down like a meteor upon the grouse, which, from the power of the stroke and the speed at which it itself was flying, spun over and over in its long slanting fall, and was found deep in the heather. Col. Bonham had an excellent little tiercel called 'Little Jack,' a famous bird for snipe; the Colonel used to go out with him before breakfast, and seldom bagged less than two or three. The same gentleman was flying 'The Countess' (a fine eyess falcon) at grouse; she was ringing at a great pitch when the old setter made a steady point. The peregrine moved on over the dog; a grouse was sprung; but as the hawk gathered herself for a stoop — which, had it sped, would have carried death — a raven, to the infinite surprise of all who looked on, intervened between the pursued and the pursuer, with the motive, however, not of intercepting destruction, but of aiding it. She joined in the chase, but utterly spoiled the stoop of the falcon. The grouse 'put in.' 'The Countess,' disdaining the society of the vulgar nigger, rose loftily; and, as the quarry was again flushed, prepared once more for her stoop. Again the raven, convinced that she alone could bring matters to a satisfactory issue, and claiming the common rights of the air, started in pursuit, placing her black body between the highborn lady and the flying prize. This was too gross. 'The Countess' came down like lightning on the back of the intruder; with one blow sent it off sick and croaking to the rocks; and then, as though she had but brushed a gnat from her path, regained her pitch for the third time, and killed the grouse at a single stoop. The Colonel, and his old falconer, M'Cullock, declared it was the finest thing in falconry they had ever seen. And now," said I, "one more, and we have done. Captain Salvin told me the following: — 'I once had a splendid flight with "Verbaea," an eyess falcon, at an old cock grouse, upon Grassington-moor, in Craven, near Skipton. The flight must have been about two miles. When I reached the spot where I expected to meet with the hawk, I found her panting and completely done, at some little distance from the grouse, which was wounded and exhausted, lying amongst a heap of its feathers. Neither could stir when I got up, and I shall never forget the pretty picture I thought it would have made. The grouse had fallen on a burn side, where the heather had given place to that beautiful short, soft, green grass which is made by the browsing of sheep and geese. Then, as a back ground, there was a sparkling stream, with rock, fringed with fern and purple heather,'" &c.

"Thank you, 'Peregrine,'" said the ladies, and Brown, Jones, and Robinson immediately said "Thank you."

* * * * * *

Put up Brown, Jones, and Robinson in their oval shaped box, made out of a great shaving that does not meet at all neatly at one side, and which is bound with another shaving, red, and thinner. They are only puppets, you know. I never knew them. Mind you don't break their legs off, or their heads, or spoil the wire that pulled them. They were very cheap and I borrowed them from somebody else; but they have lightened our toil a little — children that we are! — and I would not hurt them. We all find our playthings strewed about the serious roads of life; they get full of dust sometimes, but (thank God) we can shake it out again. I, for one, like to see them there; they do good and no harm; they may sometimes instruct, always amuse, us. Yes! I think we must put them all up, very carefully, into the play cupboard for another day.

[1] Founded on fact.
[2] John Anderson, one of the falconers employed by the ancient family of the Flemings, of Barochan Tower, Renfrewshire, frequently did this. He died in 1833, at the age of 84.

Chapter Nine - An Essay on "Sport."

People agree in their notions of what *sport* is, so far as this, — that they confess certain elements are necessary to its existence, and that, if any of these fail — these essential parts — the whole is more or less a failure. A fair prospect of success, mingled with some uncertainty in regard to the exact time when we shall be successful; an occasional difficulty, together with skill, tact, and perhaps bodily strength to overcome it; an occasional stroke of good fortune, with ability to make the most of it — all these are, of necessity, allowed places in that which is called "sport."

Still, I question if we have a very accurate impression of what it *really* is. We are inclined to see it only in its instruments. This man cannot understand it in connexion with any creature but a fox; that man weds it to a partridge.

I grant, of course, that the immediate object of pursuit, together with the implements of chase, are necessary to the existence of sport; but they are necessary only in the manner — considerable, it is true — that the body; is necessary to the mind, or the fingers of a clock to the main-spring.

Sport is not wholly material. It has material agents, but it is above and before them all. Do you imagine that, because it sits for awhile on the falcon's wing, or bounds side by side with your greyhound, or speaks to you in the music of the pack, or touches the water when' the eddy circles away, that it is the child of these? It is not the child of these. Its parentage is as high as your own; its spirit was born with your life, and will live in any house you may choose for its tenement.

Is music material? Is poetry?

I have not confused the *love* of sport with the reality. For imagine a man born amongst the objects of the chase: let his chief companions be old women, or those who, until they joined him, have spent their existence amongst streets; let him be without tuition, and do you not think that he, or his offspring, probably himself, will find a way to hunting? Aye, marry! will they, as sure as the newly-fledged falcon makes her first stoop. Such a man had never *seen* sport; he did not meet her on the wold, or in the forest: there indeed was her food and raiment; but she first sprang from his side — from himself, and came back to him clothed and armed, — the Diana of his dreams.

Now, the fair maiden may clothe herself as she lists; in other words, you, sir, may choose her dress for her, because she is sure to like it.

That which I will call the *immediate object* may be a fox, a pheasant, or a fish. The value of that object, whatever it be, is not necessarily intrinsic, — it is adventitious. This may be made clear at once by dividing sports into two classes. In one class we will place (at any rate) shooting and fishing. In these a great deal depends upon the rarity and intrinsic value of the creature taken: thus a woodcock is better than a snipe; a trout than a chub; and the "sport" is found to be very much in proportion to the *value* (as the term is commonly employed) of the bird or fish. But in what we emphatically call " the chase" — such as hunting and hawking — the value of the "immediate object," though great, does not arise from its importance when caught, but from the excitement and amusement which it affords in the catching. The fox and fox-hunting, so familiar to every one, illustrate this remark at once (the animal chased being, as a *possession,* absurdly out of proportion to the pains taken in his capture); and the simple mention of them renders other comment unnecessary.

It is the *incidents* of the chase, then, that are amusing and absorbing; these follow nobly in the train of the "immediate object;" they are created by it, whilst they are superior to it. Clearly the game *must* be valuable; yet the value need not belong to the possession, but to the pursuit.

I have thought it worth while to analyse a little our notions and feelings on the subject of *sport;* because I am about to offer my readers some remarks on the method of taking birds (with peregrines) which are treated, with reason, as vermin, or considered as worthless altogether, and can therefore be valuable to the sportsman only as they afford him amusement in pursuing them. This chapter is on magpie-hawking and rook-hawking. However amusing the magpie may be when alive and in captivity, he is worthless when dead; and falconers are, I fancy, the only sportsmen who care to pursue the rook and carrion crow, except, indeed, that the pea-rifle does some execution on the former at the beginning of every May. What I have to say practically upon this subject will be written, in great part, from notes prepared by my coadjutor, who has brought magpie hawking (introduced, or at least greatly improved, by Sir John Seabright) to what I think may fairly be called perfection.

Let us take magpie-hawking first; — rook-hawking, indeed, is almost learned from the same lesson. For this sport a "field" is necessary: it is, in fact, the fox-hunting of falconry. The quarry is the most artful of all birds which we chase; and, though his speed is insignificant compared with that of some others, the cleverness with which he shifts to avoid the stoop, the brain which he bears, and the extraordinary adaptation of his bodily powers to elude capture in anything like cover, make it necessary that the hawks should be assisted by several experienced hands. In fact, you must have a "meet." That "meet" must be very devoted and very obedient. [1] One thing it must not do upon any account whatever, — it must not bring dogs. If it forget this prohibition, even in the case of one of its members, the lives of your hawks will be in danger. Imagine a favourite tiercel, after a long and fine flight, just breaking the quarry's neck, — a tiercel that your wife, children, friends, love — the hawking community perhaps know — his name a household word among all, — imagine this fellow, docile as a dog himself, and never caring for one, run into and killed by some yelping brute! A pleasant fancy truly! "Pray you avoid" a possibility of the reality.

But you must have hunting whips. When the magpie has taken to cover, the smart crack of a whip is almost certain to send him out again. You know the effect which such a sound has on a hare in "form;" but with the magpie there is really a necessity for it Surely, if not a veritable witch, mag must imprison the spirit of some ancient caitiff who has never obeyed but at the threat of chastisement. To constitute a perfect "field" there should be horsemen and footmen — the former using their whips, the latter their sticks and staves, to drive the magpie from his place of shelter, such as a hedge or clump of trees, when he has been "put in" by the hawks.

It is not at all meant here that a falconer, with a cast of peregrines, and a friend or two (or servant or two) to help him, cannot take magpies in a tolerably open country; although, if he have never yet tried the sport, he will probably find it more difficult than he imagines it to be; but I am simply saying how the thing is to be done if it be done in perfection. In that case there certainly should be a proper "meet" — a picnic "meet," if you will. Ladies who like to ride over a little fence, and yet do not care to follow the hounds, should be on horseback; men who like riding, who like running, should be there; labourers, with a couple of hours or more of holiday, should be there as beaters; and if the "meet" be in Ireland (so says my friend from whose notes I am now writing, and who looks back with gratification — nay, perhaps I may venture to say for him — with gratitude, to the hospitality which he received in that country), there is sure to be as excellent a luncheon and as hearty a welcome as a man need eat or need shake hands upon.

Falcons are so likely to start after rooks when the magpie has "put in," and thus been lost to the hawks for a time, that tiercels ought to be used. Passagehawks would not "wait on" well — a matter in which magpie-hawks should be perfect — and would probably "carry;" for these reasons, and perhaps also from the greater facility in procuring the young birds, magpies are almost invariably flown with eyesses. A single tiercel, well supported by the "field," will take the quarry in time; but it is much better to fly a cast at him, half the beauty of the flight consisting in the manner in which the assailants aid each other, one immediately taking up the stoop which his friend has missed.

As for the sort of country necessary for the sport, it must be free from woods; not from the hedges of large enclosures, nor from occasional bushes, nor even from very small plantations, but from "woods," as one generally uses the term. Indeed, a country may be too open; a magpie, when there is no shelter near him, will take wing on the first appearance of the hawking party, and, if he is viewed at all, will be too far off for a flight. Choose, therefore, something like the following for the ground: — Grass, with leapable hedges; here and there a thorn bush, either in the hedge itself or in the large open fields; and, of course, there will be, whether you like it or not, an occasional small tree. With these advantages a falconer and four assistants may have fine sport with a cast of tiercels, but the more the merrier, and if the "cheer" may be spoken of as represented by the number of quarry killed, it will probably contradict the proverb, and not be "better" with the "fewer."

A fair sprinkling of magpies is better than a great quantity of them; the reason is, that if they be too plentiful, the hawks in pursuit are apt to fly at "check," *i.e.* when the quarry has "put in," the tiercels "waiting on" above him are almost sure to fly a fresh magpie, should it pass before the legitimate bird is driven out. It is clear that in doing so they waste their own strength without the chance of being able to fatigue their opponents, who are compelled only to a labour which, like the breaking of separate sticks, is easy when it is divided.

In this country hawks cannot be depended upon when the day is very bright and the sky azure; in such weather they like the luxury of a soar. It is not difficult then to conceive that in such a sport as magpie-hawking, when a good deal of "waiting on," and consequently patience, is required of them, they should sometimes be tempted to leave it for the amusement which, notwithstanding their hunger, nature dictates — just as you, my friend, who like luncheon and fly-fishing, would forego both, in a broiling day, for one swim of ten minutes in the deep and crystal water. And as perfect calm, accompanied by great heat and brightness, is detrimental to the sport, so is a high cold wind. The medium is right here, and perhaps anywhere; seek it, at least, here.

Let us suppose that a good falconer, with a cast or two of tiercels, and a "field" of his friends and neighbours — ladies, gentlemen, yeoman, and beaters — starts for half a day's magpie-hawking. It is a neighbourhood that affords the quarry he seeks; and one of a few scattered trees in the distance seems likely to hold it. A small but good glass is an excellent help now; direct it to the tops of the trees. There is Mr. Mag on the very topmost bough — nay, on the highest twig of all, rocking himself about in an apparently free-and-easy, care-for-nobody, American sort of manner, but, in reality, watching the little company with a most anxious gaze, and not a few nervous misgivings at heart. See how he telegraphs with his tail, in jerks whose rapidity is increasing, that all is well; while, contradicting their antipodes, his clever head is turned more quickly, and his sharp eye looks out for the refuge which he is on the point of seeking. Poor maggy! had you balanced yourself on that bough before "Highland Laddie" was blinded, I had counted you but dead; as it is, I pity you — nay, could I ride the air, I think you would be helped in your last shift, just when they come spinning past you, just as you drop one feather to their touch and expect to drop yourself when the next stoop comes.

But some one has seen you, and has mentioned the fact of your presence to the falconer. He is even now hurriedly telling his "field" to place themselves between you and that little wood in your rear, so that, should you attempt to make for it, you may be intercepted. Had you been *in* the wood (you may be interested in knowing this), the side down wind, especially if most open, would have been left clear for your exit, while the beaters went in opposite. The object in any case is to get you into the "open" as quickly as possible. I perceive that you are there already; and, indeed, that a cast of tiercels has been cast off, and is in hot pursuit of you. Do you wear the half-mourning for one of your brothers slain long ago at a great stoop? or is it put on quaintly and shrewdly on account of the doubtful issue of the present struggle, and in semi-anticipation of it? They are experienced hawks that are after you, and, had one been inferior to the other, you would have had the best first. As it is, fly! but, above all, as you cannot fly well, dodge. Pass down a hedge close to its side; just skim the ground; they dare not stoop hard then, lest they should dash themselves against it; and, if you are pressed into the open, shift backwards as they stoop. Farewell!

There are two or three methods of managing a flight. Take, for instance, the case where the country is pretty open, good for riding over, and most of the party are mounted; then a straight flight across country is most desirable. To secure it the magpie must not be headed, but allowed to make "his point," which, like that of the fox, will be straight to the nearest wood or cover — his stronghold. Or you may, under other circumstances, adopt a plan exactly opposite to this: it is common, and sometimes absolutely necessary. When cover is close by, the quarry *must* be headed at once and driven from it. He will take short flights near the ground, and from bush to bush; but his favourite course is along a hedgerow. As the hawks cannot strike him in such situations, the great object of the falconer and his field must be to drive him across the open country; at any rate, to press him over pretty good-sized enclosures, if there are any, so that the tiercels may get the chance of a stoop or two. Suppose the magpie has "put in" a hedge; let the horsemen leap it, or get on the other side by some means as fast as they can; the footmen must remain where they are. In this manner a circle is made, only prevented from uniting at two points by the hedge, which the ends of the semicircles, however, must touch, the magpie being in the middle. Let each party now rapidly approach the other, and with the crack of whips, with sticks, and voices, compel the magpie to fly free of cover altogether. As the tiercels come down, one after another, he "shifts his flight," *i.e.* turns quickly in the air, thus throwing the hawks out, and giving himself the opportunity of regaining cover. From his new shelter he must be driven as before, and that as quickly as possible, for (as the field will do well to remember) the hawks are spending their strength on the *wing,* while he, cunning fellow, is creeping through bushes and hedges; perhaps, as my notes assure us, "concocting some sly dodge to *do* his enemies."

A flight, then, may be confined to some few fields, or it may be a straightforward flight of a mile, or even possibly two miles; the latter lasting sometimes for more than half an hour. Occasionally it will be found that the magpie gains a plantation, notwithstanding every effort to prevent him. Through this he must be driven, as sharply as possible, by the cracks of whips and by beaters; but should he bury himself in a large wood, he is as safe as a fox gone to ground where there are no spades and no terriers. The "kill" is, of course, proclaimed by "whoo-whoop," at which cry all should fall back, in order that the falconer may secure the" hawks quietly: believe me he will be very angry if any one approach him too nearly at this period. The first person up at the death may claim the equivalent and counterpart of "the brush," viz. "the tail." It makes a pretty trophy to wear in the cap; and, supposing it unusually fine, and from a cock bird, it can be formed into a very nice hand screen.

Magpies are not always to be found in sufficient quantities in England to justify a stud of magpie-hawks; but they abound in many parts of Ireland; and that country, being generally free from wood, is well adapted to the sport. Captain Salvin made a hawking tour in Ireland in the autumn of 1857, having been invited there by a friend in Tipperary. John Barr (since falconer to the Prince Dhuleep Singh) was then his falconer. The tour, which lasted about four months, embraced the counties of Tipperary, Cork, and Kildare. It was very successful. The "meets" were published in the papers, and circulars were sent out, so that a "field" might be secured. The best hawks were "Assegai," "Azrael," and "Hydra" (falcons), with which sixty-eight rooks and a Eoyston crow were killed; and "The O'Donohue" and "Dhuleep Singh," (the latter hawk brother to the famous " Bishop"), which took the astonishing number of 184 magpies. No two tiercels ever varied in their method of killing more than these, though both, I need hardly say, were first-rate hawks. "The O'Donohue" always killed by a splendid stoop, while "Dhuleep Singh," though he could stoop well enough, preferred the more certain, but less grand, style of clutching the quarry the moment it began to flag. The average of each day's sport was about two or three rooks and four or five magpies; but on one occasion (the last day in Tipperary), the bird "Dhuleep Singh" took eight magpies himself! I mention all this simply as a matter of encouragement. It shows what *can* be done.

If you want to fly magpies, keep the hawks to that particular quarry. A good magpie-hawk may, however, be converted into a game-hawk by being taken from magpies and entered at once at partridges, or other suitable quarry. But the flight, which is the subject before us, gives a tiercel confidence, tact, courage, and steadiness; and when he has been well accustomed to it through the winter, he may almost always be entered to rooks in the spring. Tiercels, not being so strong as falcons, give great interest to a rook flight. A bird that is really good at magpies must have great tact and determination. Captain Salvin saw a favourite tiercel, after a hard flight, drive a magpie into a hole in a park wall; there was a good "field" well up at the time, and they had drawn round the spot. The little hawk lit near the hole, dragged out the magpie, and killed him, amidst their cheers.

I could write a chapter on rook and crow-hawking, I dare say, but it would hardly be fair to my readers to do so; for, although there might be a slight difference in detail from the sport I have just described, yet the leading distinctions can be stated in a few words, and the characters of the flights are too much alike to justify their being treated separately. It is enough, perhaps, to say, that in rook-hawking the country *cannot* be too open; that rooks are commonly flown with falcons, not with tiercels; that either eyesses or passage-hawks may be used; and that, if a tree should unhappily be in the way, and the rook takes to it, the crack of a whip will *not* drive him out, but stones and sticks, or some such strong remedies must be employed. This sport being only, or generally, followed in a perfectly open country, often admits of a good gallop; and if the quarry "takes the air" (or "rings"), which is usually the case more or less, we get a sort of approximation to heron-hawking itself. A friend of mine once had a famous rook-hawk — a falcon; she enjoyed getting amongst a flock; for, not content with one stoop or one prize, she passed several times through the whole, dealing death at each blow, and seldom descended until several victims were beneath her.

Hawks may be entered to magpies and rooks by giving them winged birds, or, better than nothing, even dead birds, in the first instance; but it is well to procure, if possible, a bagged quarry that can fly. This may be done with traps, or by rearing young birds taken from the nest. The great objection to the latter plan is that the nestlings make *friends* with you, their distinct characters and dispositions come out, and you know the little birds all by heart; you cannot find in that heart to throw them to the hawks: they have ceased to be a mass of magpies, and have become individual intelligences. You cannot select one, say good bye — and then? Or, if you can, you ought to be thrown to a wild beast yourself; and I should like to train him.

[1] Circulars should be distributed in the neighbourhood with these directions; this plan has been tried, and found excellent.

Chapter Ten - The Chivalry of Falconry

Falconry, notwithstanding its partial revival at the present time — a revival which I have some hopes may yet increase is, as has been said before in this work, still little known to the majority of sportsmen, and utterly strange to nearly all others. We find an occasional mention of it, but only as an ancient romance, in those wonderful books which, coming thick and fast from Abbotsford, bound half the modern world in a spell such as was never felt since the days of William Shakespeare. It would have been strange indeed had the magic which brought before us, just as they existed, every custom and character, every habit and manner of the past, leaving them for ever in our memories, failed to call up the great sport of chivalry itself. And yet I verily believe that the pen which taught us to cast off our merlin at a woodcock with Ann of Greierstein, or whistle the falcon to our hand with Ellen Douglas, spoilt the modern *practice* of the sport of falconry by the very charm with which it invested it. To Walter Scott, or at least to his readers, Falconry was but one ideal being in a long and sparkling pageant. She took her place only in the Past; by the arrow that split the willow-wand at one hundred paces — by the plumed helmet with the lady's glove clasped in it — and by the tall lance; with the ringing of beakers at the feast, with the "St. George for Merrie England," and the solitary Christian warrior who met the lonely Saracen on the plains of Palestine.

> "The knights are dust,
>   And their good swords are rust;
>   Their souls are with the saints, we trust."

I hope and believe they *are* with the saints: they are gone at least, but they have not taken everything with them.

Falconry is of course a mere nothing, after all. It is only a sport. I never said it was more. At any rate it need not be considered *only* a piece of the ancient pageant; but something better than the ancient or the modern perhaps. Things of the kind are in full force. They are useful, though not as matters of bread and cheese. Then let them remain; and don't be angry with me because I want to add or revive another!

I know what you, my lady, who have just thrown down that gilded volume, and are reclining there so gracefully — I know what you imagine falconry to be, — the strange, startling, beautiful fairy-tale of sport; the delicate but haughty creature that, in the middle ages, rode through Europe with a gauntlet on her little left hand, with a train of velvet robes, and plumed caps and buff jerkins behind her; the heroine who gave place only to the hero; she whose silver voice was always heard until the meeting of mace and morion, the shouting of men-at-arms, drowned it in their din. Yes, my lady, you are romantic, and falconry has taken its colour from that of your mind. And you tell us what *you* consider it, Sir Exquisite — you who, knowing about as much of field sports as the butterfly whose plumage and habit you so industriously copy; you who, with these incapacities, amongst a host of others about you, had the gross audacity to review [1] it, and, with your puny pen, to try to transfer to a subject, in which you could have no part or lot whatever, the dulness and frivolity that are so conspicuously your own!

I am a practical man, and I am about to give you, my kind readers, a page or two of *heron-hawking,* not as it appeared in the "olden time," but as it existed a very few years indeed ago; as it existed, to say the truth, among the members of the famous Loo Club in Holland. The paper which I shall present was not written by myself; it was procured by Captain Salvin, who did not write it, but received it from the writer, an eye-witness of what it describes. It is the production of a gentleman whose name I have no direct permission to give; but I may venture to say that he is an excellent falconer himself, and a very near relative of one to whom we all look up — the once fortunate owner of the wonderful hawks, "De Ruyter" and "Sultan." I shall transcribe it almost verbatim.

However, with no wish, I am sure, to tantalize my friends, but rather with the hope that I may enable some of them the better to understand and appreciate it, I shall offer a very few lines on the rudiments of the branch of the sport which it describes.

Those who have seen a cast of merlins fly a good ringing lark, have seen a portion of heron-hawking in miniature; that is, they have seen a quarry attempt to outstrip his pursuers by rising into the skies. One great element in heron-hawking, however, was omitted; the lark was very small and unarmed, whereas the heron is larger than the hawks, has formidable claws, and, above all, a most frightful dagger of a beak. With this he stabs; but the great danger is not as generally supposed, and as Sir Walter Scott represented, from a thrust in the air, but on the ground, when the hawks, having let go to save themselves from the shock of the fall, "make in" to kill the quarry. [2]

Herons (though Mr. Newcome has taken them with eyesses) axe generally flown with passage falcons; birds which, being stronger than eyesses, axe valuable in a sport in which "waiting on" is not required, and "carrying" is impossible. The heron, which might, no doubt, be killed as it rose heavily from a pool or brook by a female goshawk, supposing that the falconer stalked it to within thirty yards or so, is, when once high on the wing, a bird to try the speed of our best falcons. Neither indeed will every falcon venture at first to attack this quarry at all, even though the heron [3] is captured and offered to her. Books are the preliminary game for heron-hawks; but the real "entering" is occasionally a long and unpleasant process, a cock the colour of a heron being sometimes commenced with; also the beak of the heron (employed next) being guarded by a piece of hollow cane or elder, into which it is thrust, and raw beef fastened to its back. The fastened meat, however, is not always necessary.

When the hawk will fly bagged herons well she may be trusted, together with an experienced bird, at wild ones, but on the first trial pains must be taken to give her every advantage, and the falconer must not spare his horse, but take care to be up exactly, or as nearly as possible at the kill, in order to assist the falcons. Herons, as is generally known, build on high trees, and the place of their assemblage is Called an heronry. In the spring, they pass to and from this place to fish, much after the manner of rooks when in quest of their worms and grubs, only that herons commonly fly higher, farther, and, as their favourite water takes them in a particular direction, more entirely over the same ground than rooks do. It is during these journeys, which are called their "passage," that falconers take them. The country must be quite open. The falconers place themselves down wind of the heronry, and look out for the *returning* birds: these, being weighted with the fish and frogs they, have captured, are called "heavy," and are generally flown at; although, as will be presently seen, some hawks are equal to a "light one."

Heron-hawking has been practised even comparatively of late years in this country, both at bagged and wild herons; but owing to the draining of the land, many a good "passage" has been spoilt; one, I fear, in Norfolk. Just now it is almost, if not quite, a dead letter here. Yorkshire, too, was great once; but Clifford and Bramham Moor, of Colonel Thornton's time, are all enclosed: in fact, everywhere is either enclosed or drained — so there's an end on't.

Now for the narrative: —

"Loo, *twelve o'clock, p.m.* Scene, *a bed-room at Mother Camphoo's Hotel. Falconer enters:* — 'Not up, sir? Twelve o'clock. Wind S.W.; rain in the night, and cloudy now. Just a little wind. We must go to the Wesen field.'

"*A voice from the bed.* — 'Open the window! What a fine day for hawking! Have all the hawks out! Tell them to get breakfast ready directly; some fish "bots," which they know how to cook so well.'

"This speaker, and the rest of the members of the club, had dined at the palace yesterday, and managed, somehow or other, to get home late. However, they slept late, and arousing themselves at the falconer's call, got to the field by half-past five. The falconers had been there with the hawks an hour or more, but no heron had passed — it was too hot. However, about six o'clock one was *à la voléed,* coming over very high. The falconers looked glum and undecided. "Sultan" and "De Ruyter" were ready on hand. The fortunate owner of these hawks cries out, 'Will you have a shy, James, or shall I?' The falconer addressed thinks it rather too high for his young hawks. 'Well, then, here goes,' says the former; and having let the heron get a little past, off go the hoods. For a moment one hawk looks up, and is cast off; the other a moment or two afterwards. They both see him; now for a flight! The heron was about 250 yards high, and perhaps a quarter of a mile wide. The hawks had gone up about a quarter of the way before the heron saw them in hot pursuit. 'Now he sees them!' is exclaimed; and the riders rattle their horses as hard as they can, over deep sand-hills, down wind. The heron, in the meanwhile, vomits up his fish to lighten himself, and begins ringing up down wind. It is a curious thing to see the different manoeuvres of the birds. With his large wings, the heron can mount very fair, and has a far better chance of beating off the hawks than if he flew straight forward. This he knows full well by instinct, and puts on accordingly all sail for the upper regions, generally in short rings. Hawks make larger rings as a general rule, if, like these, they are good ones. Those have but a bad chance with a good heron if they adopt the same tactics that he does in mounting. This the two old hawks know full well.

So far they have been pretty near together, but, seeing the prey beginning to mount, they separate, each their own way, now taking a long turn down wind, and then breasting the wind again. 'De Ruyter' makes the best rings, and after having gone a mile, there is a shout — ' Now "De Ruyter" is above him!' and the hawk is seen poising herself for a stoop; down she comes, with closed wings, like a bullet, and hits the heron; it is too high to see where, but the scream the quarry gives is tremendous. Hurrah! there's a stoop for you! Both hawk and heron have descended some yards; the former, from the impetus of her stoop, much beneath the heron, but she shoots up again to a level. In fact, it was a perfect stoop. Though so near the heron she does not attempt a *little* stoop, but again heads the wind, so that the heron appears to be flying the hawk. 'Sultan' is now above both, and makes her stoop, but not so good as her partner's. However she makes two quickly, and is within an ace of catching; but the good heron will not give an inch, and 'Sultan' will have to make another ring for another stoop. But where is 'De Ruyter' all this time? She has made a long ring, and is now a long way above them. She makes another full swoop, and this time there is no mistake about it, for she hits the heron so hard that he is nearly stupefied. 'Sultan' joins in the fray and catches. Whoo-whoo-o-p! down they come. Down they all three go together, till, just before reaching the ground, the two old hawks let go of their prey, which falls bump. Before he has had time to recover himself, in a moment the hawks are on him, 'De Ruyter' on the neck, and 'Sultan' on his body. Hurrah for the gallant hawks! and loud whoops proclaim his capture. 'Wouldn't take 100l. for them,' says their owner, who has ridden well, judiciously as well as hard, and has got up in time to save the heron's life. He gives the hawks a pigeon, and puts the heron between his knees in a position so that he can neither spike him nor the hawks with his bill. He has two beautiful long black feathers, which are duly presented to Prince Alexander — alas! now no more — who is well up at the take. These feathers are the badge of honour in heron-hawking in Holland, as the fox's brush is in hunting in England. The hawks are fed up as speedily as possible, the heron has a ring put round his leg and is let loose, evidently not knowing what to make of it.

"We hasten back as fast as we can, but the weather being now hot, the herons move more by night than by day. Many anxious eyes search the horizon for another. Opera-glasses are brought into requisition, and one gentleman called *à la volée!* to a gnat which got before the focus of his glass. At last two herons are viewed coming flapping lazily along. Every one is again on the alert, and the horses are mounted. It is a fair 'hood off' for the young hawks. A pretty little flight; and the result — the hawks fortunately sticking to the same bird — a capture. He is taken after having made about six or seven rings, and in ten stoops the whoop resounds. Peter, the other head-falconer, has on hand two good hawks to fly, and all are wishing for a good heron to try their merits. In about half an hour one is seen coming rather wide; he has evidently been flown before, and now turns back down wind as hard as if the hawks were after him, being soon lost to sight. Great disappointment. In ten minutes another is *à la voléed,* and brought down in first-rate style. It is eight o'clock, and the falconers feed up. But the owner of 'Sultan' and 'De Ruyter' has a hawk called 'Rocket,' which he does not care much about, as she is sure to crab another if flown with her; besides, she does not trouble herself after two or three stoops. This waiting 'just five minutes longer' ends with the take of another heron at the second stoop. We then scamper off as fast as we can to supper, the late hour of which accounts for midday slumbers.

"The next day was just the one we could have wished for the sport; for, as we had foretold, rain came the evening before, and there were plenty of herons flying. The wind was then S.W., and the field Wesen. About three o'clock we are there, and all the hawks, good, bad, and indifferent, are taken out — some to train who are backward, either from wildness or not taking kindly to heron; some who had been beaten off after long flights, or had been lost, and wanted entering again. About twenty-eight are on the cadges: they begin with a 'train' — *i.e.* a bagged heron — on the way; but, like a bagged fox, it is not good for much, and is soon taken. A little better flight with the next 'train,' and the hawks are promised to fly a wild one to-morrow. These two herons then received their liberty, but would not fly at first a hundred yards at a time, evidently expecting to be pounced on again.

"Here we are at the field; hitherto we have been only on the way to it. The two sets of falconers, with their hawks, place themselves about half a mile apart, to intercept the herons on their passage back from their fishing-grounds. *'À la volée'* is called; it is for Peter; a pretty little flight is the result. The amateurs' horses have hardly time to catch their wind before James is seen just hooding off at another, and we have another flight of much the same sort with a catch. We have just time to light our pipes and get through the best part of one before we are disturbed by another *'à la volée.'* A heron is coming very low; immediately he sees the hawks on wing he vomits up a good-sized eel, and is trying to do the same with something else. Of course he falls an easy victim, for he has a pike of nearly two pounds in his throat, the head of which being downwards, has been digested. The eel is found entire, and is reserved by one of the falconers for supper. Another comes Peter's way, and is bagged; another to James, which escapes — for, as soon as the two hawks are well on the wing, one crabs the other, and they fall fighting to the ground. The heron goes on his way to his expectant family, not even having thought it worth while to throw up the fish. Peter has another chance, but after a few stoops the hawks give up. The truth is, they are reserving the best birds for the arrival of the royal party. However, six flights, with four catches, in one hour and thirty-six minutes, afforded some nice sport.

"The royal party is now seen approaching, some in carriages and some on horseback — a very pretty turn-out. Two casts are on hand, and, as luck will have it, a heron immediately flies close by. After a short flight of half a dozen rings and stoops, the hawks and heron tumble down within a hundred yards of the royal carriages. One amateur rushes in to secure the heron, who gives him a hint of 'noli me tangere' by striking him with his bill close to the eye — a spot herons always aim at. They must be secured by the neck. Another young gentleman, anxious to show the bird's graceful plumage to the royal party, takes hold of the heron, but not scientifically, for, after walking a few yards, he feels the heron's bill in the back part of his neck, and blood is drawn. He gets laughed at, but holds the bird pluckily. Somebody comes to the rescue and holds the bill, while the black feathers are plucked out and presented to the queen; also divers plumes to the *dames d'honneur*. The bird is then dismissed, with much pity from the ladies.

"There is no lack of herons. The little wind there was has fallen to a calm, and they come home higher. All the better, for we have some good casts to fly. One is soon 'hooded off' at, and, after a capital flight, is taken high in the air. The pet hawks are now taken in hand — 'De Ruyter' and 'Sultan;' and, as there is no wind, the owner says he will fly at the first *'light one'* that comes at all fair. All is excitement when one is seen coming *from the heronry,* and therefore unweighted. They are 'hooded off' in his face; he sees them directly, and proceeds to mount. 'Now, good hawks, you will have some work to do before you overtake him!' The knowing riders are down wind as hard as they can go. Ring after ring is made, and yet the hawks seem to gain but little on him. Still they are flying like swallows: 'De Ruyter' makes a tremendous ring, but still fails to get above him. Again and again they ring, and have attained a great height. A scream of delight is heard: 'They are above him; "De Ruyter" is at him! ' A fine stoop, but the heron dodges out of the way. Now for 'Sultan;' but she misses too: the heron is up like a shot, and three or four rings have to be made before there is another stoop. Another and another stoop, with loud cheers from below. 'Sultan' *just* catches him once, but can't hold: it seems still a doubtful victory, when 'De Ruyter' hits him *hard;* and, after two or three more -stoops, 'Sultan' catches him, amidst the excitement of hurrahs and whoops. A really good flight: *can't be better,* — two and a half miles from where they were 'hooded off.'

"We return well satisfied with the sport, and scarcely in time to see another flight going on; still they come over our heads, making a great quantity of stoops, but the young hawks are too eager, and hang at him too much; but they are good plucked ones, and at length pull him down: unfortunately the heron falls with such force that he kills himself. Another comes at a good height, and seeing the hawks as soon as they are off the hand, sets off mounting immediately, after getting rid of his fish. It will be a fine flight if the hawks stick to him, but he is very high before they reach him; they make three or four stoops and then fall below him some distance. They are so high, they look the size of swallows. One makes another stoop and then gives up; the other sticks to him, and is at last entirely lost to sight, — soon afterwards we cannot see the heron; but shrill screams are heard, and the hawk has not giv-

73

en him up yet. The other hawk is taken down with a pigeon. We stand still gazing up, but see nothing more, and the plucky but deserted hawk is taken up half an hour after. A cast or two more are flown, and 'homeward' is the word to dinner, at half-past nine.

"Thus ended as good a day's sport as any one could wish to see. Bumpers of champagne were quaffed to the health of the Royal Family, and the Royal Loo Club; nor were the healths of 'Sultan' and 'De Ruyter' forgotten.

"Alas! we shall never see such sport again; for the club is broken up, and probably the heronry destroyed."

Here ends the narrative. To me it is excessively interesting. And this is not romance but reality. I can only congratulate my readers and myself that I have been able to present them with anything so practical and so charming.

[1] Not *this* work, Sir E., — that has to come.
[2] In the spring of 1854 Mr. Newcome took several herons with "Verbsea" and "Vengeance," two excellent eyess falcons which had been flown at hack by Captain Salvln, at Kilnsey, in Craven, Yorkshire: and this is the first recorded instance of herons killed by nestlings. It has been done by another gentleman this year.
[3] Herons are caught for this purpose on their nests, by a noose drawn over their long legs.

Chapter Eleven - The Peregrine (Concluded).

This short chapter will be found to conclude all I have to say on the peregrine. We have already seen how he is to be captured, either as a nestling or a passage hawk; in what manner we ought to rear him; how train to the lure; enter at pigeons; fly at game, magpies, and herons. It only remains to speak of incidental flights, as perhaps they may be called, such as snipe, plover, etc.

The truth is, that no hawk flies well at any quarry to which he is not accustomed. Even in their wild state these birds pursue with greater eagerness the prey which is most common in their hunting ground. Well blooded to it in their youth, and having it constantly offered to them afterwards, they know thoroughly what to expect at the termination of their labour; they put out their full force on the almost certain promise of a definite meal, which they know, from long experience, will be a good one. Not that they decline other quarry; far from it. The wild hawk is remarkably liberal in his views, and leaves very little reason amongst the feathered tribe for any complaint on the score of partiality. Still, as I have said, a certain preference is observable. In the artificial state of servitude the disposition to prefer one prey to all others is strongly marked. But this is owing to the falconer; by him the natural inclination of the hawk is made use of; and, as he generally has a bird for each quarry, he acts wisely. Besides, when we come to real practice, it is found difficult to make a hawk good, or equally good, at all birds. He is entered at pigeons, because they are easily obtained; and I confess that, for the first *few weeks,* a young hawk will fly almost anything started before him; but these are not adapted to his youthful powers, and so he seldom takes them. The speed of a pigeon, however, his master can regulate by the withdrawal of a feather or two, and the young bird flies successfully at this quarry; hence his great partiality to it. You may enter him at partridges, or what you will, in the manner I have described in other chapters; but he continues to prefer a *particular* quarry, though that quarry is now partridges. In my opinion it is better to let a hawk kill but few pigeons; at any rate to get him on to partridges as soon as you can find any a little more than half grown. He may be tried at snipe also, while they are young, or else going through their moult. Mr. James Campbell, who published a good book on falconry (with, by the bye, one of the strangest prefaces in the world) in 1773, advises his pupils not to enter birds at pigeons at all. This, however, is wrong, and almost impossible. I imagine that in his time there existed a reason for his recommendation which does not obtain now; the country was full of large dovecotes, most farmers keeping " doves," and it was probably very difficult to keep a hawk, that had been entered to pigeons, at his pitch, "waiting on" for game, from which height he could see his first and favourite quarry in all directions.

I had a tiercel, last year, which I never saw leave a pigeon; but he would not look at any other quarry. He had not been properly entered. In the neighbourhood of Somerton, whither in October I had made a long pilgrimage to pay a delightful visit, I was flying this tiercel to the lure; a magpie which had been kept at *hack* by one of the villagers, but which no one can catch now, joined my bird, and flew in his wake. The tiercel took not the slightest notice of him — or, if he did, it was to hasten away: nor is this the only magpie whose presence this hawk has ignored. The case, however, can hardly, perhaps, be considered singular, for so very much depends upon "entering." All birds know when a hawk does not mean *business,* and plague him accordingly: this remark especially applies to the crow tribe.

The peewit or lapwing — the green plover, as it is usually called — affords a tolerably good flight when quite young; but there is scarcely an instance of a hawk taking a strong old bird. It is possible, however, that a cast of tiercels, if *kept* to the quarry, might succeed. This is Captain Salvin's opinion. In ordinary cases the shift from the stoop is so rapid and certain, that the pursuer is entirely thrown out, and soon discontinues the attempt. I once flew a clever female merlin at an old plover, and, as she occasionally struck her prey sideways, I thought it just conceivable she might be successful. There was no doubt about fair speed: the hawk was soon up, but the quarry flew from the stroke several times with such disdainful ease that my bird came back fagged and baffled. Of the two, I should think the peregrine would have less chance than the merlin; the sparrow hawk (though this is simply conjecture) more than either; but it could only be in her first dash from a whirl just over or round a plantation, &c.

Snipe-hawking may be successful with peregrines, especially with the tiercel, when the quarry is young or in moult, and even afterwards; but I need hardly say that the hawk must be entirely free from the vice of "carrying:" so light a quarry would hardly impede a tiercel's flight. Spaniels, or an old slow pointer or setter, accustomed to snipe, may be used for this sport. If the former are employed, they should beat close, and the falconer should know their *manner* well enough to make sure that they are on the point of springing a veritable snipe when they feather fast and begin to bustle about At that moment, and before the snipe rises, let him cast off his hawk. If the peregrine has got to his pitch, he may kill at the first stoop; if not, you may have a long flight; but this quarry is rather difficult to find when it has "put in" at a distance — at least, it must be a very good hawk that will make a point sufficiently accurate to render much assistance. Two or three good spaniels will simplify matters. If you hunt pointers or setters, the flight is regulated after the manner of game-hawking.

Woodcocks will, under advantageous circumstances, show good sport. Of course the immediate neighbourhood of woods must be avoided; but there are little nooks and corners, on and near moors especially, where we find a sort of half-ditch, half-stream, and a sprinkling of low cover. To put a cock up and" mark him down is not often, in such places, a very difficult matter. Let this be done, and the hawk cast off as soon as the cock is down. The former must be allowed to gain his pitch before the dogs are sent in to spring the quarry. The flight may be either long or short; sometimes the cock takes the air, and goes to a great distance. The following, from "Falconry in the British Isles," is a most interesting description of a flight: " A woodcock was flushed on a rough brae-side, and having been marked down in the open, a favourite tiercel was flown, and allowed to attain a commanding position; upon the woodcock being again sprung, it made a rapid zigzag flight over the broad mouth of the Clyde, but finding it could not gain the opposite shore in safety, it returned for the country it had left. The tiercel pursued it eagerly, making the most beautiful stoops, which the quarry as adroitly evaded, until within two or three hundred yards of the shore, when a fatal stroke brought it dead upon the water. The spaniels, seeing this, dashed in, and one of them brought the woodcock in triumph to land, attended by the tiercel, 'waiting on' above its head. The Scotch falconer, having taken up the bird which had been deposited at his feet, threw it to his well-trained hawk to 'take his pleasure on,' whilst the spaniels bayed around with delight — all who witnessed the scene declaring it worthy to be immortalised on canvas."

A friend in Ireland mentions a tiercel which, when flying at hack last summer, chased a heron out of sight on several occasions; kestrels also may be killed with a high-couraged tiercel; [1] the falcon is too slow at the turn.

Wild ducks are flown with the falcon. The hawk may be flown either "out of the hood" or from his pitch; but a duck would not soon rise from deep weedy water, lined with bushes, if the hawk were over her, A tiercel may be used for teal and widgeon. In all cases a small pond or shallow stream should be chosen in preference to broad deep rivers or lakes. Spaniels are necessary.

Sea-gulls, of different kinds, may be taken with the peregrine. They may be approached within a very short distance, as they follow the plough like rooks; but the distance from the sea should be considerably more than a mile. Even the herring-gull has, I believe, been killed with falcons; a peregrine must, however, be of great courage as well as power to undertake the flight thoroughly.

Black-game try a hawk's courage; young ones are easily killed; but the flight of the old black-cock is exceedingly rapid.

The Norfolk, or thick-kneed, plover affords an easy flight.

I could mention many other birds which have been taken by trained hawks, such as curlews; but these were probably killed by chance stoops; and, as they are altogether exceptional quarry, it is useless to treat of them.

We may conclude, at any rate, with safety that Providence has created some few birds, as possibly some few beasts, which, by their speed or cunning, set at defiance the rapacity of their own order.

There is one other flight, a new one in England, with the peregrine, which it is quite worth while to mention: it is with *hares*. I have myself seen even a tiercel stoop with the greatest possible determination at a full-grown rabbit; but it is evident that something might be done in earnest against hares. [2] I need not say that the birds (for there *must* be two) chosen for such a quarry should be strong and high-couraged falcons. This is, in truth, a great sport in India; and though the hares there are smaller than the European, still there is little doubt that matters might be arranged, even with our seven or eight pounders, on the open downs. It would be a fine flight. The falconer and his party would have to be well mounted, for no such course could be a short one. It seems that the falcons stoop in turns from a great height — perhaps, in a good flight, forty times; and the excitement must therefore be excessive. In training, a rabbit should be commenced with, then the birds put to leverets, and lastly to hares.

[1] In the autumn of 1858, the Maharajah Duleep Singh lost an excellent tiercel by its binding and falling with a kestrel on the sea, near Mulgrave castle, Yorkshire. The father (wild, of course) of "Comet," a famous tiercel trained by, and in the possession of, my friend, Mr. Brodrick, was drowned in the sea, having bound to a guillemot. This was in 1857.
[2] Captain Salvin has known three or four old English hares killed by a falcon; therefore the flight would be nearly certain to answer if tried upon the downs. The falcons mast be kept for this quarry alone.

Chapter Twelve - The Merlin (Falco Aesalon)

The merlin (the smallest of our birds of the chase), although a true falcon, must not be considered *typical.* He has indeed the dentated beak, and will occasionally stoop, especially after certain quarry, from a considerable height; but his wings (the second and third feathers of which are almost always, according to my own observation, of equal, or all but equal, length) are proportionately shorter than those of any other falcon, and his mode of pursuit approaches, as a general rule, to something like a stern chase. He has, perhaps, a little tendency also to length of leg; and, on the whole, it may be said of this beautiful and excellent bird that a faint suspicion of the true "hawk" attaches itself to the undoubted prerogative of classification as a true falcon.

The merlin builds on the ground — that is, the pair make a sort of hole among the heather. The number of eggs varies from about three to five; it is possible that six may have been found. These are dotted or mottled brown; varieties, I believe, exist, but I never had the fortune to meet with them. The parent birds are very careful of their offspring; and my friend Mr. Brodrick assures me that he has himself seen the female bird affect lameness, in order to draw away danger from the brood — after the manner of the lapwing, &c. An opinion that hawks, like some gulls, &c, do not breed till after the first moult, is entitled to the most entire respect; indeed, it is no doubt the correct one, though personally I have had no opportunity of testing its accuracy. An exception, however, to the rule has been known in the case of a female sparrow-hawk.

It has always been said that hawks will not breed in captivity, but I have some hopes that an experiment will be tried next summer which may possibly set the matter at rest. I say "possibly," because it could only do so by its success; failure might be variously accounted for. Certainly the merlin — the species fixed upon for the trial — is of all hawks the most adapted to the purpose. An adult male is, however, in request, and I am not sure it will be procured.

The merlin — if it were, I will not say, positively preserved, but if it were not wantonly destroyed — would be common enough in some of the northern counties to enable many a willing man to try his 'prentice hand at falconry, who is now discouraged by the difficulties he has to encounter at the threshold, I have said enough in this little work, and elsewhere, on the utter ignorance which most, though not all, gamekeepers exhibit concerning the "manners and customs" of hawks. I know that many sportsmen are in the same blissful state as their servants; that "trapping" of flying "vermin" is in itself an art, a sport, a business; that the extermination of the finest birds in the world is a feat and an achievement; that an accidental head of game is infinitely more valuable than all the claims of natural history, of a reviving sport, and of *Auld lang syne,* put together. Or, if I do not know these things, it is that I have been lately blinded to them by the noble conduct of a few great sportsmen, who have not thought it unworthy of themselves or their craft to look rather deeply into a question which late years have encrusted with prejudice, but which has come out dear enough to their generosity, because it can never suffer at the hands of sense and courtesy.

This little bird breeds is Northumberland, Cumberland, Westmoreland, sometimes in Lancashire and Cheshire; indeed, it may be looked for, though perhaps not always found, wherever we have, in the north, wild and extensive moors. Thus it is frequent in Scotland; Ireland, too, seems to suit it admirably. For autumn and winter quarters the merlin flies to the south, generally leaving England, probably for Africa, but occasionally not passing our southern coasts. It is widely distributed, being known in all the continents. At Malta it is often taken on passage, with numbers of other hawks. [1]

I have trained and flown merlins for many years, and the hours they must have stood a few inches under my eyes can only, I suppose, be counted by hundreds. Besides this, I have made it my business to examine minutely every stuffed specimen that came in my way, or at all near my way. For these reasons I give the following description of the plumage of these hawks from " Falconry in the British Isles," because my judgment, pretty well matured on the subject by this time, tells me that nothing can surpass it in accuracy, or in a brevity which is consistent with its being accurate: —

In plumage the *female* merlin differs but little in the young and adult state, the old bird having merely a greyish tint mixed with the dark brown of the back, without the light edging to the feathers which distinguishes those of the first year, the breast being similar at all ages, and marked with long dark splashes on a dusky white ground; the edging of the feathers of the back, shoulders, and scapularies is rusty, the shaft of each feather being distinctly lined with a darker tint of brown; the cere changes from blue to yellow, the legs and feet acquiring at the same time additional colour. In the *male,* the change of plumage at the first moult is much more marked. The young bird, being similar to a female, loses the brown colour on the head, back, wings, and tail; this is replaced by a uniform deep slate-blue, with black shafts to each feather, the tail having a broad black bar near the end, with a light tip, and sometimes three or four indistinct narrower bars upon each feather. In this respect individuals differ considerably, some of them having very distinct bars on the tail, while in others there is only the broad one at the bottom. The breast and throat are white, with an imperfect ring round the neck stained with buff red, and marked with oblong blackish-brown spots. The albino variety of this bird has been seen, though we have never met with a preserved specimen.

I confess, when my attention was called to the question whether there was any difference in the nestling plumage of the male and female merlin, that I saw, or thought I saw, something that might justify an answer, though a most qualified one, in the affirmative. For the first few weeks after the birds are full-fledged there is a sort of darkish bloom, clearly observable in some individuals, which is to my taste very beautiful, but which shortly disappears. When it is gone I fancy that the plumage of the hen has in some specimens a *washed-out* appearance, which one does not meet with in the male; but the difference must be slight, and perhaps altogether fanciful, when it has escaped a falconer for years; and I mention the subject here rather to call the attention of my brethren to it, than positively to assert any opinion of my own. It is quite a mistake to suppose with the Rev. F. O. Morris that there is (so I read his meaning) a *gradual change* towards blue in the males before the commencement of the moult. The moulted feathers have, perhaps, a somewhat faded appearance, but that is all. Patches, indeed, of a few blue feathers may occur before moulting time, but they are those which have replaced the true nestling plumage of which, in the spots they cover, accident has robbed the bird.

The eye is black, or at any rate appears so, except in a very bright light, when the pupil stands out as jet in the dark brown of the iris. The average weight of the male is perhaps over five ounces, that of the female full seven ounces. Heavier specimens, however, will not, I think, be found uncommon. The length of a fine female is fully eleven inches, of a male, nine and a half. The differences in size and weight between the sexes is not so great as that in other hawks.

No bird with which we have to deal is so easily tamed, or becomes so familiar, as the merlin. There is nothing more common in my practice than for one of these hawks to. sit upon my head whilst I walk the stubble, and for him to keep that place till a lark rises, A brother falconer, in Hertfordshire, bears the testimony of the same circumstance to their docility. Indeed, this is the only hawk with which I am acquainted that can by possibility be — or appear to be — *too* tame. At any rate you may so pet and feed a merlin in reward of his familiarity, that he will learn to leave the quarry, unless an easy flight, and drop on your head or hand for the food which he knows he will receive. I mention these things now simply to show the character of the bird, and not as anticipating any directions for conduct in the field.

In two chapters with which I presented "The Field" some time ago, I gave the whole history of taking young merlins from the nest, placing them in the hamper, feeding them three times a day (say at seven, one, and seven) with *small* pieces of beef or pigeon, till they are nearly, if not quite, gorged, sounding the whistle in the meantime; I described their introduction to the lure; the gentle degrees by which they should be induced to fly to it, and to the fist, from the edge of the hamper,' and then from a greater distance; the carefully feeding them with *choice* bits from the hand whilst they tug at a tough piece on the lure, so that they may not be disposed to carry, and the whole method of "flying at hack." I need not repeat what I then said, further than to recapitulate it in analysis, as I have just done; because Chapter Four of the present work, written on the eyess peregrine, will apply to the merlin, with the single exception that the latter bird should be taught to fly to the hand as well as to the lure.

Merlins may be taken wild by the clap-net or bownet. This may be done when a nest has flown before the falconer knew that the birds were ready to take; but it is possible to catch old ones on the moors with these nets. They are also sometimes taken on the southern coasts in the winter by bird-catchers, -to whose call birds they come down. The bait, of course, is a live bird, or perhaps more than one. A very singular instance of the capture of a merlin occurred last year, one of my birds being the hero of the tale. By referring to my journal, I find under the head of "Tuesday, July 21st," this short notice: — "One cock merlin missing:" this was from hack. The bird had suddenly, and with very little warning, given up his orderly habit of punctual appearance at meal times, and Tuesday was the first day on which he had not fed from the lures at all. He came no more on duty; and though occasionally doing us the favour of inspecting our proceedings from the air, or even from a wall in the neighbourhood of the house, he sedulously declined all advances made either by his relatives or myself; except on one occasion, when I very nearly had him in the clap-net. He confined his hunting ground to a circle of about three or four miles from the house; and we sometimes heard his little silver bell in the evening, when his road to roost happened to lie our way. I was sorry for his loss, because he appeared to me a very tractable bird, and just before he left us I saw him making some fine stoops at swallows. Under "Wednesday, October 21st," I find the following: — "As I am dressing, a servant comes to tell me that a hawk has been brought in a basket. It turns out to be the lost merlin, which has been away exactly three calendar months. A boy caught him four miles from here, in a horsehair noose." There, indeed, was "Ruby" in bell and jesses; the latter, having been made of strong leather for hack, were unbroken, though somewhat decayed. Poor fellow! he looked rather weak as he sat at the bottom of the basket, though I perceived that slices of bread had been offered him in the most liberal manner; nay, I almost think there was butter on them; indeed it would not at all surprise me to discover that the hospitable woman, mother of the brat aforesaid, had provided tea for him on the previous evening, and been hurt that he had not accepted it. We soon re-arranged the matter of diet, how' ever, and in one fortnight from the day I took him out of the basket he was on the wing, and as tractable as any hawk I ever possessed. The chief thing, however, which makes the story worth relating is the singular means of his capture. In the neighbourhood of my present abode, not very far from Buxton, many of the half-labourers, half-farmers, or their children amuse and occasionally profit themselves by snaring fieldfare in the winter, and thrushes, &c. in the autumn; rather, perhaps, I should say they *did* so — for the custom, I am told, is not so common as it was once. The snare is made thus: — A straight round piece of a branch is cut — from any tree of tough wood — about two or three

81

feet in length, and two-thirds or three-quarters of an inch in diameter. Every twig is carefully taken off, and the marks of the knife obliterated by a method which is rather filthy than difficult — in point of fact, by spitting on very dirty hands, and then polishing the stick therewith. At intervals of but an inch and a quarter, small holes are bored with a nail passer, into which are inserted the knots of black horse-hair nooses, each made of a length of three hairs, doubled and *twisted* so that the noose is of six hairs' strength, except at the loop. It is perhaps more than three inches in diameter when the noose is open to the full. Little pegs driven into the holes, over the knots, make matters secure. The ends of the sticks should, if that were possible, be forked; at any rate, one end forked, and the other broadly notched. Two small bunches of mountain-ash berries are fastened to the stick, some little distance apart, and so as to hang under the nooses. A rather naked tree is now selected in a spot frequented by the birds; a forked branch is found, cleared of twigs, and forced to bend apart a little in order that it may receive, when released, the inserted snare with a tight embrace. Let the operator be careful not to hurt himself:

> "He that of old would rend the oak,
>   Thought not of the rebound;"

but then he was a gentleman who once carried a bullock forty yards on his shoulders, cooked and ate him the same day. It was quite proper that he should try all those little matters, and yet he got his hand caught at last; but who would be a Milo after fieldfare?

On one of these snares my merlin was caught: nothing could have been a purer accident. There was no bait that could attract him, unless he mistook the red berries for raw meat, which is very unlikely. Of course I expected to hear that some small bird was hanging in one of the nooses, and that the hawk came to him; but no such thing. The truth no doubt was this: there were but few trees in the neighbourhood; it was perhaps about three to one against a hawk which passed within a quarter of a mile of the spot resting at all; and, given that he did rest, about twelve to one against his choosing that particular tree. However, once destined for the tree, the odds against his alighting on *that* branch were small, and for the reason that it was probably the only *horizontal* one. Most birds, and especially hawks, sit clumsily on semi-vertical boughs; and therefore, perhaps, it was about an equal chance whether the bird would settle on the one only stick which suited his purpose to perfection, or on any of the hundred that only suited it moderately. You see, therefore, that, through a great piece of luck, no doubt, the capture was probably effected without any real bait, and that the hawk happened to drop upon the only spot, and that a little one, in all his hunting ground, that could have restored him to his master!

It would scarcely have been worth while to tell this tale had it not been connected with the description of a trap, not, perhaps, generally known, but by which (a dozen should be set at once) one's table can be supplied with fieldfare in a good winter, and one's hawks half fed on them. Those that are taken by the neck, and so strangled, are for the man; those caught by the legs alive are excellent for the purposes of entering or feeding the hawk. I think, also, I see something more. Supposing I had known of the existence of this simple snare while "Ruby" came in the neighbourhood of the house, should I not have done *this?* (certainly; and I advise all those who keep merlins or sparrow-hawks, to provide themselves with such snares.) I should have chosen a very small *low* tree, as naked of boughs and leaves as possible; I should have pegged a merlin down on the ground a few yards from it, giving him a whole bird to pick and eat. The snare would then have been inserted on the tree, low down, on the side where the hawk was pegged. "Ruby" would surely have come. He might have settled on the snare as a preliminary measure to disputing the food; or, having struggled for the food (I should have pegged it down), he would have probably flown up on the tempting but delusive bough. Or, as the bird had been accustomed to raw meat, a piece might have been fastened on the snare itself. I shall always keep one or two of these snares by me; they are instantly set, have no appearance of a trap, and, as your help is not wanted, you may retire to any distance to watch them. [2]

Hoods for merlins should be home-made, or procured from Mr. W. Pape, of Newcastle-on-Tyne, to whom I will send patterns, in order that he may get some ready for next summer. I hope, too, he will collect all the young birds he can towards the first week in July, for I am in hopes the sport will have a fair trial next year. And this reminds me to mention, that merlins must be looked for nearly a month later than peregrines; therefore, if any one should be unlucky enough to miss the latter birds, he may probably be able to fall back upon the former. I was unusually successful in hooding the two female merlins I brought up this year, and the plan I adopted was this: I did not show them the hood at all till I began to fly them, or at any rate till the day before (this would not answer with peregrines). I carried a bird into a darkened outhouse, and, by the least light through a chink, slipped on the hood; I then came into the light, and found she pulled through after the least possible shaking the head. I fed her through the hood, unhooded, and replaced her on the block. The next day I did the same, giving, however, only one small mouthful when the hood was on. I then carried her to the field, and she flew instantly out of the hood, with no fear whatever at its removal, and killed a moulting lark. On our way home I succeeded in slipping on the hood at the first trial, while she was in the midst of her meal, the latter part of which she pulled through. After she had been on the block a minute, perfectly quiet, I removed the hood. The same plan was adopted with her sister, and with the same result. Now this is not what is called "breaking to the hood;" I know that. I know that, had the hoods been suffered to remain on the birds for five minutes or so after their return to the blocks, the probability is they would have struggled to get them off. But it is of no use whatever to keep merlins hooded on their blocks, or, if it be, the evil that follows is infinitely greater than the good. Every one who knows my hawks will say that I never had a feather or the web of a feather of a merlin broken by bating, and yet I never hood these birds, except when I carry them to the field, and during the latter part of the way, if a long way, in returning home. I broke the two sisters to the hood in a few minutes, as far as I cared they should be broken; they wore it in peace while on the glove, and flew quarry with eagerness the moment it was removed.

As for bells, I have never been able to get more than one with a tolerable sound, and that by accident, which I think light enough for these little birds. In lark-flying it is essential not to use any. Belling males is, under any circumstances, after hack, out of the question. When merlins are expected to fly right good ringing larks, the jesses should be made out of an old white kid glove, and well stretched and greased before they are put on. You *may* have to renew these every fortnight; but even that is better than over-weighting the birds.

On a fine summer's day these hawks may be placed on the lawn, the blocks being removed into shade during the heat of mid-day. On summer nights, the "rustic shed," described in Chapter Six, will answer very well for merlins. In rough winter nights, and when snow is on the ground, nothing can be better than a dry loft, the floor sprinkled with sand, on which is placed a block or two, while a couple of perches run from wall to wall. Here two or three good-tempered birds may be kept together at liberty; here they may have a bath, and here you may feed them with chopped meat, given bit by bit to each bird, as the set of them sit on your arm; or perhaps one on your glove, another on your shoulder, a third on the perch, and so on. You won't, of course, dream of throwing anything *whole* among them — at least if you value their plumage or their lives. I have, besides this, a large pen out of doors, most carefully made, in this respect at any rate, that everything connected with the interior should be smooth and round, so that not a feather may be broken. I often change the birds about — perhaps every two days — from the pen to the blocks, and from the blocks to the pen.

There is no use in denying that merlins are delicate. They die when in captivity, I believe, nine times out of ten, from one of two causes: they are either killed by famine or by damp. It is folly to say, that as they must be flown sharp-set, you cannot do this or that. You must feed them twice or occasionally three times a day, *if you intend them to live.* I have given a female bird, in high condition, a slight feed (no castings, of course) at nine in the morning, and killed a ringing lark with her at one or two in the afternoon! However, I do confess that even a merlin may become coy and independent, and that on occasion she may be taken down, to use the vulgar formula, several pegs with advantage. But this must be done skilfully — that is, in other words, it must be done gradually. Is it a bull to add to this, that you must not be long about it either? I think not, because I wish you to do very little in the matter at all.

With regard to damp, it is horrible; it produces disordered liver and green mutes, bad throats, tender, inflamed crops, and food discharged from the mouth like castings. Damp! Poor, poor "Pearl!" I would give good money were you alive again; and you, too, my little "Emerald," as swift as any hawk, and more brilliant than any at a catch! I could not keep the damp from your homes, my pets, though I tried my hardest, because we were sopped, and steamed, and drenched here for weeks and weeks. Oh, that I had turned you out at hack even in the rain! it would not have hurt you at liberty; and better have lost you in life than stuffed or buried you dead! It is too late; but I will yet tell people that you were brave birds, and I think they will be sorry that you were obliged so soon to leave the world and "Peregrine."

[1] There is a small hawk, similar in size to the merlin, but of very different plumage (more like that of an old tiercel), used in the East.
[2] My gardener has to-day brought in a couple of live fieldfare thus taken, which were the very things I wanted for a sick peregrine.

Chapter Thirteen - Is Entirely on Lark-Hawking with Merlins

Merlins may be flown at almost any quarry which is not much larger than themselves; but swift and courageous as they are, it must be an unusually bold and strong female which will *stick* well to a full-grown partridge; and as for wild larks, in full plumage and condition, it is only occasionally that the very best merlins can take them.

As the lark flight is *the* flight with this hawk, I shall place it first here, and enter fully into the subject. I have, a few times in my life, seen such brilliant flights, concluded by a kill, when the lark was a wild one, and in full strength and plumage, that, could the capture of such quarry happen even once out of three times, I should esteem the sport as nearly the finest in the world. But as the best merlins that were ever reared are, as a rule, overmatched by a good wild lark, falconers find it necessary to introduce an artificial element into the sport. That which the birds cannot obtain by their own determined exertions, their master must procure for them; he must, in short, *help* them, and this he can do by providing himself with bagged larks — not that every flight need be at a lark which has been previously captured for the purpose; if *that* were the case I for one should care very little for the amusement. The use of the bagged quarry may be stated as twofold; in the first place when, after a fine long ringing flight, the lark has been driven into a wall of loose stones (in which there is sometimes a run of a dozen yards), or into a thick hedge full of brambles, which perhaps straggles into the ditch — in fact, anywhere from whence the quarry cannot be shortly recovered — it is absolutely necessary to be able to produce a live lark from your bag. Merlins are persevering, and will fly a bird into the clouds; they do not grudge the most desperate exertion, but (after the first few flights) they will do none of this unless experience has taught them that the chances of success are in their favour. It may occasionally happen that wild merlins follow a ringing flight to the end, but it is a very rare occurrence. Nature will not permit her children to make such excessive efforts when the prospect of reward is worse than uncertain. Art suggests a remedy and supplies a deficiency; then Nature re-examines the matter, and gives her consent that it should be carried out. The proper way of offering the bagged lark I shall mention presently. The *second* use I spoke of is the following: — You fly your merlins, or cast of merlins, at a wild lark, which, we will say, escapes, after a long flight, by power of wing, the hawks leaving it at last in the sky. It may be taken as a rule that no merlin will continue a first-rate bird if it is disappointed twice consecutively on several occasions. Therefore, after a long unsuccessful flight, I would take the hawks up with a dead lark on a string, give them two or three mouthfuls each, without feather, and, in an hour or two, fly them at a bagged lark, in an open place, a couple of feathers having been taken from a wing of the quarry, if a strong, full-plumaged bird, and recently caught. Care must be taken, however (and this I think a very special point indeed), that the merlins don't see you throw the lark up. If they find you out they will soon be shy of wild birds, and only follow those for the easy catching of which they know you have made private arrangements.

Give, therefore, the bagged lark to your friend or servant, and let him seem to walk it up, while in reality he jerks it from him with a motion unseen by the hawks. Perhaps a better plan still is to feed your birds up after an unsuccessful flight, and reserve the bagged flight till the next day. Don't shorten the flight of the lark too much; he is pretty sure to be somewhat inferior to a wild one, and your object is not to make the flight very easy; if you do, the merlins will learn to give up birds that dash swiftly from them, and your object will be defeated, because the thing will be overdone. Another plan is to throw up a lark, its flight considerably shortened, just as your birds are coming down to you after leaving the quarry in the clouds, taking care to cheer them well as you do so. The notion, in this case, which you are to try to originate within them is that the lark you (still disguising what you do) throw up is the one they have chased, and which has been compelled to seek safety on the ground, though they did not know it. This may not seem a very clever delusion, but it is certainly better than using no bagged lark at all. I have a great notion myself that it *does* deceive the hawks, at any rate, for a time. It is certainly attended with very little trouble. By these means, because they induce the hawks always to persevere, you may occasionally kill a wild lark in *perfect plumage,* and that, though it ought to happen several times in a season, is a great feat. You will also fly bagged larks in *full* plumage; these afford good exciting flights, only there is, to me, an awkwardness in the fact that they are not wild quarry.

So much for the lark, while he is in the pride of his full power, when, in fact, he sometimes goes up whistling, out of sheer impudence, though the hawks are climbing fast. But we must inquire into his condition, prospects, and fate at another, and to him a most alarming and dangerous, period. This is the time of *moult.* From the beginning of August till the middle of September larks are moulting. Possibly they commence the operation sooner than the former month I have named; but their arrangements then are to me, practically, of little moment. I only know that they are in perfect plumage by the end of September, and so do my hawks, to their cost, poor things. [1] Now it so happens that when their quarry is in moult, the young merlins themselves, though not much more than two months old, and in a measure weak, are fast gaining their full powers; and I think their courage and determination are, at first, almost greater than we find them in older, more discreet, and more experienced birds. Therefore it is that moulting larks get most unmercifully slain. When in full moult they have really no chance with a commonly good merlin, supposing they are 200 yards from cover; nay, I would give 100 yards start in such a case. Occasionally, at this time, however, you will spring a fine fellow that will give something like a ringing flight; this, I fancy, must be an early nestling of the year, for, as such, he would be in full feather.

Unless the country is very much enclosed with impenetrable fences, you may have at the season I mention, several weeks' hawking without the trouble of bagged larks. Two out of three moulting larks will keep the birds in order; but kill four out of five if you can. Towards the end of August and the beginning of September very fine sport may sometimes be had, for the larks are nearly, though not quite over their moult, and chances are remarkably well balanced. Your birds, too, have been accustomed up to this period to look upon a kill as almost a matter of certainty. Perhaps the very finest possible flights are those which go quite into the clouds (as it seems), when not only the lark vanishes but the hawks are lost to sight also. But I fear I must say that these scarcely ever terminate in a kill; at least I was never certain of one, though it may have happened, when my birds, after such a flight, have been lost for an hour or more in an enclosed part of Northamptonshire. However, such flights as these probably will not begin, as a rule, till the end of September.

The following is a nice, quiet flight — nothing "loud" about it, as your tailor would say, but quite a neat, gentlemanly flight, sir. On Saturday, August 22, 1857, I went on the moor, accompanied by a friend, to look for a snipe in the damp pants of it. I had poor "Pearl," a female, on one hand, and "Hornet," a cock bird, on the other. I had a notion at that time that I could make merlins kill snipe. I may as well say at once that I failed, though I don't yet despair of it being done. We had hunted for snipe for an hour without finding one: my fingers ached with holding the jesses of the hawks, which were carried un-hooded, one on each hand. At last a lark got up, and I flung the merlins after him. The quarry "took the air" in a moment, and without hesitation — a sure proof that he was confident in his own powers. They did not go so *very* high; at least, even the lark was always plainly in view. They would not let him rise after a certain point, though he persisted in attempting to do so. His determination was unusual, considering that he was continually stooped at. No sooner did he fly from under the very foot of one bird than he shot up in the most gallant style, only to run the gauntlet with another. They were both good footers, but it seemed as if they could not touch him. There was some wind, and we had to run, though the continual stooping kept the flight near us. At length the three birds seemed to get into a current of air, and passed off more quickly. A bend in the moor hid them from our sight. I ran till I could hardly speak, but did not see the finish. At last we observed the cock bird on a wall. "Pearl" was underneath, in the midst of a heap of feathers; and, after preparing her meal, had just begun to eat it. She did not show the smallest disposition to "carry" on this occasion; and, on the whole, though nothing extraordinary, it was a very pretty thing indeed. I agree with Mr. Newcome in thinking that hen merlins have more perseverance than males, at the same time, I have had two, perhaps I may say three, of the latter sex which were most wonderful lark flyers, and for some time (they were spoiled at last from the impossibility of procuring bagged larks) flew their quarry into the clouds. The distance of the flight just mentioned was a good half mile from end to end; but I have had several of a mile, though not often with such good points about them as the one I have selected to record here. Very often, when a lark rings out of sight, the hawks are scarcely able to stoop at him at all, though they follow. A friend of mine, in Herts, took a wild lark the other day with a cast of merlins — a thing not to be done easily in the winter. His birds are eyesses. Mr. Newcome has taken several in the winter with wild-caught merlins; but haggards are so given to carry, that I should prefer to keep them for heavier quarry than larks.

If the field is any distance from home, it is right to hood the two hawks, and carry them on the left arm and hand. I have a *spring* swivel, with two or three inches of leash, fastened to my glove half-way between the elbow and wrist, to which the jesses of the first bird are easily hooked; the second bird has also a spring swivel, and his ordinary blockleash is wrapped round the hand. When the field is entered, I take the hawk from the left *arm* to the right hand (so that there is a bird on each hand); unhook the swivels from the jesses, holding the birds only by the latter; then I unhood them with my mouth and spare fingers, putting the hoods into a leather box fastened round the waist. It is easier, however, to do all this if you have the assistance of a friend, who will unhook the jesses, &c. The merlins learn, in a very few days, for what purpose they are thus carried. Supposing there to be little or no wind, they will sit perfectly still, only at least moving their heads quietly from

side to side, that a sharp look-out may be kept for the quarry which they expect at any moment to see rise. He will scarcely have left the ground, and
probably before you can see him, when both hawks will spring violently from
your hands. Open your fingers at once if you can, so that the hawks may not
be checked or detained; and this is easy enough when you see the lark at the
same time that they get sight of him; when you do *not* you may be forgiven
for stopping them during the fraction of a second. Give them a cheer or two,
and then let them fight it out; except that it is well to cheer any extraordinary
effort of either bird, nothing more need be said to them. Care only must be
taken, as I have observed in a former chapter, to make a broad distinction in
sound between the cry which excites to exertion after a flying quarry, and
that which calls them to the lure.

If the flight ends in a kill, you may be in time to reach the birds while they
are struggling for the quarry, each having a foot on it. In this case nothing is
easier than to take the captured lark in one hand, whilst with the other you
thrust a peg (previously prepared) into the ground, having a live or dead lark
attached to it by a string of two feet long. One of the merlins will easily be
persuaded to release his hold of the capture for the lark produced by you. If
you don't intend to fly again immediately, allow both birds to take their
pleasure on their larks, the one on the ground, the other in your hand; and, if
you wish to feed up for the day — as probably you do if you allow castings —
give occasionally to each bird a small piece of fresh beef, which has been
bruised to make it tender. If one hawk has driven the other away by the time
you get up, take that other down to a dead lark, and proceed as just recommended. Should the flight have been entirely unsuccessful, and you have no
bagged lark with you, or do not wish to throw one up, take the birds down to
the ordinary horseshoe-shaped dead lure, to which they were accustomed
during hack, and which it is better that they should not forget. If you are using only one bird, which does not plague you by "carrying," and this bird has
u put in " a lark where the cover is too dense to permit of its extrication — *i.e.*
if you cannot retrieve it — take out a bagged lark, draw most of the feathers
from one wing, and jerk it towards the hawk when she is close to you, after
you have pretended to beat earnestly for about one minute. She will certainly
think it is the quarry she "put in." But if your bird is (as most merlins are) at
all given to "carry," or if you are flying two, offer a live lark in a two-yard creance, and affect to drag it out of the bush or wall — perhaps, indeed, this is
the safer plan under any circumstances; however, I would take care that the
creance is a dirty green, and not conspicuous in any way. When, in the winter, you find that a cast of hawks have not taken a wild lark for some time,
rest them for a day or two, then choose the better one, and fly her alone
where there are *many* fences. The lark being stooped at, and missed, and seeing no second hawk underneath ready to take him should he drop, is not unlikely to cause himself to fall, like a stone, into a fence; then you are in luck,
for if you can't find the real Simon Pure, you can immediately produce a

counterfeit, as before described; and the incident will be worth anything in the world to the character of the hawk. The same experiment can be tried with your other birds.

So much for flights with merlins, which are really in order, and constantly worked at larks. But it is a duty, which I must not forget, to give a hint to the tyro that *this* may happen to him: — He may take his merlin up from hack, break him to the hood, find him most obedient to the horseshoe lure, take him to the field in the most orthodox and confident manner; possibly he may engage a few friends, to whom he has lectured on this interesting subject at almost as great a length as I have done, to witness a first but a conspicuous triumph. Up may get a lark in the most obliging manner a few yards from his feet; the welkin may ring with his first real "hoo-ha-ha-ha;" and with the most perfect imitation of that exciting cry which his admiring friends can accomplish; when lo! horror I nay delusion I — it can't be true — after six weeks of trouble and a year of hope — the lark goes off quietly and happily one way, while the "trained hawk " circles round his master's head for food, or flies off lazily another! Patience, my dear sir, you must "enter" your merlin; *that's all*; and it's soon done.

This *may* happen; but it is not every merlin that requires entering from the hand or creance; the best I ever had *did.* Still, only last year I flew two nestlings at moulting larks which rose from a field, and entered them in that way. Females are not so likely to require the artificial entering as males are. A good deal, no doubt, depends upon what the birds have killed during the end of hack, or whether they have killed anything. Before the hawks are "taken up" I would let them kill a lark in creance; you *may* capture them with it, if you please, giving a full meal, but I think I would use the common lure for that. When they are broken to the hood and made tame with what is called "handling" (which only means carrying the birds, hooding them, and so forth), throw up another lark in the open, with its flight shortened, but not in a creance, unless you think the hawk is given to "carry;" or you may compromise matters, and have a yard of fine string fastened to the lark's leg (which, by-the-way, will impede its flight sufficiently), so that, on approaching the hawk after the capture, you may secure the end of this string, and thus frustrate an attempt to "carry," should it be made. It is during these trials that the cry of incitement to chase is first taught. Any hawk that has not been spoiled will permit you, when he has killed, to put your hand within a foot of him, though he may not, at this early stage, allow you to touch his prize. After this, get on to wild moulting larks as fast as possible.

As for "waiting on," there are very few merlins indeed that will do it well, and it is by no means necessary. When a lark is "put in," these little hawks, if they are unable to follow the quarry into cover, or if they lose sight of him, *settle* as close as possible to the place where he vanished. I have stood a yard from another man, hunting with our hands in long grass for the lark which has been driven there after a hard flight, the hawk remaining on the ground between us as staunch as a pointer, and having found the quarry, which dare not move, I have given it to the little beauty who so well deserved it. I always keep the legs of wild larks taken in fair flight, and having assigned to each of my birds a particular colour (sometimes chosen in reference to its name), I tie the legs together, after they are varnished with mastic varnish, with silk of the hue belonging to the bird, and thus I know at a glance which merlin took this, and which that.

I have worked out as well as I am able the whole subject of lark-flying. In the next chapter I shall conclude what I have to say on the merlin, as well as convey to my readers all that I know about that beautiful little falcon, the Hobby.

[1] Evidently an example of a provision made for the weak by a Providence whose "mercy is over all His works." If the prey were in full vigour whilst the hawk's powers, either owing to youth or moult, were imperfect, the rapacious birds would starve. What worse than folly it is to talk of God's creatures being "greedy" or unfit to live, because they sustain life as He *intended* they should sustain it. How dare you, squeamish and morbid sentimentalist, take that fly out of the spider's web? Who taught that poor creature to weave that exquisite net for its sustenance? The same Being who, had he treated you according to your folly, would have made you break stones upon the road for your daily bread.

Chapter Fourteen - Merlin Concluded

Merlins which are used for lark flying even in August and September, *ought* to be kept entirely to that quarry; but if it be in contemplation to fly them at larks throughout the winter, their owner must make up his mind never, under any circumstances, to permit them to kill anything else. And, if, by accident, they do make a flight at a thrush, blackbird, &c, let him devoutly hope that it may be an unsuccessful one.

And what is true in this respect of lark-flying, is true also of pigeon-flying. A merlin (female of course) intended for the latter flight, and ultimately, perhaps, for partridges, should never be permitted to kill a quarry which is easily mastered. In the case of larks, the difficulty which merlins have to contend with is *speed*; in that of pigeons and partridges it is chiefly *strength*; as well, indeed, as with their own fear, which the large size of the quarry sometimes engenders. I will suppose that you wish to test the powers of a hen merlin at large quarry. You have two or three hens at hack; perhaps there is a dovecote near your house, or in its premises; do any of the hen merlins, which have been on the wing for three weeks or so, fly the pigeons? I don't mean, do they kill any, but do they chase them at all? Yes; you think they all give them a turn occasionally; but one certainly begins to take up the matter in earnest; she really strikes, while the others turn off as soon as they get very near. But she screams so fearfully, even when her meal has been much greater than her sister's, that you think, upon your word, you shan't be troubled with her. You are sure, and rightly sure, that in lark-hawking she would sit on your hand, with her feathers up, making a noise so hideous that the larks would, in many cases, either get up out of distance, or lie so close that it would puzzle you to find them at all; therefore you will part with her. Please to give me the refusal; I want just such a bird to make certain experiments with on partridges. For, be sure she has indomitable pluck; she has no eye for size, and little notion of times and seasons; she is always prepared. She may have to be flown alone, however, as she might, if sharp-set, make quarry of her own sister. I am far from wishing to say that *no* silent birds are courageous; but I never met with a merlin such as I have described which had not unusual courage. These are the birds (they occur in the proportion of about one to twelve) that, when desperately hungry, two or three times in their lives perhaps, chase a full-grown grouse (which, however, if it be unwounded, they cannot hold), and thereby convince the very logical mind of a gamekeeper, or other scientific gentleman, that merlins mostly feed upon grouse, or at any rate reject all food which has not a truly game flavour. I do the merlin, however, less or more than justice (as you will), for the hero of these wonderful tales is seldom this little hawk at all, but a bird of a larger species. Scientific gentlemen sometimes don't know very much more than that a hawk is *not* a hernshaw — at least at a little distance and on the wild moor.

Choose, then, this screamer for your purpose, which I have mentioned above; and if she chance to have size as well as courage, she is a valuable bird indeed. Her relatives I will suppose you intend for smaller quarry; let us consider how she is to be treated, with the view of making her a first-rate pigeonhawk in the first place, and a partridge-hawk in the second.

During the last ten days of hack, or as soon as she is observed to chase pigeons, call her down to a dead pigeon lure; allow her to plume the neck and to feed from it, as well as from the upper part of the breast; insert also the most delicate morsels of tender, fresh, juicy beef-steak into the breast, whilst you are helping her to make her meal, and contrive that she may pull them out, as if they were part of the pigeon. In a couple of days kill a pigeon, as the hawk is coming down to you. The muscles of a dead bird do not lose their action the instant sensation has departed, and the hawk will therefore feel the pigeon struggling under her for some seconds after she has seized it. Open this bird's head and breast, assisting the hawk in removing the feathers, and then let her take her pleasure upon it. The next day, keep your hawk waiting an hour for her breakfast (though with an eye on her movements), and when she is called, throw up a young living pigeon that can fly about twenty yards. Wait till she has found the neck, and has it firmly grasped in the terrible vice of one of her feet; then assist her, and let her take her pleasure as before. Do not even permit her to eat a lark, far less fly her at one. Try to impress upon her that there is no such thing as quarry apart from birds as large or larger than herself. It will be very easy, should you ultimately wish it,

92

to make her take blackbirds and thrushes; but if you begin with small birds you will probably be disappointed in any attempt you may make with pigeons afterwards. Perhaps this remark, however, applies only to the generality of merlins, and not so much to the extraordinarily courageous bird which I have described; but even with such a one I should undoubtedly carry it out in practice. You will find that a single good merlin, or (better still) a cast, will make excellent flights even with strong old pigeons; the struggle on the ground, however, is trying to the hawks, especially to their *tails*. A quarry as large as a pigeon is rather frightened than knocked down by merlins, though they strike and make' the feathers fly; it is almost invariably killed after it has dashed, or attempted to dash, into low cover, where it is followed and strangled. That habit of following into cover makes *good* merlins more deadly with pigeons than perhaps even the peregrine himself.

In making the attempt to get on (for it is a step) from pigeons to partridges, you will be encountered by some difficulties. You may, when it is impossible to procure young bagged partridges, select a few pigeons as nearly brown as you can find them, and rather young, so that the flights shall be easy, and have them thrown up in stubble or turnips, by some one who shall pretend to beat them up; or it would perhaps be found to be a good plan to have a pigeon-shooting trap hid in the field, the string being pulled when you are within fifteen yards of it. Young landrails, in some counties, are not unfrequently caught by the hand in the fields at the breeding season; and they attain a considerable size before they can fly. These given from the hand, as they are near enough the colour of the partridge, and very strong, may be of use. This, however, is a matter of accident, and almost of indifference; and, in truth, these are somewhat clumsy expedients when taken alone. I think I should not trouble myself with either of them until I had failed in the following: — Get some half-grown partridges marked down; take your merlin (which, remember, has been in the habit of killing pigeons — I hope brown ones) when sharp-set, if possible into the very middle of them; and may your devout wish, that the first bird she flies shall not drop into the turnips, and escape by the legs, be accomplished! If she kill, let her gorge herself on the quarry; and get on, by degrees, to full grown birds. You will find the struggle on the ground desperate indeed, and you must "make in" very quickly, or you may lose the partridge; his stout strong legs make it difficult for the merlin to throw him and reach the neck with her honest never-flinching talon. On the whole, this flight somewhat overtaxes the strength of any merlin.

When live partridges *can* be procured, and the merlin is destined for the quarry, they should be given instead of the pigeons during the end of hack. Were I commanded by a certain king to present him within a given time with a cast of merlins for partridge-flying; he appending to that command, in case of failure, several pleasing little punishments, which, while they would probably be sport to him, would certainly be death to me; — but were he in his clemency to give me the service of an eminent poacher — I should say to that slave (as soon as I saw symptoms of the merlins preying for themselves), "Procure me, oh most vile of mortals! between the rising and setting of the stars, three brace at least of live partridges two-thirds grown; in default of which offering I shall make such arrangements in connexion with thy head as shall have a very material influence upon the length of thy shadow!" After calling down my hack birds to a dead partridge, and feeding them in the manner described when pigeons are the quarry, I should on the day follow-ing wring the neck of one of these bagged young birds, as it were in the very face of the merlin (as also described in the case of pigeons), and then day af-ter day offer the "train" (*i.e.* the bagged birds) at first, with their flight con-siderably shortened, and at length in an open place, unimpeded by any re-straint whatever. This being accomplished, and the hawks having never been permitted to feed on anything but a partridge [1] (or beef out of a partridge), I should take them amongst a wild covey of young birds, having of course a live partridge with me, with which to recompense the young hawk in case the real quarry should escape in cover. Then it would not be improbable that the Grand Vizier would be decapitated, and I installed in his office, to say nothing of the offer of the dozen hands of half-a-dozen princesses, and the prospect in due time of conspiring against my father-in-law, making matters smooth and agreeable in connexion with *his* head, and finally ascending the throne amidst the plaudits of my people.

A friend of mine had a merlin which took partridges Well; it was an unu-sually courageous bird; once flew a kestrel, and once killed a magpie — both thrown up from the hand. Last spring I had a strong female bird at large; she had been at liberty during the winter, occasionally preying for herself, but generally coming down to be fed. She usually sat on a tree about two hun-dred yards from the house; and, the moment the window was open and my arm thrust out, she came to my glove. She was an excellent lark-flyer, but somewhat pf a coward, and afraid of a strong pigeon. Knowing that she was rather discreet than valorous, I was surprised, one day, on looking out of the window, to observe her dashing round a tree, in the most excited manner, the object of her pursuit being a magpie which was crouching amidst the branches. I had unfortunately, at that moment, no available help, no one within call; but I ran to her assistance as fast as

I could. We dislodged the magpie; and no peregrine in the world could have made finer stoops than she did. Other trees were near, but before the magpie could reach them, the hawk had shot up to a distance twice the height of the house, and spun down with the speed, if not of a bullet, certainly of an arrow, almost brushing the quarry's wing as she passed. She seemed to have been enchanted by a kind fairy; the very manner as well as the spirit of some dead peregrine possessed her. Rising above the next tree, she "waited on," as though she had made a pilgrimage to Ireland with Captain Salvin, and killed a hundred magpies. I was on the point of putting the quarry out a sec-ond time, when, the good fairy having left us for a moment, a confounded witch, passing by on her broomstick, and seeing that we were on the very point of accomplishing a thing not on record, [2] changed herself into a magpie, and appeared at the distance of about a hundred yards from us. Instantly the merlin went off in pursuit; as instantly did that witch take to cover; and I went on, beating out first one magpie and then another, till my hawk and myself were "beat" also. In sober earnestness, had I been supported by beaters, and had there been but one magpie instead of two, the hawk would have killed. This merlin flew a few magpies afterwards, but with no spirit at all, and I gave up making the attempt to enter her. She is not the only bird of this species which I have seen suddenly possessed of the most wonderful qualities, and almost as suddenly lose them.

The ring-ouzel has occasionally afforded me excellent sport with the little hawk under our consideration. The great and only difficulty one has to contend with in conducting this flight is the certainty that about five ouzels out of six will contrive to dash into a wall of loose stones, or into the rocks, in the neighbourhood of which they are found. I have many a time, when this has happened, thrust my hand in after the quarry, the hawk sitting on the top of the wall, and yet I have only been able to touch the tail feathers, two or three of which I have drawn out with my two fingers, and lost the bird after all. Observe that cock ring-ouzel on the wall! He sees you and he sees the hawk, but he chatters the most absurd defiance. At length he skims along on the other side; the merlin is off your hand in a moment; you hear a shriek, continued in a sort of squeal; he was taken just as he was entering a crevice. Or again, you will see a bird of the same species, and perhaps of the same sex, behave very differently. He will squat on the wall the moment he observes the hawk, his breast pressed close to it, and the white of his throat looking like a white pebble. He may even be able to slip off on the other side without the hawk catching sight of him at all. The merlin should have a live ouzel (or a blackbird will do as well) given from the hand, when it has been impossible to retrieve several from the walls, and she has flown a third or fourth to cover. The sparrow-hawk would, I fancy, be a famous bird for this flight.

Last spring we were somewhat startled by a dash and flutter against the window. A hen ring-ouzel had sought refuge from the merlin mentioned above; but she was taken just as we turned round to see what was the matter.

I may observe that, when I have wished to enter a merlin to ouzels and have been unable to get live quarry, I have taken the gun, the hawk following me; from catching wounded birds she has soon been encouraged to fly and kill uninjured ones. Merlins will take blackbirds and thrushes put out of *low* turnips or potatoes; but it will be found that, while few or none refuse a thrush, several require a proper entering to blackbirds. The flesh, too, of the blackbird, and indeed of the ring-ouzel, does not seem very palatable to them.

I think that full-snipes, when young, and found in their breeding-places, as also when in moult, might easily be killed with merlins; with jack-snipe there would be little difficulty. But it is, perhaps, worth observing, that some of my very best lark-flyers, and female birds too, have refused to follow a snipe above a couple of hundred yards, and in time ceased even to make an attempt; at the same time, I ought to say that I have seen a female bird of my own, not entered to the quarry, fly a snipe through its numberless turnings for more than half a mile, but lose it at last. However, anything can be done by proper entering; and, were snipe to be obtained alive, to serve as bagged birds, at a moderate cost, and could a store be *kept* alive, nearly as fine sport might be had with this quarry (and that, *ultimately*, in its wild state) as with larks themselves; besides, there would be a satisfaction in procuring a bird for the table, in a manner, at present, so unusual.

I have seen merlins fly the common plover, but never saw them take one. The landrail would be easily taken, in an open place, especially by a bird accustomed to partridges. Quail would make famous sJ)ort, if there were any; and in the East the small hawks are flown at this quarry with uncommon success.

I have endeavoured, in the first of these three chapters on the merlin, to give such a description of the bird, when seen either adult or young, either male or female, as must enable any one, however unacquainted he may be with ornithology or falconry, to recognise it, on a close inspection, without hesitation. And I will only add further, with regard to its appearance, that when on the wing at too great a distance to display much of its colour, the species may be detected by the manner of the flight. The wings of the sparrow-hawk are short, and have somewhat of a rounded look in the air; those of the hobby are exceedingly long, and their length gives a swallow-like appearance to the bird; the mouse-hunting kestrel is constantly balancing himself, with his head to the wind, at a greater or less distance above his prey; but the wings of the merlin are neither so short as those of the sparrow-hawk, nor so long as those of the hobby. He may be seen rapidly skimming along, at no great distance from the ground; or ringing after a bird that has " taken the air; " or following the straight, or the zigzag, line of a quarry with such wonderful (apparent) accuracy, that one is almost tempted to believe there is a path in the air by which "her way may be found," till reminded of the absurdity of such a notion by our senses; and perhaps recollecting that divine and glorious simile by which, in the Book of Wisdom, the vanity of pride and the transient nature of riches are shown: — "All those things are passed away like a shadow, and as a post that hasteth by; and as a ship that passeth over the waves of the water, which when it is gone by, the trace thereof cannot be found, neither the pathway of the keel in the waves; or as when a bird hath flown through the air, *there is no token of her way to be found*, but the light air being beaten with the stroke of her wings, and parted with the violent noise and motion of them, is passed through, and therein afterwards no sign where she went is to be found."

The character of the merlin is soon recapitulated. The bird is docile, courageous, almost intelligent. More than any hawk it seems made for the service of man; as fax at least as its inclination, though not as far as its power, extends. Individuals vary in their respective strength, but more especially in their courage, and yet I have seldom met with any that could be termed cowards. Generally they are eminently daring, though their boldness is not unlike that attributed to the ancient Gauls, and indeed to our modern neighbours; impetuous at first, it fails before discouragement. This, as I have already said, will be found when they have been overmatched, for several times, either by strength or speed. On the whole, I would most strongly recommend them to the young falconer, who will make a great mistake if he take the sparrow-hawk in preference. In skilful hands this latter bird is, as will presently be shown, very effective in *some* flights; but let the tyro commence with the merlin; and, if he will take my advice, I will pledge my credit that, with ordinary management, he shall not be disappointed.

The Hobby (*Falco subbuteo*). — I regret to say that this bird (somewhat larger than the merlin, except perhaps as to its feet) is exceedingly rare in the British Isles. I once begged its mutilated body from a gamekeeper's museum of stinking cate, stoats, rats, magpies, and kestrels; and I know the bird well, in its appearance, from having seen many stuffed specimens, and thoroughly, I think, in manner and efficiency, from the report of intimate friends who have trained and flown the species.

The hobby, an exquisitely made falcon, with closed wings reaching even beyond the tip of the tail, is found in England only in the breeding season, and then chiefly in the southern and midland counties. This species builds almost always on trees; or, to speak more properly perhaps, it occupies the old or deserted nest of some other bird, making only slight alterations and repairs. But as many species differ so much in the matter of nidification when overruled by the influence of locality, it is not difficult to believe that the hobby now and then, but very seldom *indeed*, has its nest among rocks. Certainly kestrels and buzzards (to show the converse), which breed in rocks when they can find them, breed in trees (especially the former species), where no convenient rocks are to be found. With regard to the egg, it is perhaps somewhat paler in colour than that of either peregrine, merlin, or kestrel. The merlin's has generally the lake tint more conspicuously than the others. Yarrell appears to me to describe correctly, when he makes the hobby's "speckled all over with reddish brown, on a dirty white ground." The "white," however, is *very* dirty, and has a dingy reddish-yellow tint. The truth is that the eggs of the true falcons are very much alike in colour. Hobbies arrive here in April, and leave us in October; probably they go to Africa: they have been caught *en route* to that continent (at Malta) from Europe. The bird is, however, very common in the east of Europe, and the adjoining portions of Asia.

The following excellent description of the hobby is from "Falconry in the British Isles:" —

"In plumage the young and adult birds do not vary very considerably. In the young the upper portion of the body is nearly black, the edges of the feathers alone being of a rusty tint, while the whole of the under surface is of a dingy white ground-colour, marked with long dark splashes. In the adult, the edging to the feathers on the back and wing coverts disappears, the colour is at the same time changed to a dark slate, with the head, cheeks, and primaries nearly black; the chin pure white in the male, dingy in the female, with a white ground-colour for the breast, marked in a similar manner to the young bird; the thighs and under tail coverts acquire at the same time a fine clear rusty tint, the former being in the female splashed with dark spots; this is sometimes also the case in the male; more usually however with him the rusty portions are without marks. The cere, in the young bird, is blue, which as it increases in age changes to yellow, and ultimately to a fine orange, the legs and feet altering, in the same manner, from greenish-yellow to a deep chrome. The eyes are a dark hazel."

In their wild state they take cockchaffers on the wing (as will the merlin, according to my own repeated observation), dragon-flies, and many insects; also small birds, especially larks. Whether they have the pluck — they certainly have the power — to go through the ordeal of a good ringing flight remains, as far as I know, to be proved. I have never known them flown at larks with the advantage of bagged birds; and therefore I am not aware that they have been fairly tried with the quarry. They ought to be absolutely wonderful in their flight, their speed being unquestionably superior to that of the merlin. Snipe, too, *ought* scarcely to have a chance with them. They have, however, been so stolen from Nature by people who, not being naturalists, have taken a coarse or ignorant view of matters, that falconers have no materials left to work on, in connexion with this species. Mr. Brodrick, however, killed pigeons with a haggard female, and Mr. Holford, of Ware, before he became the accomplished falconer he is at present, flew some nestlings, with only indifferent success, at larks; — he did not use bagged birds in those days. Mr. Newcome (an authority inferior to none in Europe) complains that even the trained birds amuse themselves with insect catching. I must not forget to mention that I have seen a female of this species that was shot as it rose from a dying partridge; and I did not hear, though I inquired, that the partridge had been previously wounded. Such a bird would probably be, for pluck, one out of ten; and yet I cannot help thinking that with skill, care, and perseverance, the hobby might be made, could it be procured, to show great sport with larks and snipe. I have certainly reason to suppose that a good deal was done with it in the olden time.

It [3] is hardy — much less delicate at least than the merlin — "waits on " beautifully, is very docile, and its appearance is perhaps more elegant than that of any hawk in the world.

[1] There is nothing in the *flavour* of the partridge which is attractive to the hawks; they generally like fresh, tender beef better; bat you must persuade them that this comes out of the quarry you wish them to fly.

[2] I believe there is no instance of a merlin taking a wild magpie, though it might be accomplished.

[3] Hobbies, but especially merlins, should be fed chiefly on birds: when beef is given, it should be very fresh and tender: it is well to bruise it, and some falconers chop it up like nightingale's food. Beware of giving birds that have been shot much — though I have given unnumbered winged birds with impunity. Shot taken into the stomach is fatal to hawks as to domestic poultry; the latter will pick it up if spilt in a farmyard, and die of the poison.

Chapter Fifteen - The Goshawk (Astur Palumbarius)

I make no apology for quoting the following description of this hawk from "Falconry in the British Isles" (to the pages of which I have, indeed, more than once applied for a similar purpose), because one of the authors of that book is practically interested in this; and I know that my friend, his co-adjutor, makes us welcome to anything of the kind which we may consider of service.

"The colour of the young goshawk differs considerably from that of the mature state. During the first year, the whole of the under portion of the body is of a rusty salmon colour, marked with long lanceolate streaks of blackish-brown; while the upper part is liver-brown, each feather being margined with reddish-white. At first the eyes are grey; this colour gradually changes with age to lemon-yellow, and eventually becomes orange; the cere is wax-yellow, with the tarsi and feet of a deeper tone. At the first change the whole of the under plumage becomes light grey, striped transversely with narrow bars of a dark brown colour, the top of the head, back, wings, and tail becoming of a uniform hair-brown, with five distinct bars of a darker colour on the latter; there is also a streak of light grey over each eye, speckled, as are the cheeks, with minute brown splashes. The bars on the breast of the adult birds differ considerably in width in different individuals; the under tail-coverts are pure white."

Naturalists have lately concurred in giving different generic appellations to the goshawk and sparrow-hawk — the former bird being *Astur*, the latter *Accipiter*. Certainly the difference in the length of the tarsi and the singles is very considerable; and I believe the severance of the genera is justified, if not justifiable, from that circumstance. The general appearance of the two birds, however, is so similar that, in looking at a sparrow-hawk, you might almost fancy you saw a goshawk through a diminishing glass.

The length of a full-grown male is about eighteen inches, of a female about twenty-four inches; there being, as in the case of the sparrow-hawk, a very considerable difference in size between the sexes. This bird builds on high trees, and makes a large rough nest; the eggs are a bluish-white, I very much doubt whether they are ever spotted. Goshawks appear to be very widely distributed; but those found in America, though similar to the rest, are said to have a difference which some think might be made specific. Macgillivray, however, denies the existence of this difference: I believe him to be in error; but, for the present, I am quite content to leave a matter, which is of no consequence to falconry, in doubt.

The goshawk prefers wild rugged districts, especially dark fir forests. It is not uncommon in Norway, Sweden, Germany, Holland, &c, and is found in France; the birds which we receive for training are generally imported from Germany. The excessive preservation of game, and a population which spreads itself over almost every acre of land, have exterminated it in this country; neither is it to be found, except very rarely indeed, in Scotland or Ireland. The last specimen killed in this island was however "procured" (I believe that is the term) as lately as November, 1858; this was in Norfolk. The same county afforded one in 1854, and another in 1850. But the goshawk has ceased to breed in England. Mr. Thompson mentions, in his "Birds of Ireland," that the name of "goshawk" is sometimes given to the peregrine by the common people, or by those who, ignorant of ornithology, adopt a local name, without reference to its propriety. It is indeed doubtful whether the goshawk has been seen in Ireland for a considerable period. That it was once common there we may gather from "The Gentleman's Recreation," 1677. The author, after enumerating many parts of the world in which the bird is found, says: "Yet there are none better than those which are bred in the north parts of Ireland, as in the province of Ulster, but more especially in the county of Tyrone." Also, in "A Treatise of Modern Falconry, by James Campbell, Esq.," a book of which I have spoken before, we have the following passage: "The goshawk is found in the. north of Scotland and Ireland," &c. This was written as recently as 1773, but the family must have been dying out then, and they are dead now.

The goshawk is a true hawk.

I reminded my readers, in the third chapter of this book, that there is a wide difference, both in make and manner, between the true falcons, which only we have at present considered, and the true hawks. Perhaps it may be convenient if I recapitulate shortly what I then remarked. In *Natural History* the falcons are known by two infallible marks; the first of these is the " dentated beak," or "falcon's tooth," (it will be found in the shape of a little sharp projection on either edge of the upper mandible, of which it is a part); and the second is the shape of the wing, the second feather of which is the longest; there being only one exception to the rule, as far as I know, and that is made in favour of the merlin. To these certain marks may perhaps be added the dark hazel eye and the moustache. The true hawks, on the other hand, have no tooth, but an elegant curve, called in natural history the "lobe" or "festoon;" the fourth feather in the wing is generally the longest; the eye is yellow; and the mark which I have called the "moustache," spoken of by Sir. W. Jardine as the "dark streak of the real falcon," and which descends from the corner of the gape, is of course wanting in the true hawks. In *Falconry* the manner of. pursuit is taken into consideration; also the female goshawk is spoken of as a falcon, but simply by courtesy.

The goshawk, especially the female, has not much speed: she, and also the sparrow-hawk, are flown "at bolt," or from the hand, and must be trained to fly to it. They are called hawks of the *fist,* as I have had occasion to mention before. With these birds it is proper to approach the quarry as nearly as may be, in order to compensate for the want of "stoop;" though I saw last year a female goshawk sight and overtake a hare which got up from a hill in a slight mist at 150 yards from me. She was off my hand in an instant, and rolled the quarry over, though in this instance she did not hold. I imagine, however, that in her wild state *one* habit, and that the most common, of the goshawk is to sit cat-like on a tree, ready to dash on the first unsuspecting rabbit or marmot that passes. Larger and heavier than the peregrine, and with a fright-ful power of foot, she can be trained to hold even the gazelle; but for such quarry it is necessary to "succour" her with greyhounds. This was done in the olden time even with hares. In the East, where this hawk is highly esteemed, she is used for the large quarry just mentioned, and a most interesting ac-count of these flights will be found in "Falconry in the Valley of the Indus."

It seems that so lately as the latter half of the last century, the goshawk was flown "to the river," as it was called, at herons, wild geese, wild ducks; she was also flown at rooks; but it is difficult to understand how she could be effective against any of these birds. The only possible way — and in truth this seems pointed out in the old hawking-books — was to stalk the quarry; and it was for this reason, no doubt, that the goshawk was never belled when she flew wild-fowl. Were the falconer carrying a goshawk, to creep up to the river side, through cover, or near steep banks, and in this manner get within a few yards of a heron, there is little doubt, as I have said in a previous chap-ter, that the hawk would take it in the act of rising from the shallow. I have myself marked wild ducks to a brook, when I have been shooting, and stalked them to within a few paces. When this can be done, the goshawk's work will be found light enough. With rooks there would probably be more difficulty; and I really can't imagine how the falconer is to get near geese now, even if he adopt the stalking-horse of olden times.

I have known a female goshawk dash from my hand at a snipe, which rose near, and follow it through a turn or two; frequently she has flown grouse — I need hardly say, without success in either case. For my own part, I like the hawk; there is a certain feeling of power which she communicates to you, as she is borne gaily along on the fist, derived, I suppose, from the knowledge of her great strength and courage, and from the size of the quarry you seek to kill with her. With Captain Salvin she is a great favourite; and certainly, if there be anything in intimate acquaintance, his favourable impression is a correct one. The reader is indebted to his copious notes for much of the practical part which follows on the subject of the goshawk, especially that connected with fur-hawking.

It is a thousand pities that the temper of this bird is so very far from amiable; it is, in fact, *sulky.* Its trainer must have much patience; a virtue, however, which, if exercised, the hawk will ultimately reward.

Goshawks may be sometimes procured by an application to our professional falconers; and, I believe, through the manager of the Regent's Park Zoological Gardens. If you have a choice, take a large one — especially if it is a female, and you require her for hares. Look also to the feet, for she should be well armed, as she catches by clutching; these should be large and powerful, having sharp claws. Unfortunately the goshawks which are imported into this country are much injured in plumage. They are generally, if not always, nestlings (though there is no objection to that); and it would seem that they scarcely taste food between the time of their capture in Germany and their delivery in England. All that can be done on the receipt of such a bird, preparatory to training it, is to feed it gradually, and keep it as clean as may be. The feathers which have been broken, either by the hunger-streak, or by its constant beating against a cage or pen on its voyage, or by both, may be left unimped until the bird shall be, in a measure, reclaimed. The tail, if perfect, is sure to be destroyed by violent bating, even from a bow-perch. The cost of an untrained nestling is about 4*l.*

But before detailing the proceedings which are recommended with a goshawk just delivered at your door, a few advantages in the use of the bird shall be recounted, which may tend to reconcile you to your purchase, should it look ragged and miserable: —

1st. It can be used in. an inclosed country, where it would be impossible to fly a falcon.

2nd. Its flight being short, it is never far from its master, and is therefore in little danger of being lost.

3rd. Its feathers are very elastic, and those of the wing, at any rate, are scarcely ever injured. (Proper treatment is, of course, taken for granted here.)

4th. It is very hardy; stands our climate well; is not subject to frounce or kecks; and will thrive, if necessary, on the coarsest food, such as rats, cats, &c.

5th. It need not be flown at hack.

6th. It does not, like the falcons, deteriorate by standing idle; but will become all it ever was by a week or ten days' attention.

7th. It improves with age, which, to say the least of it, is a very doubtful matter with falcons.

8th. Desperate courage.

The drawbacks are the following: — 1st, want of speed; 2nd, uncertainty of temper; 3rd, the impossibility of flying a cast together, as they would "crab," and injure or kill each other; 4th, a habit of leaving quarry after a few unsuccessful attempts.

I will now suppose the untrained bird on the hand of her master for the first time. She will probably feed there by candlelight; indeed, when very sharp-set, she will scarcely refuse to feed by daylight. Her food should be given by small pieces, and a sufficient quantity for a meal spread over some hours. This may be arranged by giving the legs of rabbits which have previously lost a portion of their flesh, and indeed the toughest pieces that can be procured. It will take the hawk some time to pick them clean or to tear them to pieces. Thus you will have induced her to sit on the hand for a long time without overmuch bating. Let her be carried, if possible, by at least two people during the day, each person having her for three or four hours; she should be stroked with the wing of a bird, and by degrees made to endure the presence of strangers. As she progresses, introduce her to every possible scene likely to be new — as the fields, the stable-yard, the noise of a camp, the sparks of a blacksmith's shop. Falconers in the East often tame their hawks by carrying them into the busy streets of a large town after dark; this is an excellent method. If the goshawk should bate excessively, when, during the first week or two, she is committed for a short time to the bow-perch in the day-time, a person to whom she is accustomed may remain close to her; this may have a tendency to console her, and he will of course try to attract her attention by a little judicious feeding. Total darkness is the only thing that will keep a wild hawk perfectly quiet.

When the bird becomes a little reconciled to the fist, she should be placed on a wall close to it, and induced to jump to hand by the offer of a tempting piece of meat. One mouthful having been taken, she must be again placed upon the wall; there will probably be no difficulty in making her return to the food. She may then be carried for ten minutes, pulling at a stump from which very little meat can be obtained. Again the wall; again the fist, a few inches further from the wall; and again a more substantial reward than she can obtain from the stump. And so, day by day, the distance of the jump is increased; at last it becomes a *fly;* and six, eight, ten yards is done easily. A creance is, of course, used during this part of the training.

During training a full crop of food should not be given; neither should the bird be made weak by too much fasting. Beef is more supporting than rabbit; but very much here must be left to the judgment of the trainer. All hawks differ in temper and constitution, and must be treated accordingly. Scarcely a day should pass without your hand having been run along the breast-bone — there is no objection to it being a little sharp; but if the sides of the breast seem to have fallen in, give more food.

We do not hood goshawks in these days. How they ever could have been hooded, as we are told they were, I, for one, cannot understand. As I shall have to observe, in the chapter on the sparrow-hawk, the great secret (to many I believe it *is* a secret) with the short-winged hawks, is to let them see all it is possible they can see; they want taming — emphatically *taming* — nay, they must be *kept tame*; they require this far more than the falcons do; and it can only be effectual (as far as my friends and I see the way to it) by the continual recurrence of new scenes, other people, fresh dogs, as well as by all sorts of sounds. We cannot comprehend the wisdom of Mr. James Campbell's remarks

Female goshawk and hare.

on the subject of hooding the goshawk: "Beware of carrying her bare-faced; ... no hawk demands the hood so much as the goshawk, which she ought never to want but at weather and bath."

The bow-perch, on which the short-winged hawks are kept, is a very simple contrivance. For the goshawk it is an ash or oak sapling, four or five feet in length, or something of the kind, bent to a half circle, in which shape it is kept by means of a strong wire fastened to either end of the bow, about seven or eight inches from its points; these points may be shod with iron. A ring, which will run easily upon the perch, is placed upon it, and this is, of course, done before the wire is used. To this ring the hawk is fastened by the leash, the perch having been firmly fixed in good and level turf. Some falconers make matters more secure by attaching the middle of the wire to an iron pin, which is driven firmly in the ground. This precaution, if not necessary, is advisable; for should a goshawk escape in the neighbourhood of hawks on their blocks, she is not unlikely to kill them all, one after another. Great care must also be taken that the leash, jesses, and swivel are very strong. Do not, however, make the jesses of harsh thick leather; your own judgment will decide upon what is the happy medium. I have had a goshawk's foot made very sore by hard coarse jesses; the fault was in the leather, which was continually greased, and ought therefore to have been soft.

There is a state to which the short-winged hawks must be brought before they can be flown with effect, called *yarak*. It may be known by the erect crest, a certain eager straightforward look, and occasionally by the cry of hunger. The plumage too is slightly puffed up, and the bird looks anxiously round for the expected quarry. When, together with these symptoms, the hawk sits quietly in the hand, looking suddenly at every bush which you kick, and occasionally — as it were in a moment of repose — rousing and pruning, there is no doubt that she will fly, and fly in right earnest. But if, on the contrary, she bate from the fist, not daring, as it seems, to look you steadily in the face; if she make herself small by keeping her plumage close, uttering perhaps a sort of twittering chirp, be quite sure that she is better on the bow-perch, for she will not fly that day.

The process by which this necessary condition of yarak is arrived at; the entering to pheasants, rabbits, and hares, together with the actual flights at these quarries, I must reserve for another chapter.

Chapter Sixteen – The Goshawk (Concluded)

When the young goshawk has been treated in the I manner described in the last chapter for a fortnight ' or more she will begin to show signs of "yarak." This is the time to enter her. But before we proceed to that necessary part of her education, I will dispose of "yarak" altogether — at least as far as detail is concerned. A goshawk which has been trained, but which has been allowed to stand idle even for weeks, may (supposing her bow-perch has been in a tolerably public place) be brought into "yarak," and therefore into flying order, in from five to ten days. And this process is so exceedingly like that of training a young bird (though the absolute carriage may be confined to two or three hours a day), that it is only the great importance of the subject which induces me to risk the appearance of repetition. Let your walk be in the fields, taking a companion with you, and occasionally going within a short distance of labourers, talking to them, as the hawk seems disposed to bear their presence; but this comparative publicity is only an introduction to frequented roads, where horses, carts, women and children are continually met. Neither should the flying to hand from a wall or gate be forgotten. If the bird has become very fat during her long sojourn on the bow-perch, her flesh must be slightly reduced before you carry her at all. This precaution is to avoid the risk of a fit, with which she might be seized if she bated very much from the hand in her obese state. Still I would trust *chiefly* to the time she is carried for bringing her into condition. The great matter, of course, is to keep the hawk neither too low nor too high; and the happy medium will probably be attained by giving rather more than half a crop of rabbit, or rather more than a quarter of a crop of beef daily. However, for the reason mentioned in the last chapter, no fixed rule can be laid down, hawks differing in temper and constitution. I think that, when a goshawk has been fed rather too sparingly for several days, and is indulged with a hearty meal early in the morning, she will be very likely to fly in first-rate style at twelve or one o'clock on the morrow. The full meal will have given her pluck and tone, and yet she will be very sharp-set. The. usual and, no doubt, the best plan, is to continue the small meals, given with regularity both as to time and quantity, for a week, or until the hawk exhibits the symptoms mentioned at the conclusion of the last chapter; and then allow the bird to kill something, taking care that she has a full meal. On the following day she is to be fed very slightly, and on the third day taken to the field and flown. Once in "yarak," she may be kept in that state by very little carriage and judicious feeding on the *few* days she is not used: she should have a warm gorge once, or sometimes twice a-week.

But to speak more immediately of the young bird whose taming, rather perhaps than training, we may now consider complete. She bates towards you for food, when she is sharp-set, as you approach the bow-perch; she comes to fist ten or twenty yards from a tree or wall; and you safely conclude she has arrived at "yarak," all the symptoms of which she unmistakeably shows. We must now come to active operations, — to actual use in the field.

The goshawk is used in Britain chiefly against rabbits, hares, and pheasants, or even partridges. It will also take landrails, water-hens, and coots. The first of the trio last mentioned can only be flown when the grass is not very high; and Ireland seems to be the country which affords the best opportunity for the flight; water-hens, when found in hedge-rows, at a little distance from water, are easily taken by the goshawk; and coots, which are not very common, can only be dealt with in a frost. These, however, must be considered incidental flights; and I shall confine myself in description to fur, pheasant, and (to a glance at) partridge-hawking.

In describing the course of training necessary for the bird before us, I have just reached the point when it becomes proper to enter the hawk. Now to what quarry do you wish to enter her? Do you aspire to pheasants with a male or female, to partridges with a male, or to hares and rabbits with a female? I will suppose you have a large hen bird with powerful feet, which you intend to enter at rabbits at once, and perhaps to hares hereafter.

Lay in a stock of live rabbits, which are easily obtained by nets and ferrets. Give one in a string to the hawk at the perch, the string passing through the eye of the hawking-pin, which has been spoken of, as securing the bow-perch at the middle of its wire. The falconer can thus draw the rabbit — one about two-thirds grown — within the reach of the goshawk: the leash of the hawk may be lengthened, and indeed every precaution taken to prevent the bird being disappointed at this her first attempt at killing. If she seize and hold on, go in and kill the rabbit at once; the thrust of a long blade is to be recommended, care being taken of the hawk's feet. [1] Open the head of the newly-killed rabbit, and feed from the brains, eyes, &c. This will teach the bird in flight to make for the head, which is the only sure place to hold a strong rabbit or hare with a goshawk foot. After this let her take her pleasure on the rabbit. The next day, or perhaps on the two following days, she must be fed sparingly; then a second rabbit may be given.

At this time, if not before, let the hawk be belled — on the *tail*. It is much better, for short-winged hawks, to place the bell here than on the leg; it is less in the way (a fact, by-the-bye, which applies to falcons also), and it has an excellent chance of being heard, as the trains of goshawks and sparrow-hawks are constantly in motion. The process, however, will require explanation. The bell itself must have a shank of peculiar form; Messrs. Benhams and Frond make it. You have the bell in your hand; take a piece of strong leather, about as long as the bell is broad, and which tightly fits its shank; at some little distance from either end punch a hole large enough to fit a feather of the goshawk's tail; cut a passage, giving it a little breadth, from those holes to the ends of the leather; insert respectively, by way of the passages, into the holes the shafts of the two middle feathers, and make all secure with waxed thread. If the leather widens abruptly at the ends, the thread will have a firmer hold. If this description be not clear, reference may be made to a plate in "Falconry in the British Isles," which is exceedingly so.

Your bird may now be flown at liberty at a bagged rabbit, whose speed is impeded thus: Put a light collar, with a yard of string attached to it, round the rabbit's neck, to the loose end of the string fasten a shorter piece at its *middle,* and tie the ends of this second piece to the ends of a piece of cane about a foot in length. A light splinter-bar is thus formed, which, besides slackening the speed, prevents the rabbit, should it escape the hawk, from entering any cover or hole from which it would be difficult or impossible to retrieve it. This of course is not intended to be sport; on the contrary, it is the very unpleasant part of its preparation; but there is certainly no more cruelty in it than in the chase of a greyhound after a leveret; in either case the pursued is over-matched. The rabbit, as a matter of policy as well as humanity, should be killed as soon as the hawk has taken it. In a wild state the goshawk must put her prey to a prolonged suffering.

When this experiment has been repeated with success, the hawk may be considered **trained.** I should recommend that she should now be taken to the roughest possible ground on which rabbits can be found lying out, were it not that ploughed fields, &c. would injure her feathers; but, at any rate, I hope the hawk may have an easy flight to begin with, and then all will be well. She will soon kill on grass. It is a good plan to take young hawks, as much as possible, to fields free from trees; because, until they become steady by work, they are apt to take perch when they have the opportunity; and then, turning rakish and wild, they may give an infinity of trouble. As no one, however, can altogether guard against his young goshawk taking to a tree, it is as well to make het acquainted with live pigeons at her perch and to a string; one of these is easily carried to the field, and the pegging it down near the root of a tree may possibly save hours of toil. There is another plan which may be advantageously adopted when a goshawk declines to come from a branch to hand — a piece of red but tough beef (exceedingly tempting always) may be fastened to a string and thrown into the tree; then hawk and meat can be pulled down together; or a dead rabbit may be used with effect in the same manner.

Rabbits, as is generally known, may in most places be found sitting out in rough grass fields and the like, particularly after windy weather, and for a day or two after their holes have been ferretted. Where this is the case, the falconer may often kick them up, and a considerable number may be killed in a day with one bird. Still it is advisable that they should not be nearer any hole than 80 or 100 yards. When the first is caught by the hawk, make in and kill it. Open the head, or give, at any rate, the eyes and tongue, with perhaps a small mouthful of cheek. Bag *that* rabbit, and proceed. The goshawk must be slightly rewarded after each successful flight; and, if she be really good and in *practice* (that is the great matter) she will go on killing till those mouthfuls have made nearly a meal, or till she is over-tired with much work.

Where rabbits do not lie out much, they can be ferreted: the hawk will, however, bate at the ferret, and care is necessary to prevent a catastrophe. If a fight took place, the hawk might possibly suffer, and the ferret would be killed. However, by using the two together, a sort of armed neutrality may be established — nay, perhaps a certain alliance.

If the bird is intended for hares, enter her at leverets; it is unnecessary to have them bagged, supposing your pupil tolerably perfect with strong rabbits. She should be flown on a sort of "graduating scale," beginning with small leverets, and ending with large hares. Also let her be kept as much as possible to the quarry; that is, do not *purposely* fly her at rabbits. I shall never forget a flight I had last year at a hare about three-fourths grown. It was in a thin plantation. I did not see the hare jump up, nor indeed was I aware that anything moved. "Vampire" knew better. She was in almost screaming yarak, and shot from my hand gloriously. There were occasional bushes, and a little underwood, and when the hare passed through them the hawk rose as high as the tops of the trees, coming down the instant there was an opening. It was one of those happy occasions when your bird seems to go beyond herself, and surprises you with a manner which is scarcely hers. This flight was very parallel with that of the merlin and magpie, described in Chapter Fourteen. "Vampire," owing I confess partly to the position of the trees and bushes, *stooped;* she was a falcon for five minutes. The flight occupied a period not very short of that time; hawk and quarry passed twice over a stone wall; a bird which generally gave up after four unsuccessful strokes, struck twenty times. As for me — "what was the world beside?" — it was sport truly, but it was ecstasy also. It won't do *again*, even if I should ever see it again; but I had never seen it before. I dashed down the hill to find them; they came back and met me. "Stick to her, my girl! you shall have a rich feast." They were out of sight. "Once more above the tree, 'Vampire?' Down! — the well-known cry of a hare; she has really done it!" I flung myself in with open knife. Talk of the "beauties" of sport: look at *that* picture! They were as still as statuary; they only breathed. The quarry had pressed forward on being taken; the hawk lay back, one foot over the head, the other on the shoulder of the hare; the fine second plumage of her long striped thigh lay like black and white mosaic; her head leaning towards that of her victim; one of its hind legs was inserted through the feathers of her wing. I have the hare's foot in my study here. "Vampire" is dead, much further south. [2]

But I will now tell you what Capt. Salvin has done, armed with a good hawk, and in a good country. He took two 8lb. hares and one rabbit with "The Bushman," a strong four-year-old goshawk, during an evening's walk; on another occasion he killed with the same bird, five hares, three-parts grown. About the same time (the autumn of 1857), at Cloughton Hall, Lancashire, the same bird caught in one day ten rabbits, most of them old ones, of which she held nine — one breaking off and gaining its hole. Some years before he caught eight old rabbits with a goshawk in one field, not one escaping. He has seen a hare leap up three or four feet to free itself from the hawk; rabbits roll right over with the hawk, which retained its hold; a goshawk turn upon a dog, in a passion at missing its quarry, though previously they were friends and allies. These are some of the experiences of an indefatigable friend of the goshawk.

All flights are not straight, short, and easy; far from this. Sometimes, from the frequent doubling of the hare or rabbit, the hawk becomes exhausted — occasionally, undoubtedly, sulky — and she stands panting on the ground without looking at the quarry, which disappears. Again, hares and rabbits are taken at a headlong dashing flight into cover, just as they are dwelling for a second on entering it. At other times they break away, and are recaptured. When near many spectators, they sometimes turn from a straight course, and are taken amongst them. A rabbit may be caught at the mouth of a hole by one foot on the head, while the other is employed by being firmly pressed on the ground to save its possessor from being dragged in with the prey; the position strengthened by outstretched tail and wings.

It must be understood that the female goshawk only has been spoken of as yet; the male is too weak even for rabbits. He has been used, however, with success against both pheasants and partridges.

Captain Salvin has been very successful in taking pheasants with the male goshawk; he found that the bird required no entering, but flew and killed even old cocks, threading his way curiously, rapidly, and beautifully through the trees.

Col. Thornton was perhaps the last falconer who used the goshawk, *together with spaniels* (clumbers are the best), for pheasant-hawking. The hawk was trained to fly this quarry when it had taken perch, as well as on the wing. Mr. Campbell gives the following directions: — t€ Take a brown chicken with you to the woods in the evening, and, having broke its neck, erect it on the top of a long pole, high enough to be seen by the hawk; then stirring the pole, so as to give the chicken a fluttering appearance, and at the same time calling to the hawk, she will come directly and pull it down. Let her eat the head and neck among the dogs as her reward. By following this method you will bring your hawk to be so bold that she no sooner shall see a pheasant go to perch than she will seize him and bring him down." More recently a bagged cock pheasant, in a creance, has been placed upon the bough of a tree, and the hawk allowed to seize it, when both were lowered to the ground amongst the dogs. These in their turn had to learn a lesson, viz. that of keeping at a respectful distance from the hawk when she was lowering amongst them. It must have been a pretty sight, and I hope it will *yet* be a pretty sight, to see the spaniels barking round the goshawk and quarry in a bit of fine wood-side or picturesque glen. Howett, the artist and etcher, published some plates on hawking in 1799. One of these gives an excellent idea of pheasant-hawking. And as he was a sportsman, and came from Col. Thornton's neighbourhood in Yorkshire, there is little doubt that he had frequently seen what he represented with his pencil.

It is scarcely expected of the goshawk, in partridge-hawking, that he should actually take the quarry on the wing, unless indeed at the beginning of the season, when the coveys are young and lie very close. "A great many partridges," says Sir John Sebright, "may be killed *by the means* of the goshawk in the beginning of the season, when the birds are young, and particularly in a dewy morning, as their wings becoming wet from their having been driven into the hedges, they will be easily taken by the dogs. In fact, not one in ten of the partridges brought home by those who use these birds has been actually taken by the hawk." In an open country even the male would have no chance with partridges; where there are hedges he drives them into cover, and then takes his stand on a tree, or even on the ground (in this latter case he should be called to fist), and waits till the spaniels have flushed one of the partridges; he is then off a second time, and if the quarry is wet and draggled, he may take it in the air.

The goshawk is excellent with fur, good with pheasants, and only tolerable with partridges. He may also be used, with effect, in the "incidental flights" mentioned before. The general character of the bird has already been given in the balancing of the advantages and disadvantages attendant upon his use.

These birds may be moulted either in a room or out of doors. If a room be chosen, care must of course be taken that there shall be no *edges*, but that all shall be round and smooth, so that there may be no danger to young feathers. There must be a perch opposite the light, and an occasional, bath given. If the bow-perch be preferred to in-door moulting, it should be placed on smooth level grass, and occasionally moved. Let it be taken under a large out-door shed in *very* wet, or very hot, weather.

It is necessary to exercise some patience during the end of moult; for the bird must not be put into training until the last wing-feather is quite down and hard; neither must she be made to lose flesh rapidly when taken up. In fact, what I have previously remarked concerning a gradual lessening of food, while the hawk which has been standing idle is yet confined to perch, holds good in drawing her from the mews. From over fatness, coupled with exertion, you have to dread a fit. It is, perhaps, the only illness to which a goshawk is subject; but if it attack her, it will be her last.

[1] Or the hawk may be taken off on a dead rabbit, the live one being instantly knocked on the head.
[2] Mr. Holford took fifteen *bagged* rabbits out of seventeen with "Vampire" in one day.

Chapter Seventeen - The Sparrow-Hawk (Accipiter Nisus)

This is a very beautiful and a very capricious bird. It has a great deal of ability and a great deal of vice. I intend, in the course of a page or two, to enter thoroughly into its character.

Its natural history, as far as appearance and habits are concerned, is generally known; at any rate, it may be told shortly. Perhaps this bird may be considered, in reference to the merlin, very much what the goshawk is in reference to the peregrine. It is the little hawk to the little falcon. Whether the sparrow-hawk, which is widely distributed, inhabits America seems a doubtful point with ornithologists; but so simple a matter ought to be cleared up. In different parts of the world its size and colour will probably be found to vary: the difference may be specific, or it may belong only to races. The male is about twelve inches in length, the female fifteen inches. "In plumage the female sparrow-hawk, in the nestling state, differs but little from the adult bird, the principal change being, that at the first moult the feathers on the upper surface of the body lose their lighter edging, and become of one uniform brown. The colour of the breast differs very much in different individuals; even in the same nest, one or two of the young birds may have the ground-colour white, with dark brown transverse narrow bars, whilst the others may be entirely of a rusty colour, with uneven markings of a darker tint. The *young* male bird resembles the female, but after the first year the brown colour of the back and shoulders is changed to a dark slate blue;

whilst the breast is finely barred with rusty brown upon a light ground, the under tail-coverts being pure white. Whilst very young, the hides are of a greenish-grey; this colour changes with age to a lemon-yellow, and eventually becomes of a bright orange-tint. The cere is of a greenish-yellow, and the legs and feet gamboge, with very black claws." — *Falconry in the British Isles.*

This bird builds a large rough nest, having broad sides by way of a platform for the young to creep on when they are strong enough. It is *generally* its own architect; but this, I believe, is not, always acknowledged. The nest should be looked for, and may be easily found, in the tall trees, especially the fir-trees, of a wood. The eggs, like those of all other hawks, are roundish; colour a skim-milk ground, with reddish-brown blotches, chiefly at the larger end. The number is generally four or five. I have always believed that the sparrow-hawk feeds almost exclusively on birds; I am disposed still to believe it. A respectable man, however, whose former occupation called him much into woods, assured me that he had seen the sparrow-hawk seize and carry off small rabbits. The man is so honest that I quite believe he has seen *some* hawk do this; and that he knew the sparrow-hawk by sight (at any rate, on inspection) at the time he refers to, I have convinced myself by many questions. His testimony, however, does not amount to demonstration. But a far more wonderful thing is told us by a modern author, whose opinions I am, for many reasons, unwilling to attack; still I complain bitterly that one who has undertaken to give instruction on ornithology, not only to ordinary mortals, but to the highest personage in the land, should commit himself to so many errors in his chapters on the birds of prey. He tells us that small birds are devoured *whole* by the sparrow-hawk, even legs and all! This is monstrous. I am sure I do not say so unkindly, neither do I wish to affect superiority over a naturalist whose scope of study is wider than my own; but surely a writer on a scientific subject should be careful in dissecting evidence, and thoroughly armed against asserting as a fact that which is a physical impossibility!

In considering the disposition and character of the sparrow-hawk, we are met, on the threshold, by an apparent difficulty — a difficulty, at least, to those, if there be any, who will not admit that a creature may have two distinct and opposite points of character. At the first glance, too, it might appear that a rule already given is faulty, viz. that a state of semi-captivity helps to bring out, or bring to our knowledge, the true disposition. I hope to explain these things satisfactorily. My present proposition may look like a paradox; it is this — the sparrow-hawk is the most shy hawk in existence, and yet is of so bold and reckless a disposition as occasionally to approach voluntarily its most dreaded enemy, man, and to place itself in his power. There is perhaps no bird which is more disposed generally to give us a wider berth than this hawk; it is "as wild as a hawk," and a shade wilder. Except in the breeding season, he must be a clever fellow who creeps within gun-shot. And yet, on *occasion*, few birds are so daring in the presence of man. I am speaking as yet, of course, of the unreclaimed and uncaptured state.

The general wildness will be admitted; there are numberless instances of its *apparent* opposite. Such as a cage containing a canary, or small song-bird of some kind, and which hung on the wall of a house close to a window, seized, and an attempt made to tear out the occupant. A bird, which had dashed through a window, positively pursued into a room. A sparrow chased and killed in a *town*. I was myself a witness of the following occurrence last winter. A fieldfare was caught alive in a snare of the kind described in Chapter Twelve. A female sparrow-hawk struck at and hung to the captive. I was attracted to this state of things by the almost diabolical clatter of a couple of magpies, which never ceased to jump and fly from twig to twig all round the snare. The hawk did not notice them, but dropped from her hold of the poor fieldfare only to cling again. I was in hopes that she would ultimately settle on the top, and be taken in one of the nooses; this, however, she declined doing, not, I am convinced, from any fear of a trap — she was too much excited for that — but simply because the thing did not occur to her. But the magpies, I doubt not, were calm amidst their clamour, and had weighty reasons for not settling among the horsehair. At length I was humane enough, or weak enough, if you will, to feel for the poor wretch who was suffering torture, and I despatched the gardener to the rescue. He killed the fieldfare; but, as he was taking it from the snare, the hawk coming "from somewheres or other" dashed at his hand, which in his descent of the tree was near his head, and nearly knocked his hat off. That, however, was the last we saw of her.

The species — or if, so to speak, but *one*, the genus [1] — under our consideration has, then, as I set out by saying, two distinct, and perhaps antagonistic, points of character; but it is clear that they can exist together. These are — to restate them concisely — (1.) an intense appreciation of danger; and (2.) a courage and recklessness great enough, at times, to overcome and override that appreciation. Now, in training, we observe the first point *only*. That comes out clearly enough, as I fear some of my readers may find to their disgust. The sparrow-hawk is, in my opinion, the wildest, in some sense the most intractable, the most ungrateful, the most provoking and temper-trying, of all birds or beasts that were ever taken under the care of man from the beginning of the world. But, when training is over, and the hawk is in *constant* practice, in continual work, there is no bird more fearless in the field, nor any with which a greater head of quarry can be taken in a single day. A trained sparrow-hawk has been *cut out* of a blackthorn bush into which it had forced itself after its prey. So perhaps the paradox is broken altogether; and also training, with its results, are shown to assist, even in this instance, the inquiry into character.

I think, moreover, that I observe in the sparrow-hawk a want of *intellect*, if I may so express myself. She is governed by present impressions, which are wonderfully evanescent. Under the circumstance which I am on the point of describing, she will forget Nature with tolerable rapidity, and in a few hours she will return to her utterly. I am now speaking of "training" in a great measure incidentally, as it tends to prove character and disposition; I shall soon do so systematically, and in connexion with the practice of the sport. Pray observe the following: — Sir John S. Sebright tells us that he once "took a wild partridge with a sparrow-hawk of his own breaking *ten days* after it had been taken wild from a wood." There was a time when, having kept spar-row-hawks for two years — flying them at young pigeons — I was terribly puzzled by the above quotation. It was with me almost a balance of opinions whether a man of spotless integrity, and a great falconer, should, in the in-tense desire to accomplish a certain matter, have dreamed or fancied he had accomplished it; or whether the sparrow-hawk, in an hour of amiable eccen-tricity, had made a vow to confuse and confound her foes, while, in point of fact, she had rendered herself insanely agreeable. Such were my feelings then; they have changed now; I accept the account literally, and see my way to its explanation at once.

Ten days, [2] if *every hour* of them be employed, is a sufficient period to leave on the brain of a bird, peculiarly organised as the sparrow-hawk is, a certain strong though passing impression. When I speak of "every hour" I do not wish to dwell so much on number as on continuance. Of course you must have a certain time; but what you must *not* have is intermission. When Sir John Sebright tells us that he trained this bird himself, he probably means that it was trained partly with his own hands, and partly under his immedi-ate orders and superintendence. Probably it was kept awake for the first three or four days and nights, there being a relay of watchers; carried as long as it could be induced to pull at a stump or pinion, and returned to its perch when it had obtained what was considered proper; made continually to jump to hand for food — at first in the house, afterwards in the garden, then in the fields; never left with less than two or three people, and those *moving;* cer-tainly never, except for a few hours at night during the last five or six days, left alone. I imagine it was flown in the *afternoon,* having been quietly carried during the morning, tearing at the skinny bits of partridge's wings, without being allowed to swallow a feather; and I should think it killed a bagged par-tridge in a creance two days before the flight, on which quarry it was permit-ted to make a tolerable meal. Then mark! — it was flown, not at a blackbird, or small bird of any kind, but at a partridge, which it could not carry, and which could be sprung under its master's feet if the period chosen were the beginning of the season.

This description, a little modified (no sitting up at nights, for instance), may serve for training a haggard in real practice; but I mention it here to show that an impression, a habit, must be *kept up* (more or less, according to the time you give yourself for the training, but certainly kept up) if you are to succeed with the sparrow-hawk. The habit and the impression in the case of a fresh-caught bird will, if you withdraw the means which created them, pass faster than caloric from boiling water in a frost, if you take the fire away. Nature will rush in if they are absent for an hour, quickly as the frost will take away all that is *artificial* from the water. I say it advisedly, if, after but ten days' training, close as it must have been, Sir John had lost his hawk for a day, perhaps for half a day, he would scarcely have taken her again *only* with lure or fist, even if she had procured but a poor meal in the interval, and though she had flown well to hand in the morning. Nature would have touched the bird in every breeze, and spoken to her in every sound, and beckoned to her in every waving tree, and wearied herself to re-assert her dominion before that sun was half set.

> "Naturam expelles furcâ, tamen usque recurret,
> Et mala perrumpet furum fastidia Victrix."

A haggard sparrow-hawk may be taught to fly to hand at ten or twenty paces for food, and from it at quarry in about six weeks, moderate attention being given to her training; but to effect even this the bird must never be left alone in the daytime, and, when she is carried (which may be for an hour and a half in the morning, and an hour and a half in the evening), she should be constantly introduced to fresh scenes, and made to fly for food to several people. All wild-caught hawks, however well trained, have a tendency to "carry;" and, this being the case, it is better to enter them to heavy quarry: in the case of a large female sparrow-hawk, I would suggest partridges or land-rails.

Having disposed, then, of the haggard, a bird not so frequently trained as the eyess, we will lose no time in climbing the tree containing a nest which has lately been guarded with more care than if it had been a pheasant's in a hedge-bottom near a path. There are four young ones; two hens and two cocks, the sex being easily distinguished by the size. Now, the male, or musket, is seldom trained, though I really do not see why he should not be flown at blackbirds; he would be quicker than the female, and perhaps less likely to "carry." At least the only explanation which suggests itself to me is this: — it is found that even the hen bird is disposed to prefer sparrows, chaffinches, &c, to blackbirds; and this tendency might be even greater in the male. However, let us carefully convey from the nest the two hens: they have a brown and white appearance — feathers and down— the brown predominating. In a week, perhaps, they will fly. Even at this early age they suspect you. The sparrow-hawk always is suspicious — you know it by the wild eye, half-open beak, and panting body. They may be brought up either at hack or in a room; but if hack be chosen, it should be of short duration. This hawk soon preys for itself, and every day may well be grudged that it is allowed to be apart from its master. I should say, take it up as soon as it can sit erect and firmly on the fist. Of course my readers remember all about the hamper into which nestlings are placed. If you determine to have this in a tree, care must be taken to cover it well with something waterproof, for sparrow-hawks are very subject to cramp, induced by wet and cold; and if the attack does not kill the bird, it will probably paralyse a leg for life. But there is no place better for the hamper than an unused outhouse, having a *large* door or window which fronts the morning sun. Many falconers would confine the bird in this room till the time for training arrives. Hack is certainly not necessary with sparrow-hawks. What has been said in Chapter Twelve on the merlin, with regard to the *times* of feeding and the use of the whistle, applies also to this bird. It is of the greatest importance, however, that there should be two or more feeders. The nestlings may become so familiar with their master as to fly readily to his hand or arm; but if they are not accustomed to others also, they will be as dreadfully frightened at the approach of a stranger as if they had never seen a human being. Nay, it is all the better if they are fed, from the first, by men, women, and children; and accustomed, also, to the presence of different dogs.

As young sparrow-hawks sometimes contrive to fall out of the hamper before they can fly, put a little straw underneath it when in a room, and a little fence round it out of doors. I should certainly choose a dry room, free from damp and rats, and put them on the floor with plenty of straw. They must be well broken to fly to the fist as soon as they can use their wings; but I think they should also be made acquainted with a lure. For this reason; — a sparrow-hawk, like a goshawk, may take a fright in the field, and hesitate about coming well to hand, and yet the lure may bring her down even from a high tree; if she be properly trained, though not in actual yarak, a *live* lure will be found to answer when the ordinary one has failed.

The time, I will suppose, has arrived when it is considered proper to take up the nestlings and to commence their training. Carriage on the hand — absolutely necessary to their proper tuition, for they will *have* to be carried — will at first have a tendency to make them wild; presently, if properly managed, it will make them tame. The young falconer will naturally be disappointed to find the bird which came so well to hand yesterday, now, on the first day of its being carried, stare wildly with its mad eyes, and bate violently. It will probably even hang at the length of the jesses and swivel, and dash off again the moment it is quietly replaced. More than this, the very power of standing will appear to have left it; the claws will be clenched and distorted. The whole creature will be changed; instead of a tolerably bold and Very handsome bird, the transition of a few minutes will present you with a terrified, crouching, vicious, abject wretch; a horrible mixture of fright and feathers. My very kind compliments, dear sir; it is with pain that I am compelled to bring you to this pass; but I thought that probably you would like to know the truth — the worst. It is indeed as I state, though I confess the nuisance is transient, and appears in a modified form when the nestlings have been much accustomed to many people. Some people think that the helpless look of the feet and legs arises only from temper, and that it is a sham; it may arise from temper, but it is not a sham. It appears to me that this bird's brain is overcharged with electricity, or something fearfully subtle; and that, on the smallest provocation, these fluids shoot through the whole frame, overturning and deranging everything that is healthy and regular. Well, it is very unpleasant to have to deal with a lunatic, whatever be the cause or explanation of the lunacy; but it must be done here. The sparrow-hawk's legs are, during these fits of fright and passion, in a temporary paralysis. Still, it is of exceedingly short duration; and, when the bird is trained, it passes away altogether. For fear of fits, and for the obvious reasons connected with training, the bird must not be carried after a meal.

This hawk should be belled on the tail, in the manner described for the goshawk. Its whole training bears a close resemblance to that of the larger bird; and up to the time of entering it would puzzle a writer to point out any difference. However, training, when applied to an eyess, may be learned from a glance at the directions in this chapter on that process as it refers to the haggard: not only the nature, but the details, of the discipline are alike; less *time*, perhaps, may be employed with the young bird than with the old one. The actual rearing the nestlings done with, he who can train a haggard can certainly train an eyess. I would only warn my readers not to make "carriage" an annoying or painful process. It is a great mistake to suppose that you can train or tame a sparrow-hawk by fastening her to your hand for two-thirds of a day; and, when this horrible and senseless arrangement is over, turning her into a room, where she can see no one, till it is time to "walk her out" again on the morrow. How is it possible that a bird can do anything else than take a disgust to your hand, and to you, when you have done all in your power to induce her to consider the "fist" a prison or a pillory, and yourself a jailor or an executioner? No; carriage is absolutely necessary, but it must be done with judgment. From the bow-perch, on which the nestling just come to her strength is placed, she must be taught to fly to your hand for *food* — for something which she likes — for something which is ultimately to make her like you, and the spot and position in which she received it. She is to remain on the hand some time. It is for these reasons that I have insisted so much on tough pieces of meat, on the stumps of wings, &c., for the meal is prolonged by the difficulty of obtaining it, and "carriage" should scarcely last longer than the meal. *This*, however, may be done with great advantage; in fact, I am convinced that it must be done — viz. when the bird during carriage has pulled for twenty minutes or so at a "stump," quietly withdraw it, concealing it in the right hand. The hawk, if in an advanced stage, will put her head on one side, at first quite in a facetious manner, as she tries to peep into your right hand; or she will look eagerly underneath her talons and between the fingers on which she is carried. I would keep her attention to the food as long as possible, by occasionally giving her very small pieces of it. Presently she will begin to notice objects near; bate at a passing bird perhaps (that is good); after a pause, look restless, almost frightened. Now, don't go beyond this point. She has had some excellent experience. You have every reason to congratulate yourself. During the actual pulling and eating she was taught to like the fist in a measure; I say in a measure, for she was so eager and excited in tugging for food, that she hardly knew where she was. After the withdrawal of the food she had more time to consider matters: the first, natural, and (as it happened) correct notion was, that food is not far off — somewhere about *you*. So far, very good; the proper feeling was still being kept up. She looked, as I have said, round her, and felt that the position was an awkward one — alone, without an object, on the hand of her natural and most dreaded enemy! There had been time to recognise and appreciate this; for, the feeding having been stopped, her attention was released. But the truth came gradually, and it came out of *good* — out of chicken's wing, or some such delicacy. It came fast, however, at length — too fast. I will suppose that moment this one. Stop the truth before she connects her position with pain: you have gone quite far enough for to-day; out with that same chicken's wing! She will forget her climbing sorrows in it.

Now, a sparrow-hawk treated in this way will not only learn to like her master and his society, but, while she is learning such things, will be accustomed also to the motion of being carried, and to the appearance of trees, hedges, &c, as she is made to pass them on her chariot. But remember that you struck down the scales in favour of yourself the moment doubt began to merge into fear, or the moment before; and the position on your hand, which was fast appearing new, unnatural, frightful, was rendered expedient and desirable by the opportune re-introduction of the meat. With the recurrence of such a fear on another occasion, there will probably come the recurrence of a circumstance vastly agreeable to a hungry hawk — there will be a recollection of dinner. And so, by degrees, good-bye to Nature, or, rather goodbye to the teaching which *she* gives her children: you have induced her to permit you to succeed in something that is new and opposite. Habit is not a "second nature," nor a "new nature;" there is no such thing: it is nature in another garb, perhaps in another form.

Your young hawk is pretty sure to receive several frights in your morning's and evening's walk. So much the better: she must get *use* to be frightened, or, rather, she must be taught by practice to recover instantly from her fright. Something under three hours a day — the time divided between morning and evening — is long enough to carry an eyess in training, *provided* she is always in the society of human beings, and is called to hand several times during the middle of the day for small but tender pieces of meat. For my own part, I think it is almost as difficult to reconcile a sparrow-hawk to the bow-perch as it is to the hand. I give, occasionally, a small bird, or a portion of a large one, at the perch, standing close by the hawk while she is feeding, and once or twice offering a tender piece of beef at the tip of the finger; but this is a point upon which, after practice, I wish my readers to form their own judgment. There is another plan, to be used in a somewhat advanced stage of the education, which I have found exceedingly useful in *taming* the bird; and, as it is so very difficult to tame her at all, I ought to mention it. It is this: fasten your hawk, when she is somewhat sharp-set, on the "perch or screen," described in Chapter Six. In wet weather, this is of course done indoors; in fine and very *still* weather out of doors. Place in the garden or the hall, as the case may be, a small box containing tiny pieces of meat, which have been squeezed three or four times in cold water, in order to extract a considerable portion of nutriment. (How much more quickly birds would be trained if they could eat twice as much they now do, and yet have an appetite!) Instruct every one who passes — ten minutes or a quarter of an hour intervening, we will suppose — to abstract one piece of meat from the box, and, quietly walking up to the bird, present it on the tip of a finger or short stick. The hawk bates off; but with her little leash she *must* come up again in the same place, or nearly so; don't move the finger; the meat will soon be taken; now pass quietly away. The consequence is, that in time the bird, so far from being alarmed at the near approach of a stranger, will rather hope for it. Something of this kind was done when the nestlings could only just fly; however, it ought to be continued. The only objection to the above plan is a possible sacrifice of *tail;* but who can keep that perfect even on the bow-perch?

I have but glanced at the natural history of the sparrow-hawk, or what is usually called the natural history, for most people are tolerably familiar with it. In this chapter my chief anxiety has been to place before the reader *character* and *training*. In the next I shall touch lightly on the method employed by successful hawkers; show my readers this bird in the field, and append a little history which I hope they may find interesting.

[1] There are, however, to say the least of it, foreign *varieties;* perhaps they may deserve the dignity of species; if so, it is incumbent upon Science to find some other specific name than *"nisus"* for her other children.

[2] Nevertheless, some merlins could be trained in the same time and -with less trouble, but only to short low flights, like those of the sparrow-hawk. No haggard peregrine, with even night and day watching, could be put upon the wing in *anything like* ten days; but this is not attributable to her disposition (which is far more tractable than that of the sparrow-hawk), but simply to the range and height of her flight. Sir John, no doubt, was fortunate in the temper of the bird which he trained.

Chapter Eighteen - The Sparrow-Hawk (Concluded)

There are now in England several gentlemen who fly the sparrow-hawk most successfully. I have before me two letters from Barmston, near Hull, the contents of which will, I am sure, induce my readers sincerely to thank Mr. Bower, who so kindly wrote them for this work. He says: "I allowed my nestling hawks to fly at hack till perfectly strong on the wing; and, during the early part of the training, showed them every new scene I could; I never allowed them to feed except on or from some one's hand — as many different people as possible. I found this of great use, as the hawk on the approach of a stranger rather expected food than showed any fear. My present sparrow-hawk is far the best I ever had. I don't remember her ever having refused to fly at a blackbird within thirty yards; and frequently she has killed a black-bird with, as near as I could tell, 100 yards' law. Sometimes, but not often, a thrush has beaten her to a hedge, and I have been unable to drive it out. I flew her a little at partridges the early part of September; altogether she killed seventeen, all full grown, and six old birds amongst them — all sprung within ten yards, except one old one, which passed about forty yards off, as she was sitting in a tree; she pursued and killed it in the middle of a large seed field. I had capital sport at thrushes in the turnip-fields. I believe she would have gone on killing partridges well, but I kept her more to blackbirds, as I think they afford better sport. I commenced flying her on the 23rd of July, 1858, and from that time till the 7th of September, I flew her about three days a week. She killed, in the time mentioned, forty-three blackbirds, thirty-six thrushes, seventeen partridges, seven sparrows, four hedge-sparrows, and one starling. I never let her kill a sparrow if I could help it, and always fed her on blackbirds. Her best day was six blackbirds, three thrushes, two partridges, and a sparrow. She has been on a bow-perch during the winter, under a shed, and put out on fine days, a bath of chilled water having been occasionally given her in the sun. I have another sparrow-hawk that has been at large in a room; both have been well and regularly fed, and are in perfect health. I never trained a male, or haggard. My hawks are broken to the hood, but they never wear it unless when travelling. I think that by always feeding a sparrow-hawk on the hand, you prevent any disposition to carry; I never had any trouble in that respect. The great thing is not to attempt to fly a sparrow-hawk till it will come well down to the lure from a tree; for if these birds get a habit of *sitting,* it is hardly possible to break them of it." This ex-cellent hawk is now in perfect health, and moulting nicely. Mr. Bower further says of a sparrow-hawk which he trained in 1857: "I killed my first bird with my little sparrow-hawk (called 'Teddy') on the 23rd of August, 1857, and up to the 20th of October she killed 327 birds, consisting of sparrows, black-birds, thrushes, a few partridges, and linnets — more than two-thirds spar-rows. She unfortunately got drowned by getting into a pond, having pulled her bow-perch up. In all probability she would have killed as many more if this had not happened, for she was quite as keen as ever, and got very shifty." (By the way, does not this misfortune show, at least, how *desirable* it is to peg down the wire of the bow-perch, as recommended in the chapter on the gos-hawk?)

Sir Charles Slingsby, Bart., has been very successful with this bird. Major Verner, too, who had seen it used by the Sikhs some years ago, when his reg-iment was in India, caught 150 birds in about three months with a single hawk; and I doubt not he has done even better since that time. I believe I represent his opinion correctly, when I say that he is no friend to a *great deal* of "carriage" during training, but that he trusts very much to keeping his young birds in a public place, and to calling them to fist frequently.

Sir Molyneux Nepean, Bart., has most kindly interested himself on the subject of this chapter. As long ago as last September he wrote me a letter in which he described the management of sparrow-hawks, by John Gale, hawker to the late Baronet. I quote from the letter: — "You are quite right in your surmise that the landrails were taken with the female hawk; she was chosen as being superior in size and strength to the cock bird. The hawks were always kept at perch (a moveable bow-perch, the bow fixed into a flat heavy board), either in Gale's cottage or about the premises, where people of all ages and sizes were constantly passing in and out. Threats of instant vengeance were, however, always held out if the hawks were either fed or bullied. The dogs we used, which were *small* spaniels, were continually about the place where the birds were at perch: they attended the hawker when the birds were fed, and, indeed, were sometimes fed themselves in their presence. With regard to the wild nature of these hawks, ours were not particularly wild unless neglected or kept from society, but they were always distrustful with a stranger, and would not stand teasing. The treatment was this: The birds were taken from the nest quite young, and as soon as they had sense and strength enough they were compelled to creep to the edge of the place they were kept in to get their food. As soon as they had a little use of their wings they were taught to fly from the perch to the fist holding the food, beginning, perhaps, with a foot in distance, and gradually increasing it to the length of the room. When quite accustomed to this, they were taken on the green, and (with a long and light string attached to the jesses and perch) taught to fly to a stuffed bird for their food, which was fastened to the back of the neck. After this the stuffed bird was gently swung at the end of a string (like a lure), which taught the hawk that she must not only strike and bind, but that she must do so when the quarry was in motion before she got her dinner. The hawker *always* whistled in a peculiar way when feeding his birds, or, indeed, going near them; and they got so accustomed to it, as a sort of dinner-bell, that if they did stray, the whistle would almost always bring them to fist. If they missed the quarry they would sometimes fly off to a tree, but were seldom if ever lost. They were always kept in the *highest possible condition*, and if they seemed dull, the old man's grand specific was cayenne pepper put into a bit of meat, which they could swallow without inquiry. Old Gale used to refuse to fly his birds if there was a breeze; he said that they would not and could not fly if there was wind — 'If afore 'em they could not face it, and if ahind it turned 'em over.'"

It seems also that Gale's birds were always to be depended upon when sharp-set; they would follow a quarry sprung at thirty yards or more; he never hooded them; they occasionally, but very rarely, flew partridges —

landrails were the quarry. People in those days did not shoot landrails; they hunted them up with little spaniels, and flew the hawks as the birds rose. At the time to which reference is made, a great deal of hemp was grown about Loder's Court, Dorsetshire, and hemp is a favourite resort for landrails. *Many* country gentlemen, in that county, forty or fifty years ago, always took those birds with the sparrow-hawk, for the sake of the sport, and also because shot often injures the delicate flesh of the landrail.

I will place at the end of this chapter a paper containing the particulars of poor John Gale's death (father, I believe, of the present Gale, who is still on the estate); it will have a melancholy interest, but I trust may not be considered altogether out of place in this work. The narrative has been forwarded to me by Capt. Salvin; but it is in the words of one of the family in whose service Gale lived and died.

However, I must not in the meantime forget my promise to show the sparrow-hawk in the field. After the letters already quoted, that will be soon done.

For real sport, blackbird-hawking is probably the best. It is conducted very much after the manner of magpie-hawking, and altogether resembles it. The hawk must be kept entirely to the quarry. Several assistants are required; they should be armed with long sticks, with which to force the blackbird out of cover when he has been "put in" by his pursuer. If the quarry is found in one of many bushes in a large field, it is flown at as it leaves one cover for another. The hawk, it is assumed, has been accustomed to fly to *any one's* hand for food, having only perhaps a slight preference for that of her master. In the excitement of the chase, supposing her in thorough yarak, she will perhaps settle on the head of the beater who happens to be nearest the spot where the quarry disappeared, and dash off in instant pursuit at the proper time. Beating hedges must be conducted in this way: a beater is placed near the hawker, but on the opposite side of the hedge, while several others are sent forward to prevent the blackbird from escaping by creeping up the fence, or by flying out on the wrong side of it. They make a large circle a considerable distance ahead; unless they do this, it is very possible that no flight will be had. If the country is very much enclosed, the flight (or rather, perhaps, forty flights after the same bird) may last for more than half an hour; the master and his assistants having had almost as much to do as the hawk herself; having had, at least, as much healthy exercise as they can well stand. A hen blackbird is usually killed in a few minutes, but a fine old cock affords, as a rule, a very exciting flight. Four or five — taking cocks and hens as they come — is good work for a good hawk in one day.

I have no doubt that, in Ireland, much sport might be had even now with landrails, but in this country they are not found in sufficient numbers to justify the hope of anything like a good day with them. This flight has been already described. Mention has also been made of excellent sport with thrushes out of turnips. Last year a gentleman in Ireland flew a female sparrow-hawk at a woodcock; the hawk, which had lost a considerable portion of her tail, seems to have stuck well to the cock, but did not take it. However, a sparrow-hawk, though in complete plumage, must have been overmatched, in such a case, if she missed the first dash.

Partridges, half or three-parts grown, may be easily taken with this bird; nay, as shown above, even when strong and old, a good hawk has speed and power to kill them. A steady old pointer, or a couple of very small close-hunting spaniels, may be used; but where game is abundant, it is, of course, possible to walk the birds up. The old hawking-books tell us that magpies were flown at with the sparrow-hawk; this one can easily credit; but rook-hawking with this little creature, mentioned also, is entirely out of my comprehension. Water-hens may be killed with a strong female, but I never saw the flight, though I believe it is a pretty sure one. I once flew an excellent hen merlin at a water-hen; the hawk knocked it down, but could not get to the throat At -last there was an entire shake off, the quarry gaining its feet; and very well did it deserve the escape which it effected, for, rising erect on its long green legs, the little tail stuck up, and lifting high the red-capped head, it stood in the attitude of defence assumed by a game-cock. The assailant stared, paused, and flew quietly away. The sparrow-hawk, however, has certainly more power than the merlin.

In April 1859, the Maharajah Dhuleep Singh took three sparrow-hawks (which had lately arrived from Syria) to Italy for quail-hawking. The hawks were flown from seven to ten in the morning, before it was too hot for the sport; and in seven days they killed 117 quail. The gipsies in Wallachia use it for this quarry. Had we but quail here, what fine sport could be had with the subject of this chapter, and also with the merlin!

The advantages and disadvantages in the use of this bird have already been rather elaborately, though in a measure incidentally, laid before the reader. I need only add that it is the *favourite* with some excellent falconers now living, and that in the old time it held a very fair position. It was assigned to a priest in *this* country; but in the late Manchester Exhibition there was a portrait, by Titian, of the Duke of Milan holding a sparrow-hawk upon his fist. However, had he been an English nobleman, there is no reason why he should not have carried a hawk *below* his station.

I now offer the story of which I have spoken; it is called...

The Dead Hawker. [1]

One fine morning in February 182-, an old man issued from his small cottage, situate in a village in the West of England. Though the snows of more than seventy winters had fallen since his birth, Old Time had dealt kindly with him. He was, in spite of his great age, still hale and vigorous, his eye glittered like a diamond, his pace, though not quick, was firm and regular. His square shoulders, well-set head, long arms, and immense bones, showed that in his early days few of the best wrestlers (in a country famous for that athletic game) would have selected the rustic Titan as an easy playfellow. His head had no appearance of baldness, but every hair was as white as snow, and hung in curls over his neck and shoulders, giving an appearance and dignity to the old man that might have well become one of the patriarchs of old. In his right hand was a "quarterstaff" or stick, used for beating covers or as a weapon. It was between five and six feet long, and somewhat thicker than a man's thumb, of which weapon (now almost extinct as such) the old man had been a distinguished professor in his youth. On his left arm (which up to the elbow was protected by a long glove, of antiquated appearance and curious work) sat a hawk pluming its feathers in the bright sun, and occasionally picking at its master to obtain a caress, or playfully endeavouring to pull off its bell and jesses, the badges of its servitude. The veteran had that unmistakeable look about him which belongs exclusively to those who have spent their lives in the field, alike indifferent to the scorching sun and the wintry hail-storm. He was, as his appearance denoted, "a *hawker*" nearly, if not quite, the last of his race or profession in the once merry West of England, and was in the service of the lord of the manor in which his cottage stood. He was followed by five or six spaniels of the small cocker breed, which were used to spring the game, principally young partridges and landrails. These dogs were always reared with the hawks, and were carefully broken when young to hunt within twenty or thirty yards of the hawker, so that when the quarry was roused the hawk might get a fair flight. Half a dozen chubby, curly-headed urchins (under pretence of asking after his health, and where he was going) hung about his heels, well knowing that the kind old man in his progress through the village seldom failed to stop at "the shop" and spend his odd pence (if he had any) in the purchase of choice "lollipops," or those wonderfully-shaped quadrupeds made of gilt gingerbread, which delicacies he distributed for the special gratification of these youthful allies; nor were they on this occasion disappointed, and consequently old John Gale, or " Jan," as the provincials call him, was greeted with their lusty cheers as he left the village on his way to visit an old gamekeeper in the service of a neighbouring squire, who lived about twelve miles from Jan's home. That day and the next passed over, frosty and clear; on the second evening the clouds gathered round, and at night there was a heavy fall of snow. On the third day, although the morning was bright, and looked more like settled weather, a snow-storm burst with terrific violence over the whole tract of high, bleak down and deep valley, of which that part of the country is principally composed, and continued until the morning of the next day, which was a Sunday. That day was fine, although the storm still raged in the distance, and the whole parish assembled for morning service; and when that was finished the church-goers were grouped about the doors gossiping, &c., when a very tall, powerful man, whose huge whiskers and badger-skin cap were congealed into one mass of frozen snow, and who appeared exhausted with fatigue and exposure, burst into the circle, and was at once recognised as head-keeper at the Squire's, to whose place the old hawker had gone, and son to the old forester with whom he had sojourned. He at once demanded whether old Jan had been heard of. "No," said his astonished and wondering auditors, "he be'ant comed whoam yet!" "Then vur zartin zure," said the keeper, "he be smothered up i' snow, vur his dogs be coomed back alone and whining — that be as yesterday's sundown. I've been zarchin for un since grey o' mourn, but the very dog couldn't veace the curl o' the storm," pointing to a large bloodhound that lay panting and footsore at his feet. In less time than I have been describing this fearful interruption, the news had spread like wildfire through the village that old Jan was lost in the snow, and three or four hundred stout men (the flower of the lordship) had hurried home to doff their Sunday garments, and start, headed by the keepers, to scour the country in search of their old friend. On came the night, and with it the return of the almost exhausted villagers, whom the renewal of the storm had most unwillingly compelled to relinquish the search. Next morning, at daylight, they again started with better hopes of success, for the day was beautifully clear, and they were reinforced by a score or so of keepers, with their retrievers, from the neighbouring manors, who, as soon as they heard of the news, came forward at once to show their good feeling towards one so universally looked up to as old Jan. Some hours had passed without a trace being discovered, when one of the sons, who was rounding the shoulder of Eggerdon hill (which his father might have gone over as a short cut) fancied he heard the cry of a hawk, and partly by chance, and partly from habit, gave the long shrill whistle used to lure the hawks by his father, and a hawk instantly replied to the well-known call. The stout countryman sat down in the snow, and covering his face with his hands, said to those with him, "Zumthing do tell I that be poor feyther's bird. Go ye up, two or dree of you, and seek the drift." They did as he bid them, and, guided by the occasional cries of the hawk, soon came to the spot where the old man had laid down to his last sleep. Not a part was visible through the snow but the hawk-hand, to which the bird was fastened by his leash. The poor creature, not being able to escape, had (to the horror of the men) fairly ripped up the glove, and, in the extremity of hunger, fearfully mangled the hand of the dead man. Sorrowfully they bore the stiffened corpse to their village, each tiny hamlet, as they passed, turning out to offer such consolation as they could to the old man's mourning family. His funeral was wonderful; many came from the heart of the neighbouring counties who had long known "Jan the Hawker," and many whose skulls had in youthful days been cracked by Jan's unrivalled cudgel at the village fairs came to show that though their heads might not be quite sound, their hearts were. To this day his rustic virtues and accomplishments are never-failing themes of gossip and admiration; and many a stout fellow would give his ears to be likened to "Jan the Hawker."

[1] Hawks proper, or the short-winged hawks, require a different treatment from that necessary for the long-winged hawks or falcons; and this applies not

only to their daily management at home, bat to the sort of country in which they are flown. Thus we find those who, living in an open country, kept falcons, were called *falconers;* whereas the men who (in wooded districts, &c.) trained and flew only hawks proper, were described as *hawkers.* They were frequently quite ignorant of the management of the nobler birds.

Chapter Nineteen - Jer-Falcons

If, as I have hinted before, the old writers on falconry, either directly or by looseness of expression, laid themselves open to the suspicion that they supposed specific distinctions where none existed — as, perhaps, in the case of the peregrine — their error with regard to the jer-falcon was entirely on the other side. An Iceland, a Greenland, or a Norway falcon were all jer-falcons to them, and probably nothing more. They are jer-falcons to us also; but many modern naturalists have begun to recognise a specific difference between the Norway bird and the others, while some class even those two as different species. [1]

Let us dispose, first of 'all, of that bird about which there is not very much dispute. "We are indebted," says Mr. Brodrick, in "Falconry in the British Isles," (S to the kindness of Mr. John Hancock for the means of giving a figure of this noble bird (the Norway falcon). His specimen is a male bird of the second year, showing the change of plumage from the nestling to the adult state, and presents very much the appearance of a large peregrine. This species might be obtained from Norway at the present day, and would probably well repay the trouble and expense of seeking. The male bird, from which our drawing was made, was (with the exception of the greater length of tail) almost of the same proportions as a large female peregrine, though with a less powerful foot; but this must have been a very small specimen; for, upon the authority of several falconers, we find it generally of the same size as the Greenland and Iceland species. The tarsi are partly feathered, similar to the other northern falcons; and in colour also it is intermediate, between the adult peregrine and the darker varieties of the Icelander; the legs and cere in the young bird are blue lead colour, becoming yellow when adult. This species, though possessing great power of wing, appears to be very local; and we have never heard of a specimen, in any stage of plumage, having been met with in these islands." It seems that in August, 1839, Mr. Newcome netted in Norway three young birds of this species, two tiercels and a falcon.

With regard to the large falcon found in Iceland and that found in Greenland, the question is, whether they are distinct in species, or only dark and light varieties of the same bird. To enter into this subject at any length would be simply to copy in words, or, at any rate, in substance, the admirable remarks upon it (would that I could give the author's invaluable drawings!) contained in "Falconry in the British Isles." With that book before me, and with the aid of Mr. Hancock's last paper (from the Annals and Magazine of Natural History for February, 1854) "On the Greenland and Iceland Falcons," I can offer a short analysis of the argument, which may perhaps be found interesting.

The two and *only* difficulties — the former perhaps at first sight considerable — with which the upholders of the specific-difference theory have to contend are, that "both species are precisely alike in size and comparative proportions, which is perhaps [but there is a suspicion of this in the case of the Norwegian bird] more than can be said of any other two distinct species known;" and also that "even in colour some of the adult birds of the two species *approach* very closely to each other, viz. the darkest of the Greenland and the lightest specimens of the Iceland birds."

On the other side we have the following very strong and important evidence: — The darker bird, for which a specific name, *Icelandicus,* is claimed, breeds only in Iceland; the lighter coloured bird, *Greenlandicus,* only in Greenland. This has been proved by observation. The *nestling* plumage of the latter is always lighter than the *adult* plumage of the former. Now, in both instances, there will of course be a change of colour in the first moult; but the dark bird of Iceland will not appear as the light bird of Greenland. *After* the first moult there is scarcely a visible change in either species — or so-called species — perhaps none at all. It is a mistake to suppose that the plumage of falcons becomes lighter each year after it has become adult. Mr. Hancock, premising that (this was in 1854) he had seen at least 150 specimens of both "species," writes as follows on the Greenland falcon: —

"The mature Greenland falcon is distinguished from the young, not so much by its greater whiteness as by the character of the markings, which on the back and scapulars are always cordate, inclining to sagittiform; the head, under parts, and tail are frequently unspotted, but not by any means constantly so. The young is characterised by having the upper parts marked with large oblong spots, and the head and under parts with long narrow dashes. In both old and young the markings are of a dark warm grey, almost black in the former, which is also distinguished by the cere, beak, feet and toes being of a pale yellow or straw colour; while in the young these parts, with the exception of the beak, are of a light livid blue. Some of the young are very white, so that they can be distinguished only by the form of the spots, and colour of the naked parts. In such the spots or dashes on the head and under parts are reduced to mere lines, scarcely wider than the shafts of the feathers, and the tail is not uncommonly devoid of all markings. Other nest birds are comparatively dark, with the spots large and crowded. The former, on maturity, are very little spotted, and have all the under parts, head, and tail not unfrequently pure white; the latter never attain the same degree of whiteness, but change into the dark and richly marked varieties of the adult. There is no doubt with regard to the mature and immature state of this species. I possess several specimens with the large oblong markings of the nest plumage, which are moulting, and in every case the new feathers have the cordate spots of maturity; and to show that no change takes place afterwards, it is only necessary to refer to the beautiful specimen which was kept alive in the Zoological Gardens, Regent's Park. This individual was a male; it had the plumage very light; and when I first saw it in 1849, it exhibited both mature and immature feathers, the old and faded ones, on the upper parts, having the oblong spots of the first plumage, the new feathers of the back and scapulars being all marked with cordate spots. I took a drawing of the bird in this state. On completing its moult it was one of the whitest specimens I have ever seen. It lived until May 1852, and must consequently have changed its plumage twice after having assumed its mature dress; but no further alteration took place in the form of the markings, and *the bird was as white on its first moult as it was when it died.* Another living specimen, which I had in my possession some years ago, moulted once. This was mature when I received it, and it was as white then as after its moult, and no change whatever took place in the character of its plumage. It may also be stated that I have several specimens in the mature plumage, which have partially cast their feathers, and those coming are exactly like the old ones — neither darker nor whiter — the feathers of the upper parts bearing the same characteristic cordate spots. Thus there appears ample proof that the birds with oblong spots on the upper parts change at once into those with cordate spots, and that the latter undergo no subsequent alteration: the one is therefore evidently the young of the other, and is undoubtedly in the first or nest plumage, unless this species be an exception to the rule, that all the true falcons get the mature plumage on the first moult: the Iceland falcon, peregrine, merlin, hobby, redlegged falcon, and kestrel all do."

Mr. Hancock then proceeds: —

"*Falco Graenlandicus,* then, differs from *F. Icelandicus* in both the mature and immature states, and is characterised by its greater whiteness of plumage. The former, in fact, may be stated to have white feathers with dark markings, the latter dark feathers with white markings; besides that, the mature Iceland falcon is further distinguished by conspicuous transverse bands above and on the flanks, and by the blue colour of the beak, and bright yellow of the cere and feet."

I copy a further description of the Icelander from "Falconry in the British Isles": — "The weight of a female Iceland falcon is about 3 ½ lbs., its length from bill to tail about 23 inches, the spread of the wings being above 4 feet; the length of the male bird is about 20 inches. In colour and markings both sexes are alike, as well in the young as in adult states; individuals differing only as they assume the light or dark varieties of plumage with the intermediate gradations... The tarsi are feathered about half way down, and the naked parts are, in the young birds, of a blue lead colour, as are also the cere, and skin about the eyes. This colour changes to yellow in the mature birds, and deepens with age. The young birds are,' all of them, on the upper parts of

128

the body, of a dark greyish brown colour, each feather being margined with dusky white; the under surface is of the same dusky white, marked thickly with longitudinal blotches of the dark colour of the upper parts; the thighs and under tail-coverts having long streaks, which, in the adult plumage, are changed into transverse bars, similar to, though not as distinct as, those in the peregrine. The colour of the irides is dark hazel."

With regard to eggs, I can do nothing better than copy the following from a letter which Mr. Hancock was obliging enough to write to me, the other day, on these birds: —

"In my opinion, the egg of the Iceland and Greenland birds will neither differ in size nor colour. Description of the egg of the Iceland falcon: about the size of that of the barn-door fowl, but of a rounder form, blotched or spotted all over with red-brown; colour varying from light to dark in different specimens."

The broad differences in plumage, detailed above, between the nestlings bred in Iceland and those bred in Greenland, together with the particulars of the first moults, are simply *facts*, obtained by observation. They are the data upon which naturalists must determine if in these great [northern birds we have different species; or whether one is but a variety of the other.

Of the three birds already mentioned, the Iceland falcon is that which has been used most frequently in this country. I imagine, however, that when we read of a very great sum being given in olden times for a cast of jer-falcons or white falcons, the Greenlander is intended; for it is rather a difficult matter to procure this bird at all; and individuals are occasionally met with so slightly pencilled, that it would hardly perhaps be an error in language to call them "white." In 1545 there was a certain battle fought in Scotland called "Lilliard's Edge;" at the commencement of it (says Sir Walter Scott), Lord Angus, as he led his Scots against the English horse, saw a heron rise from a marsh close at hand: "Oh," said he, "that I had my white hawk here! we could then all join battle together." As the Greenlander was *not* there, the heron escaped; but Lord Angus cut the opposing cavalry to pieces.

Till the end of the last century, the Iceland falcon was used for flying the kite. This quarry was frequently found at a great height — only, perhaps, just within sight. To bring it down a curious expedient was adopted. Sir John Sebright gives it thus: — "A great owl (*Strix bubo*), to the leg of which the falconers usually tie a fox's brush — not only to impede its flight, but to make it, as they fancy, more attractive — is thrown up to draw down the kite." Poor *Milvus* probably considered, from his height, that there, near the earth, fluttered a bird that he could bully, slowly carrying off some heavy and valuable prey; so *Milvus* came down just in time to see a great grey hawk dart from a man's hand by a hedgeside, and chase him for his life. The forked-tail kite was once very common in this country, and was, we are told, protected in London in consequence of its services as a scavenger. I need hardly say to the enlightened men of this generation how unworthy it would be of mankind in the "nineteenth century" to accept anything directly and at once from the hand of Nature. We are too wise, and too foolish in our wisdom, for *that*.

Recently, the Icelander has been flown at hares and herons; even at so small a quarry as partridges. Mr. Newcome "succoured" those trained by him with a slow dog for hares. The flight was not very successful. The hare was repeatedly rolled over by the falcon, and left an easy prey to the dog. It was seldom, if ever, that the hawk did the whole. [2]

A tiercel turned out a very good heron-hawk; and one which the late Duke of Leeds gave my coadjutor was good at partridges. For black game I can imagine nothing better than a jer-tiercel.

These hawks — the jer-falcons altogether — are generally netted soon after they can fly, or as old birds. In either case they must be trained precisely in the manner recommended for peregrines; and, if it were possible to bring them over as half-fledged nestlings, they would still be treated like the smaller falcon. Sir John Sebright speaks of the Icelander as being esteemed for its great powers and *tractable* disposition. I have heard from more modern falconers that the tractability is not so conspicuous. This gentleman makes a distinction between the gyrfalcon (or jer-falcon) and the Icelander, assuring us that the former is less than the latter; but I have no idea what he means (in this comparison) by the "gyrfalcon;" for the Norway bird is probably all but, if not quite, as large as either Greenlander or Icelander; and these are — one the size of the other. To the Saker he was probably an entire stranger.

In "Falconry in the British Isles" we have three most valuable plates (to say nothing of that of the Norway falcon) of hawks not known in modern or European practice — unless, indeed, *possibly* the last; these are of the *Saker,* the *Lanner,* and the *Barbary* falcons. No naturalist can afford to ignore these pictures and the letter-press belonging to them. For myself, I have no language to express my admiration of both. Mr. Brodrick has placed himself out of the reach of flattery — for even a friend cannot exaggerate excellence.

Of the *sacre,* [3] Before says that in colour it is something like a kite — a sort of smoky red, the dullest in plumage of all the hawks used in falconry, with blue legs and feet (when young): that it is a bird of passage, and was taken by falconers in the islands of the Levant, Cyprus, Rhodes, &c. The "Gentleman's Recreation" gives the following description: "She is somewhat larger than the haggard falcon; her plume is rusty and ragged; the sear of her foot and beak like the lanner; her pounces are short; however she hath great strength, and is hardy to all kinds of fowl; she is more disposed to the field a great deal than to the brook, and delights to prey on great fowl, as the hern, the goose, &c." It seems that this bird flew the kite well. The quaint writer proceeds to say of this flight — "if well observed, together with the variety of contests and bickerings that are between them, it cannot but be very pleasant and delightful to the beholder" (what a shocking sentiment! and yet methinks I would have walked barefoot some miles to have seen those same contests and bickerings); "for," he continues, "I have known in a clear day, and little wind stirring, that both the sacre and kite have soared so high that the sharpest eye could not discern them; yet hath the sacre, in the encounter, conquered the kite, and I have seen her come tumbling down to the ground with a strange precipitancy."

Both sacre and lanner differ from all the other European falcons in this particular, that "neither of the sexes alter the colour of their plumage in the first and subsequent moults." The female sacre is about the size of the male Iceland falcon.

The *lanner* seems to have proved somewhat of a slack-mettled hawk, though it is far from being without its share of praise. I have several times seen the female bird at the Regent's Park, called a lanner, and I believe truly called so. It is certainly not a peregrine, nor a bird of any species which I have met with elsewhere. The lanner breeds, we are told, in France, on the highest trees in the forest or in the loftiest rocks. Possibly it might be procured without much difficulty; but for *practical* purposes the peregrine is doubtless superior. For further information on this bird I must refer my readers to "Falconry in the British Isles."

The *Barbary falcon* is, I may venture to assert, almost unmatched in speed, strength, and courage by any hawk of its size in the world. Some pains have been taken this year to bring the bird to England, but I don't know, at present, with what success. I should exceedingly like to see its powers tested; perhaps some day I may do so.

The following is a description of it: — "This beautiful little falcon, in colour and marking, is a perfect miniature likeness of the peregrine, and might be taken for a dwarf variety of that bird, were it not for its proportional difference. It forms, in our eyes, the *beau idéal* of what a falcon should be, and is a perfect model of strength and speed combined. For, although smaller, by nearly a fourth, than the peregrine, it has the organs of destruction — such as the beak, feet, and talons — fully as large, united to longer and more pointed wings in proportion to its total length; in this respect almost rivalling the hobby." — *Falconry in the British Isles.*

The Kestrel is a beautifully-shaped little falcon; and has no fault in make that I can see except a want of length in the foot and singles. It was occasionally trained in the olden time, but assigned to a "knave" or servant. Nature has played a prank here, and has condemned one of the most beautiful and capable of her children to be the victim of a grovelling instinct. Why should this little Hercules wash out the stables? Why should this Arachne, who could work tapestry with Minerva, be made to do a spider's task? I cannot tell. The kestrel or windhover (*Falco tinnunculus*) contents itself, as a rule, with mice, with a beetle or two, but will attack a bird in a snare, or a wounded bird unable to fly. I have been at the trouble to prove these last facts by experiment: a male kestrel seized a fieldfare, and a female a pigeon. But there is no *making* it chase for many yards; and it was probably carried of old as a badge, and for the amusement of seeing it fly to the lure, which it may very easily be taught to do. There could be no nicer pet for a lady than this bird, were it not that the merlin, which is rather smaller, is useful as well as beautiful. The kestrel generally builds on rocks, occasionally on trees; neither is it scrupulous about appropriating the old nest of another bird, a few alterations and improvements being made. Its eggs are in colour much like those of the other falcons.

As this work professes to treat only of those birds which are or have been used in falconry, it would be out of place to attempt any description of the buzzards, harriers, &c.

The next chapter will conclude this treatise. It will be devoted, in some measure, to the diseases and moulting of hawks; but will contain also some *Indian Hawking,* which I hope may relieve the tedium of details that are more necessary than amusing.

At some future time I may perhaps give a detailed account of the British birds of prey, from the largest to the least. It has been the object of the present work to make natural history subservient to falconry; in the next the sport must only be servant to the science.

[1] Such recognition was subsequent to "Falconry in the British Isles."
[2] I believe it has been done since by the hawk alone.
[3] A friend of Capt. Salvin has lately seen the Arab Sheiks use both saker and lanner: for a trained sacre £40 was frequently offered and refused.

Chapter Twenty - The Ugliest and The Last

I must apologise for this chapter — it is the last, and, in some parts, the ugliest of all; not, perhaps, that the former fact will distress many, but my readers must try to forgive the latter. However, the dish is served up with some excellent Indian pickle, which will be found in due course. This is an appendix, and will stand on its privileges. I have tried to be systematic and methodical through nineteen long chapters; let us, in the name of mercy, have a nice, complicated, lazy, refreshing jumble to end with!

During the publication in "The Field" of the aforesaid "nineteen," I received a very considerable number of courteous letters from strangers; containing, in the first place, a little incense which I was begged to burn at the shrine of Vanity; and, in the second, a list of questions on the Art of Falconry which the writers hoped I would be kind enough to answer. I was — not *kind* enough, but — grateful enough to reply privately to most of those queries; and, in doing so, I had occasion to remark to many who propounded them, that the required solutions might be found by reference to some former chapter. Still, I know that, when a small work like the present drags its slow length through more -than a year and a half in the periodical in which it appears, the best memory cannot always retain the whole of the facts recorded, to say nothing of the order in which they were written. In their present form of a volume, and with the advantage of an index, I trust these papers may not be considered incomplete; but I make it my business now to attempt to supply any omissions which I may have made during their composition.

"What," says one correspondent, "is a "makehawk," — A "make-hawk," my dear sir, is an old and experienced hawk flown with a young and inexperienced one, in order that the latter may be incited to perseverance, and instructed in manners. Such a help, however, can only be employed when the birds show no signs of "crabbing." Again, "How do you prevent two birds ' crabbing ' in the air or on the lure?" You cannot prevent them from crabbing in the *air*; but, if you use but one lure, take one of the birds from it to your hand with a piece of beef as soon as both bind. "How to hood a hawk without disgusting or alienating him thereby?" Cultivate a manual dexterity, which comes to some men sooner than to others, but which in any case can only be acquired by practice. Work away, if you *like*, at a kestrel for a fortnight. Also, rather drop the left hand, and turn it outwards; this will oblige the hawk to keep his head tolerably steady, and also to thrust it towards the hood. When the hawk is tame enough to feed from the hand "barefaced," he may be made to pick a few pieces of meat out of the hood, which is to be of course held in the right hand. Other directions may be found in their proper place.

With regard to cats killing hawks in captivity, my own experience has been that they will not touch them. I know that an immense wild tom-cat was in the habit of prowling among my merlins at *night*, and that he did not hurt them. At the same time the fate of Mr. Brodrick's goshawk shows that cats, in this matter, are not absolutely to be depended upon. My friend's bird was attacked in the garden, in open day, and was so injured that it was mercy to kill it. I have no further information on this subject which is not negative. I have heard of a rat or rats injuring merlins, and of a male sparrow-hawk having been killed by a stoat or a weasel — I forget which. Mr. Brodrick had a peregrine tiercel knocked off its perch, at night, by an *owl*; really "by a mousing *owl* hawked at, and (I think) killed" — more probably by the hanging than the blow. Foxes have been known to pass by trained hawks at night, leaving them untouched.

And now a few words on an important subject, viz. moulting. Hawks, as I need scarcely mention, change all their feathers once a year. For instance, the nestlings of this summer will begin to moult in 1860; young peregrines, if kept fat at the time, will probably drop the first feather — the seventh in the wing — between the middle of March and the middle of April. Merlins are later; but they are in full plumage again by the middle of September, as are often young peregrines. By taking care that a hawk is in flying order, and by constantly working him, you may so postpone the *important* part of the moult that he will fly well till September. Captain Salvin has several times done this. In point of fact, it is quite possible to fly hawks — I don't speak of the same individuals — all the year round. The second and subsequent moults always commence later than the first moult.

The birds may pass their period of moult at liberty in a room, or confined to blocks out of doors under cover of the shed in very hot or wet weather; but, when out of doors, on fine soft grass. The fatter they are kept, the sooner the moult will be over. If they are moulted in rooms (the most expeditious, but not always the most convenient way), great care must be taken to cover any angles with double matting, in order that no feathers may be injured in case of a hasty flight round the room, or towards the roof. Each bird should have a room to itself. [1] Large, round, smooth stones will serve as blocks. The floor must be covered with sand to the depth of several inches. Every falconer should have some room or loft which will answer the purpose of mews — the larger the better. Here he may, if he choose, moult his hawks; and here also he may place them to protect them from stormy and snowy weather, when they are in flying order (plenty of straw in such cases being round their blocks). It is obvious that two or more such rooms are necessary to many falconers. As for shape, that will probably be left to chance; for I certainly shall not discourage the young falconer by telling him that he must have mews *built*. The room must be ventilated by its own chimney, or, if it lack that, by some device which will not let in the day. There must be a window and a close-fitting door, through which no stream of light can enter. The window must have the closest possible shutters, all, of course, to be opened and closed at pleasure. I have mentioned in a previous chapter under what circumstances it is necessary to make the room quite dark, and I need not recapitulate them. Hawks require a bath at all seasons, and in very hot weather it may be offered daily. Let them have, as a rule, more food during the cold than during the hot months; when in moult, however, they can scarcely have too much, and some peregrines may be fed twice a day; merlins at *least* twice, better perhaps three times; sparrow-hawks and hobbies twice; goshawks once, and *well*. When the moult is over, and the hawk fit for getting into flying order, he must be carried and almost rebroken to the hood. Eeduce the quantity of food for two days, but return to it *thoroughly* on the third. If beef be used, it may be dipped once in cold water, and squeezed nearly dry. The little weight which you intend the bird to lose must be lost gradually. Give castings daily, and once, perhaps, during this preparation for flight, a couple of grains of rhubarb on an empty stomach, without castings. Do not trust only to "carriage" for bringing back good order and training; but before the hawk is put on the wing at liberty, let him bate to the swung lure from his block, on which he has been placed unhooded, on thick fine grass, immediately putting the food within his reach when you find he is sufficiently eager. He may also be flown once, in an open place, in a fifty-yard creance, to the lure. During the period of moult, the hawks — I assume — have been fed from the *hand*, as they sat either on the fist or block. It will never do to throw the food in amongst the sand, and leave the birds to fight it out. But I ought to beg pardon for seeming to think it possible that such a thing could be done.

And now for the pharmacopoeia. You must sometimes throw a little physic to hawks as well as dogs; but very little, and very seldom. I have been asked a great deal about diseases; but they are either very few, or not readily recognised. Our ancestors had pages on pages of recipes — very elaborate, very curious, and very incomprehensible. Take the following nice little remedy. I don't mean, swallow it yourself; Heaven forbid! but take it — it's a very easy way — as an *example.* In point of fact, "Take germander, pelamountain, basil, grummel-seed, and broom-flowers, of each half an ounce; hyssop, sassafras, polypodium, and horse-mints, of each a quarter of an ounce, and the like of nutmegs; cubebs, borage, mummy, mugwort, sage, and the four kinds of mirobolans, of each half an ounce; of aloes succotrine the fifth part of an ounce, and of saffron one whole ounce." [2] This is to be "put into a hen's gut, tied at both ends." I hope it may be found agreeable.

I suppose all this means that a happy mixture of purgatives and stimulants is occasionally desirable.

Let us look seriously into the matter; but I know that I shall disappoint the reader, for there is really little or nothing to add to the last pages of "Falconry in the British Isles."

Cramp. — This attacks hawks in their extreme youth, when they have been taken from the nest too soon. [3] It breaks the bones of peregrines, and paralyses the feet of sparrow-hawks. There is no cure for it. Should nestlings unfortunately be sent to the falconer when they are little more than out of the down, the only thing which I can imagine as likely to be of service, is the keeping them in a very warm room, amongst a depth of straw, and perhaps, if they are very young, placing a flannel over them. But this is only conjecture, as I never had occasion to try the plan.

Apoplexy. — This disease has been found by some of my brother falconers to be very fatal to merlins. I am not aware that it ever killed a bird of that species in my possession. When I have lost these little birds, by disease, they have died, in damp weather, of some affection in the crop: symptoms — perfectly green mutes, sometimes changing to black, accompanied by an erect position on the block, with (often) a stretching up of the neck and head. There is no further convulsion; and this cannot be apoplexy. It is probably inflammation of the crop. A grain of rhubarb may be given to the smaller hawks when ill; they must be fed frequently, but somewhat sparingly, with light food, such as live sparrows, &c.; no beef, unless it is pounded to a paste. But when a *merlin* is seriously ill, one can do little more than hope against hope. Mr. Holford had a famous merlin which died in *fit,* when in the act of killing a thrush in the field. *This* probably was apoplexy, and it is not the only case of the kind which has reached me. I have seen a favourite sparrow-hawk of my own die in a fit, and over-fat goshawks may be killed by apoplexy, especially if they are allowed to bate in a hot sun. Peregrines, if ordinary care be used, are exempt. In the case of nestling merlins, which have flown at hack for some weeks near the house, I am quite convinced, from experience, that the best plan is, on the first symptoms of illness which are at all decided, to give a slight purge; two hours after it, half a crop of light food; to put on a couple of hack-bells, and give the hawk its liberty: after a few days' hack, it may probably be taken up, quite restored to health.

Epilepsy may attack peregrines, but I am not aware that any *special* treatment belongs to it.

The Kecks, also called the **Croaks,** is a sort of cough which may attack a peregrine, and is generally produced by damp. *Remedy:* Six or seven bruised pepper-corns, given in the castings; keep the bird dry, and fly it to the lure three times a day. High feeding, and frequent; but the food easy of digestion.

The Frounce. — This disease is said to be very similar to the thrush which sometimes attacks young children. Like many others, it proceeds from damp. If taken in time, it may be cured. *Remedy:* Scrape off, with a clean quill cut for the purpose, all the diseased coating with which the swollen tongue and palate are covered. The bleeding parts are to be dressed with burnt alum mixed with vinegar. If a rod of nitrate of silver be used, it must be used very slightly, or it may occasion sloughing.

Small Tumours, or swelling on the feet and toes, which are occasioned either by accident or by long standing on a hard block, may generally be removed by opening them carefully with a sharp knife. Of course the bird must in future be placed upon a soft, perhaps a padded block. This complaint is generally spoken of as "corns."

Inflammation of the Crop. — *Symptoms:* Throwing up the food after it has been some little time in the crop. The appetite is tolerably good; but the bird loses strength, and may soon die. — *Treatment:* Give two or three grains of rhubarb in the morning, fasting, and repeat the dose every second or third day. The hawk should have rather frequent but small meals of light food. No castings. The warm flesh of rooks or pigeons is good.

Worms. — Give river sand upon the meat, and every other morning, fasting, a dose of rhubarb.

Bangle. — Falconers of old gave their hawks small stones, thrusting them into the throat. This is not done now; but experiments are being tried on the *voluntary* system, and they seem to succeed.

The Blain. — It "consists of watery vesicles within the second joint of the wing, and is supposed to be peculiar to passage-hawks." The swollen part may sometimes be lanced with advantage; but if the disease is of long standing it may produce a stiff joint. No thorough cure.

Fractures. — Curable in the leg, especially if below the joint; almost incurable in the wing, "Where the bone is simply fractured, as far as the restoration of the bird's power is concerned, it will be necessary to have the bird held firmly by an assistant, and, after the careful adjustment of the broken surfaces, to secure the bone in its proper position, either by a bandage of cal-

ico, previously dipped in strong starch, which hardens in drying, or by forming a neat splint of gutta percha to fit the limb. This is easily done by softening a strip of the material, about the thickness of ordinary shoe leather, in warm water, and while in that state moulding it to the limb, and when cold and hard trimming and rounding the edges, and sewing on tape-strings. This form of splint will keep the broken parts immovable, and after about three weeks' time may be removed, when the limb will be found straight and sound again; the plumage acts as a soft wadding between the splint and skin, and thus prevents the latter from becoming chafed. When, however, the fracture is a compound one (where the broken ends of the bone are forced through the surrounding muscles), and the flesh much lacerated, the part should be bathed repeatedly with warm water, and not bound up tightly until the inflammation and swelling have in a manner subsided; after which it must be treated as in the former instance. The wounded bird should be kept as quiet as possible, in a darkened room, and fed twice a day upon a light diet, such as the flesh of rabbits cut into small pieces, and given from the hand."
— *Falconry in the British Isles.*

Parasites. — There is a very curious flying tick found on young merlins, which does them no harm and soon leaves them. It comes from the moors. I have seen it also often on the peregrine, on young grouse, and I *think* on plover shot in the neighbourhood of moors. Once I was introduced to a highly respectable bullfinch, in Northamptonshire, which was said to have been attacked by one of these creatures, and it was found a very difficult matter to catch the parasite: considerable warmth, if my memory serves me, was resorted to in order to induce the vermin to show himself outside the feathers. It is wonderful how quickly the hard flat body, with flat wings, disappears before you can touch it. *Lice* may be got from rooks, or partridges of a late hatch, during the time the hawk is killing the quarry. Frequent bathing is the best remedy; should this fail, a decoction of tobacco mixed with spirit may be applied to the neck and shoulders. There is also a species of *acarus* which burrows in the nares, and which must be got rid of as soon as possible; it is a sort of dark red mite. A fine camel's hair pencil and the tobacco-wash are remedies; in bad cases the red precipitate of mercury ointment should be applied. The hawk affected with this worst of all parasites must be kept from his companions till he is pure.

For a Purge. — Two or three grains of rhubarb given (to a peregrine) in a piece of meat, on an empty stomach, without castings. If only a laxative is required, pounded sugar-candy rubbed into meat acts well; also water, conveyed by dipping in it several pieces of meat. Thick lumpy mutes show that the bowels require an artificial relief. I like to see mutes full; not very thick, nor very thin; white, with no. rainbow streaks; but a little lump of black in the middle is quite admissible. Beware, however, of being fanciful, and of giving too many drugs. The whitest and most healthy-looking mutes come from fresh beef, castings having been given. These castings, which will be found under the block or perch, should be looked at; all is right if they are free from indigested food or slime, of a nice oval shape, without smell. A small piece of the skin of a young rabbit, the hair inside, is a good casting to convey pepper. Peregrines and goshawks, if fed and flown regularly, and kept dry, and yet out of the scorching sun, have seldom any serious ailment.

I confess that the old falconers would have laughed at my simple doctor's shop and very unassuming kitchen. They would have ridiculed the absence of the "complexions" — black, blank, russet, &c. — with the cock's flesh for "melancholic" hawks, and lamb's flesh for the "choleric:" they would certainly have been angered that I did not "incorporate" *incense* and *mummy* with my castings, and add *cassia fistula* to my purges.

I once wrote to a dear friend of mine to ask the question, "What is mummy?" His answer was, I have no doubt, correct, but perhaps scarcely explicit; "mummy," he said, "is *mummy.*" In candour, however, I should add that he proceeded to observe: "It is often used as a paint, the asphalte with which bodies were preserved being probably the colouring matter, and perhaps the medicine." So much for physic!

I said that this chapter was a medley and an appendix; so perhaps the following may be not much out of place. In itself it is exceedingly interesting. I offer it in the form of *scraps,* which I took from the letter of Major R—, an officer in India, to Capt. Salvin.

Indian Hawks and Hawking

The Lugger. — This is a beautiful falcon, not so large as the peregrine, but with a longer tail. It is very dark; the female's breast nearly black — not a speck of white; the head, light coloured, like a light peregrine's, contrasts curiously with the dark plumage. The adult bird is like a *young* peregrine; for, instead of assuming the transverse bars on the breast, the dark breast changes to white, with *longitudinal* markings. The back never becomes blue, but the head gets darker and very like a young peregrine's. In the first year the feet are bluish, but the mature bird has a very beautiful bright yellow cere and feet. Strange to say, they do not bear the heat well, and sometimes die in their hoods of sun-stroke. They are not quite so swift as the peregrine, but good footers. Pigeons and quails were the quarry. No implements for hawking were to be met with at Cawnpore. The Indian birdlime is very good, crows and kites being caught with it; it is a difficult matter to get it off the feathers — oil is used for the purpose. Cawnpore is not a good place for sporting; a man can only get out from 4.30 A.M. to 7 A.M., and from 5 p.m. to 6.30 p.m. Eagles are a great nuisance to the falconer; they follow the falcon, and make her drop the quarry. It is necessary, therefore, to let your servant carry a rifle.

Hawks in India are much tamer than those in Europe. A falcon was seen to fly a tiny dove, which had a very narrow escape by slipping down an old well. The falcon lit on the top, just over, and Major R— spiked down a pigeon within thirty yards of where she stood. He took out about 100 yards of line, made a noose over the pigeon (after a way described in a previous chapter), and caught the hawk directly. At another time he saw a merlin eating a pipit; immediately a quail was pegged down, a noose and pull-line arranged, and the merlin transported to his house. [4] Major R— continues: — "A sparrow-hawk did what I never saw a sparrow-hawk do before. It is a female, of an Indian variety, smaller than our bird. I shot at a blue rock pigeon, near an old castle, and knocked feathers out. The bird would have gone off, but this little beggar dashed out from a tamarind-tree and caught the pigeon. For once in a way I had no materials for catching hawks. Here was a got I badly wanted a sparrow-hawk; here was a stunner, which I was sure to catch if I had my things. Well, I was determined to have her, so I left my groom to watch, and keep her from eating too much, and galloped off to a village on the river, hardly hoping to get anything, as string is bad and scarce in Indian villages. Luckily, however, I went into a house where they had some fishing-line. I easily got a trowel and spikes. The hawk was still there, and I caught her the moment I left the snare after arranging it. She will be a clipper. She takes a pigeon without hesitation, no matter how big it is.

"I shot a curious sort of eagle the other day, and in its crop it had four snakes, each of which the natives tell me would" kill a man in an hour. I have given away my tame eagle to H—; it is still a great pet. H keeps him at hack: he sleeps every night in the verandah, in front of the door of his room. The merlins — I have another which I took from the nest a month ago — are rum little birds. They would be beauties were it not for their chestnut-coloured heads, which I don't like; otherwise their plumage is exactly that of an old peregrine. They are very plucky little hawks, and very swift.

"I *heard* much of hawking at Lucknow, but found none.

"This morning I caught a beautiful falcon; I had watched her for three days. It settles a point about the plumage of luggers. In the second year, after the first moult is completed, the lugger only loses her white head; the breast remains, black. This falcon is just finishing her moult, and very beautiful she is with her new feathers — such a bloom on them! Her legs are not so yellow as the old hawks. I now fancy my oldest falcon is five years old. This new falcon will fly first. I am now feeding up the others like fun, to get them through their moult. I forgot to mention that the day before I left Cawnpore I caught a falcon — the one I say I fancy must be five years old. Her breast is a fine clear white without a speck, except at the sides."

The following communication from Major R— has been received subsequently to the foregoing, and is crowded with interesting matter: —

"I find that here, as everywhere, there is no bird, on the whole, better than a peregrine. The *shabeen* I have not seen, or even its skin. The falconers I have questioned have never seen it, though they have heard of it. The falcons best known and most generally used in the parts of India I have visited, from Calcutta to Delhi, are the *cheskh*, which is like a very large lugger, swifter and pluckier than that bird, and flown at the heron, black curlew, hares, &c. It is considered inferior to the peregrine for most quarry; but a peregrine, for what reason I know not, is not flown at the black kite, whereas the cheskh is. The falconers admit that a peregrine would most probably take them if tried, but they have never seen it done. I have never seen a trained cheskh; indeed, only one specimen of the bird at all, which I shot, not having at hand means of catching her, and wishing to inspect it. The cheskh in its wild state feeds almost entirely on small ground game, a large sort of lizard, and rats; it rarely kills birds, except in hard weather. Its plumage is not so bright, hard, and clean as a peregrine's. The foot is much smaller. Next in size is the peregrine. Most falconers in India, about Lucknow, -and Oude in general, will tell you that the peregrine (or *bhyree*), is the finest falcon in. the world. They have heard of the *shabeen,* and s*afed cohee,* [5] and *coquila,* tiercel of the safed co-hee, as they have heard the *jer-falcon* and *her tiercel* called, but they don't count these birds, but seem to consider their existence as almost mythical. The peregrine is always used in India as a passage hawk — literally a pas-sage hawk — as they are taken only for about four or five months in the year when they come, following the flights of wild fowl in the winter. Chiefly red hawks are taken. The bird is quite undistinguishable from our European birds. I have seen them of all sizes and shades of colour. In India they seem to prey almost entirely on waterfowl, and live near great lakes.

"Next comes the *cohee.* My men tell me there are three varieties of the co-hee. I have only seen one. The one I know is, in the young plumage, exactly like a young peregrine, but that the plumage has a red glow, the cere and feet are much deeper yellow than in the peregrine, and the feet are larger in pro-portion to the bird's size, as is the case with all the varieties of cohee; and the cry differs. In the adult plumage the head is of a chestnut red, back and wings of a light slate colour, and the breast gets transverse bars, as in the peregrine. It is a visitor as far south as Lucknow. It is said to breed in the Nepalese mountains, and near the Raptee river in trees. Its chief prey is parrots and doves. It is very swift, though not so clever at repeating a stroke as a pere-grine. It mounts very high, and generally kills at its first stoop. I have only one cohee now; I had two, but one turned out useless, and I let it go; the one I use is an adult bird. I will not fail of securing you some skins of the cohee.

"Next comes the *lugger,* which I described in a former letter. It preys, like the cheskh, on ground game, and rarely kills birds, except such as are weakly, in its wild state.

"Next, the Indian merlin (or *turmutz*), a beautiful little falcon, quite differ-ent from our merlin in everything except size and proportions of wing and tail, which are precisely the same. Its colour is totally different. The head is red, and the back and wings and tail blue, and the breast marked with trans-verse black bars on a white ground, like an adult peregrine. It is an exceed-ingly swift hawk; some falconers say the swiftest of all. It is used in India for flying at the roller, which is an exceedingly difficult bird to take. Very few peregrines can do it. It mounts to a great height, and tumbles about in the air in a wonderful manner. By the way, the turmutz is the only hawk in India of which two are employed at the same quarry. The season for merlin flying is shortly coming on, and I shall soon look out for some. The hobby I have not seen. So much for the long-winged hawks.

"The goshawk is held in India in higher estimation, perhaps, than any other hawk. It is exactly the thing to suit a native — never being lost, and killing such a quantity and such a variety of game.

"Next comes the *basha,* a short-winged hawk, which I consider identical with our English sparrow-hawk. It and the goshawk are migratory about Central, and probably are not found in Southern India. They come, like the peregrine, in the cold months for a short time, and are said to breed in the hills of Nepaul. It, the basha, is thrown from the hand.

"Last comes the *sicara,* or Indian sparrow-hawk, a wonderfully plucky little brute: — thrown from the hand. In the young plumage the bars are longitudinal, as in the young goshawk. It is highly valued by natives, but I don't care a rush for the bird. It lives all the year round in India, and breeds here. By the way, the lugger and merlin are the only other species which breed in the hot parts of India. The sicara sparrow-hawk is flown all the year round, and takes an infinity of game. It is valued by the rich, but chiefly it is in high favour with the poor, who cannot afford the valuable migratory hawks. I have seen them take hundreds of crows, jays, &c.; and I am told that a male sicara will actually seize on a white heron, and hang to him till the bird comes down and is caught, though many are killed by the heron's beak. I do not doubt it, from what I have seen. For this purpose it is necessary to sneak very close to the heron while he is feeding, and throw the hawk with all your force at him. The sparrow-hawk (basha and sicara) never kill except when thrown; and when trained to be thrown, never attempt to catch anything without this assistance.

"I broke five falcons and four tiercels; but lost a tiercel and caught a falcon immediately after, and I let the young cohee go. Since I arrived at Delhi I caught a young tiercel and two falcons, and I had one falcon brought to me. Magnificent hawks! but what on earth to do with them I don't know. One is six years old. These I do not count in my establishment, as I am undecided whether to kill them for their feathers, which I cannot bear to do, or to turn them loose; and I have a hankering wish to keep them, though of course they will be useless when the hawks come in at the beginning of the cold season. Indeed, I believe that the wisest plan would be always to turn out the hawks in March, and catch fresh hawks every October; but I do not like turning out my good hawks, and shall at all events keep them to look at. It is quite impossible now to work a peregrine, and, except a few days in the rains, when they may be flown at easy quarry in the early mornings and late in the evenings, they will be idle till October. Natives only keep the very best. Hawks are never clean moulted till December. Most of these peregrines were caught by myself; some two or three were brought home by native bird-catchers. One peregrine was taken from the train of the rebel Begum of Oude, by one of the loyal Zemindars, together with a goshawk, and the commissioner of the district got them for me. The falcon has evidently been selected for her beauty for the Begum, and has been taken the greatest care of. She is two years old, and has not a blemish, now every one of her nestling feathers has fallen. She is a perfect picture of a peregrine; very bright blue, with a bloom on it, and a fast hawk. The goshawk is three years old; was a present from Benee Madho to the Begum; she is clean moulted, and a nice hawk. My best falcon, 'Tigress,' is an old falcon (two years old), which I caught myself at Bijnow. She had moulted clean before she was caught — is a very black hawk. She was the first old falcon I had in my mews, and native falconers were strongly advising me not to have anything to do with her, and break none' but young red hawks. I insisted, more on account of the beauty of the falcon than anything, and she has turned out the pluckiest and swiftest falcon I have ever seen. Now, though my men and the Nawabs have been falconers all their lives, and are first-rat fellows in their way, yet everything they do is by rule. They did not speak, as they told me, from experience, when they tried to dissuade me from training the wild old falcon, but on principle; and I heard Peerbux, my head falconer, say to another near him, while the falcon was going up to a heron, 'I will never reject, an old falcon again, if I get her clean moulted.' Certainly it will never do to stint a hawk in her grub, &c., when she is yet moulting; and if I found an old falcon very fractious, I would not break her, as one must fly her so light that the young hawks would be better; but I often thought, and this season's experience has confirmed my opinion, that provided an old falcon be clean moulted, and very carefully dealt with, she is swifter and more powerful than young hawks.

"Falconers are in the habit of saying the young hawks are the fastest; but this is surely impossible. It would be absurd to say a young grouse can go like an old cock; and with other birds the same argument applies. Undoubtedly old hawks are much the most difficult to manage at first. A young falcon, — very like your falcon 'Assegai' in appearance, only much handsomer, never having *been in a basket,* &c, — is the next best: she is capital at black curlew; and I have frequently seen her take the long-billed curlew. This she would do, turning from a heron in the most provoking manner. She is nearly as fast as the old hawk. I have two clipping tiercels, — splendid plover-hawks: it is capital sport, plover-hawking! none but passage-hawks, I am sure, could do it.

"My falcons are *flying* at herons, white herons, black curlew, wild ducks, spoonbills, and one has killed a crane. The tiercels fly white herons, teal, plover, and paddy birds, a sort of bittern (I should say were flying, as they cannot work now).

"The goshawk is now killing partridges, and occasionally a hare; but in the cold weather she killed no end of peacocks, hares, wild ducks, little white herons (it won't do to fly a goshawk at the big white Heron, because, as you know, she does not secure the head and neck as quickly as does a peregrine, and will get stabbed). A good goshawk in the young plumage takes eagles and kites. My goshawk catches crows like fun; but of all quarry she prefers partridges and hares.

"I will now give you the results of a morning's hawking, on which occasion I killed 28 head, viz.: —

3 herons			3 partridges	
8 white ditto			2 hares	
7 paddy birds	killed with		1 peacock	killed with
3 plover	the peregrines.		—	the goshawk.
1 wild duck			6	
—				
22				

"I don't wonder at Mr. Barker imagining he could take partridges in England with the goshawk. One would not think there was much difference in pace between our birds and the Indian; but there must be, inasmuch as I am satisfied no goshawk could touch an English bird, and I see here they never miss an Indian partridge. I have not tried the black partridge as yet.

"*April 20th.* — Last night I was out with the goshawk between five and seven p. M. She refused all the hares, but killed two and a half brace of partridges. I see she will not go on flying much longer: she is dreadfully punished by the heat. She affords great sport to those who do not understand much of hawking: they are pleased with the large bags of game, and the hare-killing.

"Natives never think of flying two falcons, either peregrine or cheskh, at a heron: no falconer I have met with ever heard of such a thing. I said I would do it, but I never have: all my falcons have killed herons single-handed. No peregrine falcon, say they, ought ever to fail in killing a heron, unless from some such obvious cause, as the heron falling into a large sheet of water. I have never seen a long flight at a heron, even a light one: when the hawk is hooded off at a heron at a moderate height, say two gunshots, the hawks generally kill at the third stoop; or, say the falconers, 'the falcon is playing with the heron' (if she is a good hawk), and fly her no more that day, but physic her next morning, after feeding her on washed meat the same evening on which she is flown. I have seen some splendid flights at lofty herons, however. The hawks here have far greater determination and dash than I have seen shown by hawks in Europe. Mine are all very nice hawks, — such a pretty show! — no broken feathers; and, being all passage-hawks, no "singers" among them. I have one tiercel and one falcon which mantle over their food, which trick I detest: I shall get rid of the falcon for it, but I would not part with the tiercel on any consideration.

"The black curlew is, next to the heron, the best quarry my falcons have flown at. I like this sport well enough; but the worst of it is that the black curlew has got an abominable trick, when he is well aloft, and finds he must give in, of using all his remaining strength in a dash at a village. He is five times out of six taken in the air during this effort; and the consequence is that the hawk is liable to be in a scrape with a cur-dog, or, if she is at all shy, disappointed of her quarry by being obliged to let go. However hard you may ride, and however well-mounted you may be, it is impossible always to guard against misfortunes at this work. It is much better when you are stationary at a place, as then you can warn the villages all round; but at the time I had the best of my curlew hawking I was marching up country, and consequently going into a new country every day. I never had an accident to the falcon, by luck, but on several occasions they were disappointed of their quarry, and had to be taken down, as it won't do to let a passage-hawk be wheeling about in the air till you can get up to serve her, more especially in such a country as India.

"I had an unlucky accident with a tiercel in the early part of the season; he has, however, quite recovered now. He had bound to a night-heron in the air, and got struck by its beak on the pinion-joint. For a few days he could not fly at all, and I feared it was all up with him; but he got better, and killed paddy birds. As he got still better he killed white herons, and at last took plover again; and when I left off flying peregrines he was the swiftest tiercel: he mantles. He takes wild pigeons, which is a most unfortunate habit, and makes it dangerous to fly him, — at any rate till some peregrine has been on the wing near at hand. Pigeons do not avoid the lugger or cheskh. The night-heron is good quarry for a tiercel, so is the white heron in all its varieties, egrets, &c. One species is bigger than the great grey heron. But I like plover-hawking best of all for a tiercel: his speed and activity are more severely tested. Hawks are rarely made to wait on in India; natives do not care about it Wild ducks and teal are the only quarry for which they are made to wait on: a hawk is never flown out of the hood at this quarry.

"I saw a curious thing near Billore lately. A young falcon of mine, very like 'Assegai' of yours, had flown a black curlew. She killed close to some natives, unfortunately, near the edge of a river. She was at this time rather shy, having only just completed her training. The crops were very high, and there was no open place large enough to give her a good sweep at the lure; and, after striking at it a few times, she sat down on the bank, the far side from us. I was preparing a live pigeon with a long string, that she might truss it in the air, when five or six wild geese came over from some other part of the country, high in the air, and passed over the falcon; and to my horror I saw the falcon look up, open her wings, and rattle away after the geese as hard as she could go. 'They won't stop under four cop (six miles),' said Peerbux, my falconer. He was mistaken. They went till they were specks in the sky (a good distance on a clear Indian morning): the falcon was undistinguishable. I had given up hopes, when the specks looked larger and larger, — so we all said. There was very soon not much doubt the geese were returning, but the falcon was not to be seen. At last they got within easy sight of us, when all of a sudden the geese opened out in all directions, and the falcon shot like an arrow through them, marking her course with a cloud of white feathers, leaving one goose staggering, while the others made the best of their way off. The falcon was up again in a few seconds, and at him again, with the same effect as before. At the third attack she bound to him, and fell about 200 yards on the other side the river. One of the Nawab's falconers swam over and lay by the falcon. I galloped off to a bridge about a mile off, as I did not want to get wet under a hot sun with ten miles to ride afterwards, and came up before the falcon had done feeding, — most fortunately, as she would not let the naked falconer get within ten yards of her, but jumped off the goose. That was the most extraordinary and the luckiest, flight I ever saw. Peerbux tells me he has in his life lost six or seven heron hawks by their going away at a disadvantage straight on end at wild geese, but never saw a kill like that before.

"*April 21st* — I went put last night with the goshawk. She had plenty of chances at hares, but only took one leveret and a brace of partridges. She is very much oppressed by the heat. In a very few days flying her will be out of the question. I let two magnificent old falcons go last night, after levying a a small tax on them in wing and tail feathers. One of the falcons instantly killed a parroquet when she had got up. The other rattled away after some teal, over the Jumna, at a great distance off. Pigeons are exceedingly cheap here. I sometimes buy them by the hundred, in the large towns, at from two to three rupees a hundred. In the country I have hired a day's services of a bird-catcher for a few pence, and received a hundred and fifty pigeons. Grain in abundance; to feed them is exceedingly cheap. Wild ducks are excellent food for hawks. I have bought them near Delhi at one rupee for fifty. Pigeons swarm all over the country; common blue rocks. They breed by thousands down the shafts of dry wells; the same kind is found in equally large numbers, breeding about the houses of crowded cities, as in the loveliest parts of the jungle. I fancy peregrines in India prefer wild ducks and waterfowl to all other quarry. When they come fresh from the wild state they well know the whistling of their wings as they pass over head. I have often seen the falcons sitting unhooded on the falconer's hands near a fire, before it was light enough to hawk or even to shoot a duck going over, but the moment the sound of wild ducks' wings was heard, all the hawks rose up and stared into the sky, and if they caught the least view they baited furiously, being in trim for flying. The bird-catchers tell me that they have seen a peregrine go in chase of a flight of wild fowl before it was well light, heard her kill, and found the duck.

"*April 23rd.* — My falcons are suffering tremendously from the heat; I do not expect they will all live. Only one, the Begum's falcon, is in the highest health and spirits; she never gets any physic. The others would soon be dead but for physic. They throw their meat (not from inflammation of the crop however), refuse it frequently, and bait furiously, although tame. 'Tigress,' I am glad to find, has not very much the matter with her. I long for the rainy season. I think I shall go on leave to the hills on the 23rd July.

"I have not mentioned hoods. Indian hoods have no ties; they are very nice hoods — most excellent for flying a hawk '*out of the hood*;' but a hawk must *never* be allowed to *pull off* her hood, even once, for some two months, or I should think no hawk would keep one of these native hoods on her head a moment when put on a block. They are far more easy for a hawk to feed through, not that I consider that much of an advantage. I think it a very bad plan to allow hawks to feed through their hoods after they are broken, or unless there is some necessity for it. It makes them pull and bite your glove in a tiresome, foolish manner. I should be for using Indian hoods in England, on those hawks which do not throw them off. They are lighter than ours. I decidedly think the absence of bands is a very great advantage. The hood goes farther back under the falcon's chin, and leaves the upper part of her head more uncovered; it is something  in this shape, [6] very much bossed out at the eyes, and the plume is stuck right at the back, which, at first, had an ugly appearance to me, but I now am used to it; as also to the handling of it, which at first I found rather difficult.

"Natives always carry a falcon on the right hand.

"Winged game for hawking and shooting also abounds: partridges, black and grey; peacocks; quail; wild ducks and snipe; geese; herons; cranes; curlew; white herons; egrets; bitterns; night-herons; plover, &c. I am sorry to find Mag. is never seen, but hawking him could last but a very short time in the year if he were; and none but old hawks could be used, as no young or old passage-tiercels would wait on for a magpie two months after their capture. Hawking in this country has suffered a very severe blow by the recent mutiny, as you may imagine, — perhaps not so great as the last war inflicted on the hawking in Europe; but the demand for falcons in the great cities, Lucknow and Delhi, Cawnpore, &c., has dwindled to nothing. I was the only person to whom falcons were brought last season at Lucknow. Formerly, I am told, so lately as two years ago, not less than 200 peregrines were disposed of every year in Lucknow.

"Probably somewhere about this number came to Delhi, Cawnpore, and Benares. Now the birdcatchers do not catch them unless specially ordered to do so, as they have no earthly use for them and cannot dispose of them. This is rather lucky, however, for a poor man like me: my hawks cost me nothing, or next to nothing; and I have a large choice, by catching more than I want, and turning out those I do not approve of.

"I shall end by a few remarks on the sport itself. Hawking in India, although it sounds very well when you hear that one can get any number of hawks, and kill herons, black curlew, cranes, &c, is, I have come to the conclusion, on the whole, inferior to hawking in Britain. Many, I have no doubt,

146

would not think so; but I cannot get over the climate. It is true, I see a few days' most brilliant sport, and some days in the cold weather you can work all day, but you cannot take the hard exercise, — the atmosphere and country are not so enjoyable as in England.

"A goshawk, properly speaking, is not fit to fly much after the 1st of March or before the middle of November, — that is to say, to kill handsomely hares, peacocks, &c. She will go on early and late at partridges, *voilà tout*, in April, but the greatest care must be taken of her. Again; with a peregrine there is such a variety of nasty troublesome birds she can so easily take, that your sport is very frequently spoiled. If a peregrine once takes to killing crows you had better get rid of her. Paddy birds, and minors, and doves, and parrots are eternally in the way, — ducks also. 'Tigress' took to killing ducks a good deal. Luckily, she is such a fast falcon that it did not much signify; but many hawks are lost by flying out of the hood slap at a flight of ducks. These take a falcon half a mile, we'll say; she puts them into a pond; she is a passage-hawk. As she recovers from her stoop which she made at them over the water, which foiled her, she sees others; before getting a sight of the lure, away she goes again, perhaps with the same result; and a third time kills, goodness knows where!

"One day's absence in India is the certain loss of a lately caught passage-hawk, — she can so easily kill. Only the Par Sal hawks, as the natives called the intermewed hawks, are to be trusted. I have only one, — the Begum's: she will wait on and kill a wild duck, or kill a heron; but she is much inferior to 'Tigress' though she is a very good falcon.

a in figure B is a small flat bar of brass, about 1 ½ in. long, with three holes punched in it. (1 2 3) *b c d* are three round bars of brass, about 1 ¼ in. long, each having a ring at one end, and a knob at the other.

"When put together, figure A, the two right and left ones, as *b* and *d*, should have their rings and knobs on the same sides as each other of the bar *a* and *c*; the centre one must be reversed. To the ring of *c* is affixed the hawk's leash, to the rings of *b* and *d* the hawk's jesses. The holes in

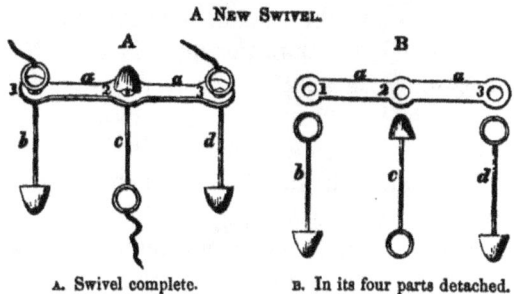

A New Swivel.

A. Swivel complete.   B. In its four parts detached.

the bar should allow the rods of *b c d* to play very easily from knob to ring.

"Inconvenience of course attends the fastening and unfastening the jesses to the rings of *b* and *d*; this is the only difficulty. I have no doubt you will find a way to manage it; otherwise this swivel is perfection."

The following paper is from the pen of Capt. Salvin:

Management of Hawks at the Camps. — Hawking is such a fine manly sport, and is so particularly adapted to a military life, that we hope to see it taken up by officers; and this we may reasonably expect, since there are now some keen and good falconers in the army, who must give others a taste for it. As we have had some experience as to the management of hawks in our camps of Aldershot, the Curragh, and Shorncliffe, &a, where they must be more or less exposed, and have to ' rough it' like everything else, perhaps a few hints may prove acceptable. The two great evils to be avoided are wind and sun. For the first evil, observe which direction the wind *generally blows* from, and cut it off by erecting a wall of canvass supported by stakes, from the top of which stakes run out ropes, and peg them down tight, as an additional support. Hawks should be taken in at night at our camps during the winter. If at any time of the year the weather is very severe — that is, if it is too hot or too cold, or too wet or too windy for hawks to be exposed to it, we should advise their being taken in even during the *day*. When taken in they are to be placed upon the perch. If it should be a very hot day they would be cooler hooded, with the windows thrown open, but generally it is better to keep them unhooded in the dark. A window is easily made dark by covering it with a frame of wood, to which must be nailed some of that oil-cloth which is used for table covers. This frame maybe easily fastened by means of 'leather hinges, and a wooden catch or button. It should be so contrived that it will not interfere with opening the window. To keep the mews clean, cover the floor with fresh clean sawdust, and place sheets of newspaper (supplement to the *Times*) over that portion where the mutes will fall. Little stones put upon the paper will keep it from moving. The paper can be burnt, and fresh put down as it may be required. Though goshawks, from their being so hardy, may be kept out both night and day in most weathers, they must occasionally be taken in when the weather is very severe. When this is the case it is better to put them in a stable upon the bow-perch, with plenty of straw round it to save their feathers, or if this cannot be done, hood them, and place them with their tails inwards upon the box-cadge. A 'hot meal' should occasionally be allowed your hawks; and, as you may wish to save your pigeons, which are expensive household goods, you may economise in this way. In every regiment there are to be found men who are fond of field sports, even in the humblest branches, and for a slight reward and the loan of a steel trap or two, &c, they are delighted to trap you rats, mice, sparrows, &c. Then, again, rat and rabbit catchers often visit our camps, and are glad to sell both their live and dead stock. 'The little staff gun,' sold by Messrs. Hancock, Bridge-end-street, Newcastle-on-Tyne, is most useful to the falconer, especially at the camps, where it is a great help to the larder. For instance at Aldershot (the worst camp for hawking), this little gun is invaluable to the falconer, for many rooks will gain the trees, in which case it is better to shoot them with the gun whilst they are kept in the tree for fear of the hawk; you thus get food for the hawk, and he is not disgusted at missing his quarry. If the trees are near or down wind, you may generally anticipate the rooks going there, and therefore it is better to be there before the hawk "leaves the hand," Though this gun will only carry shot some fifteen or twenty paces, it is a deadly weapon for small birds and for rats, which are generally found about camps. You can never make hawks too public, since ignorant people will kill them. You should therefore put out notices about them, and these notices should be sent to the canteens; and this should be occasionally repeated, as when a new regiment comes in. It may be as well to observe that at the Curragh tiercels will be required for magpie-hawking; and at Shorncliffe you may fly tiercels at magpies and partridges (having of course obtained leave); but at Aldershot you have no quarry but rooks, and therefore you require nothing but falcons. We have found it an excellent plan to put out damaged corn in open places in order to bring up the rooks. Some would imagine that the camp itself would interfere with the flight, but it is not the case — indeed, some of the finest flights we have ever seen have been amongst the huts of the north camp. We have seen as many as fifty or sixty stoops at a strong old rook, and we well recollect — and hundreds must remember it too — that on one occasion the rook and falcon 'Assegai' mounted all but out of sight; from which immense height both came down amongst the lines of the 36th Regt., and at the next stoop the quarry was taken upon the roof of a hut, to the delight of every one. A horseman is necessary, to keep dogs and men off the hawk when he kills.

"In concluding these hasty remarks upon hawking at the camps, we must observe that there could scarcely be a better place for lark-hawking than Aldershot; for though birds in general are very scarce, larks abound in every direction."

It is time to bring these chapters to a close. I am sure I do so unwillingly. Their first form of publication, in a periodical, is one which suits my taste, and I certainly had some kind readers. 1 hope to have some kind readers still. Many of my old friends will, I think, meet me in the pages of this book, and I may perhaps hope for some new ones. Collected papers are certainly more convenient for reference than the odds and ends which one snips and shears out piecemeal; and mine have lately had great advantages — as mentioned in the Preface — from the experience of Captain Salvin.

It is difficult to say "Goodbye!" but it must be said sooner or later; and I leave all my readers with thanks which I do not know how to express, but I am quite sure that they are not the less sincere because they are not long and not eloquent.

Peregrine.

[1] Goshawks should be moulted either on the bow-perch, under a shed (where there is plenty of grass), or separately in rooms.
[2] "Gentlemen's Recreation," 1677.
[3] Capt. Salvin, however, has seen *tetanus* produced in a falcon by the sudden loss of a claw, as she was taken roughly from a rook. She died from the attack.
[4] An officer of the Rifle Brigade sent me an old female sparrow-hawk, a month or two ago, which was caught at his house in Scotland, by the butler, in the man-

ner alluded to above. The hawk had killed a wood pigeon. She was put off it, the snare set, and she caught on her return. I trained this bird in a few weeks to fly to hand at any distance. I also killed bagged starlings thrown from the hand with her. She was on the point of an introduction — or re-introduction — to wild quarry when she was lost by an accident.

[5] Literally, White cohee.

[6] The original sketch was unfortunately too indistinct to copy, and consequently all that could be done was to represent an Indian hood from the Punjab. This hood however has two ties, but its shape is exactly that of the original drawing which was so obscure in its details. From the text we may infer that the ties are done away with altogether in some districts of India. — F. H. Salvin.

Fishing with Cormorants

Chapter One - Introduction

The most ardent lovers of the rod cannot, we trust, begrudge a little cormorant-fishing during the heat of summer, when fishing with the rod is impossible. To such as possess a good reach of river, or who can get leave for an occasional day's fishing with these birds, it will be found a very delightful summer's amusement; and as it comes in just at the time when most rural sports are at a standstill, it deserves some encouragement, particularly when carried on by sportsmen and gentlemen who will not abuse it. Should this little treatise fall into the hands of those who generously invited me to fish their waters some years ago in the northern counties, I take this opportunity of thanking them for their kindness and liberality, through which I derived so much amusement myself, and which, I believe, at pleasure. They are fond of perching or standing upon a rock in a commanding situation, and therefore they should have a rockery, mixed with roots of trees and branches, in the centre of the yard. As a pond, or rather a large tank sunk in the ground, is very necessary for them to bathe in, and must be kept very clean, it should be so contrived that the fresh water can be let in and the foul let out at pleasure. The tank should be made of thick planks of wood, two feet deep, by ten long and four broad, well covered with pitch. The floor of the shed should be covered with litter, which must be frequently changed; and each bird should have a stone to perch upon, at such a distance from his neighbour's that he cannot bite him. The yard also should be daily cleaned and covered with sand; and the "guano," which is not to be despised by the agriculturist, may be saved.

Chapter Three - Training Cormorants

You must fix your cormorants' dinner-hour so that it shall not be too late in the day; for as they *always* take their bath after dinner, there would not be time for them to get dry before going to roost were the meal late. Teach them at that hour — which must be kept exactly — to come to the call and to the rattling of the tin box you carry their food in. This may be called "making them to the lure." As they are clumsy [1] birds on land, those that require lifting to your arm (it is a good thing to accustom them to be lifted) are to be laid gently hold of by the head, neck, or beak, the forefingers being passed down the arch of the neck to support it. Indeed, whilst training them, and afterwards, this is the best and safest way of lifting them up and of putting them down; in doing which throw them also a little forward, at the same time drawing them slightly towards yourself, which will break the force of their coming to the ground. If this (rather extraordinary manoeuvre) is not attended to they are apt to pitch upon, and to break up, their tails, which it is a great object to keep as perfect as possible, being of the greatest assistance to the bird in diving. Cormorants' feathers will come again, so you may sometimes pull out a feather, but they will not imp. Hot water will sometimes straighten them. [2]

You must now begin to "carry" them for two or three hours every day for nearly a week, just as you do hawks, with this difference, that in the one case you are constantly hooding and unhooding the bird, whilst here you have to be hooded *yourself*; that is, you must wear a *fencing mask*, otherwise the bird will take out your eye to a certainty, to say nothing of biting your face. Your ears and hands may not escape, as you cannot cover them, [3] but should they suffer, the cut, being a very clean one, soon heals. By "carrying" they see new objects, and as they at the same time acquire confidence in you, it tends wonderfully to tame them. Some will be much more wild and savage than others, but "*nil desperandum*" must be your motto; and be sure to turn your face to them whenever they strike the mask, which will soon convince them that the jar it gives them is more disagreeable to themselves than to you. "Carrying" is useless unless it is *continued*, and as it is tedious work where you have several birds, an assistant who can be fully trusted must be procured. It is conducted thus: — Being masked, take up the bird, and having placed it upon your hand [4] put your thumb upon its right foot. Whenever it bates from your fist hold it if possible by your thumb, then by yielding a little to it, and with a peculiar backward jerk of the arm, and at the same time balancing the bird, it will regain its seat upon your hand. Whilst thus carrying it about, occasionally offer it a morsel of fish from your tin box, which, if not too sulky, it will eat. Such attentions, especially if offered after it has tried to bite you, will gain the bird's affections, which lie more in the stomach than in the heart. Whilst training you must keep its appetite sharp-set. The next thing to be done, after having made cormorants to "the lure" and to "the fist," is to enter them in a large tank, *without* their straps (which shall be explained) at live fish, a good supply of which you must have netted for this purpose. After repeating this lesson two or three times put leather straps, five inches long, and nearly half an inch broad, with a small one-tongued buckle, upon their necks, like a horse's lip-strap.

The oesophagus or gullet, having a bottom formed by this strap and being very elastic, is turned into a capacious bag for holding the fish. [5] Feed them, with the straps on, in their yard. This will teach them to hold their fish, for whenever they disgorge it, it will be stolen by another bird, and in their eagerness to be fed and to hold it they will allow you to handle them. This tantalizing ordeal should be repeated three or four times. The birds will be now ready "to enter." For this end choose a small moor-side stream which you know to be full of trout. Trout are slimy, and consequently better than scaly fish to enter the birds at, for the scales irritate the gullet or pouch, which at first the birds do not like. If you have an old steady cormorant ("a make bird ") it will save you much trouble, for it will both teach the young ones to hold the fish they catch and to come out of the water.

It is often no easy matter to catch young cormorants, and much tact is required in wading round them, and putting out your arm, or the whip, on the side on which they are likely to pass you, &c, which experience and patience alone can teach. When you make a bird disgorge always give it a small piece of fish for its reward. Cormorants are lazy birds, and must be made to dive by cracking a whip, and by throwing soft earth at them, which frightens them. If an old bird tries the water well, and then flaps and washes itself, you may rest assured there are no fish. When once entered keep them at work daily for a week, and as it is of great importance to tire them well, choose a small rough stony-bedded stream, that by walking from one deep to another they may be well fatigued, which will greatly help to tame them, and is an excellent prescription for any other wild subject.

When only one cormorant is kept, "noose jesses" are put over each foot, to which jesses a cord is attached, to serve as a leash, and the bird is carried either on foot or on horseback to and from the field, &c, upon the fist, [6] just as we carry hawks. When several cormorants are used, they must be carried in a palanquin, which must have a *separate* chamber for each bird, otherwise they would fight and injure each other. It will be necessary here to describe the palanquin. The framework of this conveyance must be of light wood, covered with tarpauling; the cabins into which it is divided must have a door on each side, opposite each other, that the bird may go in or out on either side. These doors are of tarpauling, and open half-way up the framework, like an apron, being well *stayed* to prevent their slitting up. They are fastened at the bottom, on each side, by leather straps and one-tongued buckles. The four *legs* of the palanquin must be long enough to allow of their passing through openings in a thin wooden platform, which forms the bottom or floor, and is quite separate when the iron pins which pass through holes in each leg are withdrawn. It is thus easily washed and kept clean. The palanquin is to be ventilated and kept cool by means of holes along the sides near the top, and by an opening round the bottom, which also allows the birds' tails to come through. The palanquin should be 2 feet wide by 5 long and 2 deep. Whilst fishing down a river, the birds are to be rested and worked in their turns, and the tired ones carried *outside* the palanquin, where they will spread their wings and dry themselves. A sponge must be kept in a pocket at one end, for the purpose of keeping the top clean. The poles by which it is carried must be *flat*, and in order to pack in less room they should have a hinge in the middle. They require to be well padded where they rest upon the men's shoulders.

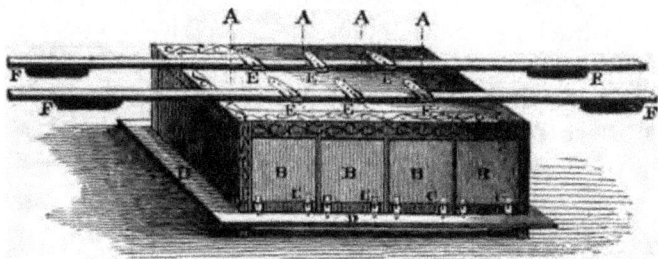

A A A A, the four cabins, B B B B, their doors, C C C C, the straps. by which the doors are fastened, d, a light wooden floor, at the corners of which are four openings through which the palanqain legs pass, and the whole is made firm by the iron tongues which pass through its holes. E E E E, four strong broad straps, with rollerbuckles with one tongue, by which the poles are fastened to the palanqnin. The middle straps are to pass over the pole hinges, by which the hinges are prevented from moving. A leather washer must be nailed on between the division, to prevent the hinges from being strained, F F F F, padding on the poles, to protect the carriers' shoulders. [7]

Leather fishing-boots will be found to stand the hard work of climbing up banks, running, jumping, and bushing through rough places, better than Indian-rubber. In order to change your boots from one foot to the other, and thus prevent wearing them down on one side, they must not be made "rights and lefts." There should be rough nails in them, to save the wearer from slipping from atones, &c. To prevent the legs of the fishing-boots from coming down, I find it an excellent plan to have a single-tongued buckle about the middle of the outside of each boot, from which a strap with a loop is to be run upon another passing round the waist above the hips. Long warm thick stockings should be worn with the boots. A tin box, say 4 inches wide by 3 broad, and 3 deep, and made in the shape of half a circle, so as to fit the side, should be worn in front, upon this hip belt, for the purpose of holding rewards or lures, consisting of pieces of fish, of which more hereafter. This box can be easily run upon the belt by having a loop of tin on the flat side. The master of the cormorants should also carry a fishing creel or pannier, and perhaps the best costume he could wear is a sailor's jacket and shepherd's plaid trowsers. I shall now wind up this chapter with a few observations upon the daily management of cormorants. Although as active and swift as swallows below water, they are, as I said before, very awkward upon land, and in this artificial state they are apt to break their feathers, particularly their stiff whalebone-like tails. This is to be avoided as much as possible. It is advisable, therefore, to keep their larder *out of sight*, for their endeavours to get to it would cause them to pitch upon their tails and break them. [8] After the young birds are full grown, they are fed but once a day, about noon.

The feeding and conditioning of cormorants is a very important duty, in order to insure health, strength, and obedience in the field. Like hawks, they must have a full "gorge" on Saturday, with very little on Sunday, so as to create a sharp appetite for Monday. If they are not in full work they should be sparingly fed for two days in succession — say a quarter of a feed the first day and a little more the next. They should not be fasted longer than this. On the third day they should be well fed, otherwise, by getting them too low you may sicken them. Good condition and health all depends upon judicious feeding. Cormorants will eat meat greedily, [9] as sheep's and beast's livers, hearts, rabbits, &c.; but meat brings on disease resembling scrofula, which attacks their joints as well as their interiors. Fish of every kind [10] is the best, because the natural food of these birds. Perhaps the safest way to feed cormorants, in order to prevent their biting each other or breaking their feathers, is from the fist, to which some will spring like hawks; but when they decline jumping to it they must be lifted, as described at the beginning of Chapter Three, or you may throw them the meat, which they will catch with great dexterity. After dinner, in lieu of taking a nap, they take their bath, and then, having ascended some elevated position, they flap and dry themselves, and finish their toilette by oiling their feathers from the oil gland, which I have repeatedly seen them and hawks do when upon my fist. "Old Isaac" did this so deliberately, that you could actually see the "macassar" squeezed out; and after applying it with bis bill, he rubbed it in with his throat.

[1] My cormorants used the bills like parrots, for pulling themselves up banks, &c.
[2] In drawing a feather out, let an assistant hold the root, whilst you pull it out with pliers.
[3] Spirits of turpentine is the best cure for such cuts. It acts thus: The oil forms a coating and keeps out the air, whilst the spirit evaporates and cools the part.
[4] Cormorants can throw back the hind toe of each foot, which enables them to perch.
[5] The Greenlanders float their fishing-nets with them.
[6] That part of the arm upon which you carry the bird should be guarded with leather, in the shape of a gauntlet with the hand cut off.
[7] To take off the ugly appearance of the palanquin, it may be ornamented with a little colour, à la Chinese.
[8] Imping does not answer with cormorants, for their tails are constantly used, as in the woodpecker, &c, to balance their bodies: and this strain upon such coarse feathers is too much for the needles to bear. I think they might be mended, as the Eastern falconers repair hawk 's feathers, thus:— Cut the bird's feather where it is hollow, then put a feather down the hollow, and, haying passed a fine needle and thread two or three times through and round the shaft of both feathers where they are joined, tie it fast and cut off the ends.
[9] I have frequently caught water rats with cormorants, and upon one occasion I witnessed one take a water, or moor-hen whilst it was diving. The cormorant, however, did not detain it long, for, appearing annoyed with its feathers, it let go the poor bird, which lost no time in making off.
[10] At present it is not ascertained whether fresh-water fish will keep them in health, or whether it is necessary to feed them chiefly upon sea fish.

Chapter Four - Field Management

Like most sports, cormorant fishing requires a peculiar country and certain circumstances, in order to enjoy it in its fullest excellence. The essence of a fishing-place is one consisting of short deeps, clean sloping sides, gravel beds, and streams; or in other words, a brisk wadeable river or brook, which has generally these requisites; [1] and lastly, there should be plenty of fish of a certain class, upon which I shall presently offer some remarks. Weather, too, is an object which must not be lost sight of, particularly in making an appointment for "the meet," inasmuch as heavy rains might suddenly come on, and so swell and discolour the water as to prevent the birds from working or seeing the fish.

With regard to fish, it is necessary to observe that certain fish cannot be managed by the birds, and, in fact, it is running a great risk to attempt it.

Perch, and all such fish as have a similar back fin cannot be disgorged, and if the bird is not speedily allowed to swallow them by taking off the strap, there is great danger of the fin lacerating the pouch. Cormorants are so fond of eels, that where they are plentiful they will catch nothing else, preferring them to all other fish; nor can they take large eels on account of the great difficulty they have in killing them. Eels, when small, often pass into the stomach, which of course makes the birds still more independent. In short, where eels abound, cormorants "run riot" and are unmanageable, and soon get tired from the eels repeatedly escaping by riggling up again out of the pouch. It is quite clear, then, that where such fish are it is impossible to use cormorants. Ponds and mill-dams, and all water having, like these, a muddy bottom, cannot be fished successfully, because the fish know their green-eyed foes by instinct, [2] and all fish, even trout, will disappear in the mud in order to hide themselves. "Wearing," or "fendering" (as it is sometimes called), weeds, roots, walling, cracks in rocks, and large stones, will afford so much shelter to fish, that where these exist no success can be relied upon. Having considered everything necessary for fishing, I will now prepare for starting. The first thing to be done is to put on the neck-straps, which are not to be too tight, then put the birds into the palanquin and send them with two trusty men to the place of meeting. [3] Arrived at the brook or small river to be fished, turn out one or two of the birds, according to the size of the stream, for like dogs they assist each other. Whenever you come to a likely place where you wish them to dive, crack a whip, and cry "Get away, ah!" or throw a little light soil at them. Young birds are shy of being taken when they have caught a fish, particularly if it is not a large one, when it will give them little trouble to hold it.

As we before observed, it is sometimes a good plan to wade round the bird in order to get it out of the water. If it is inclined to turn back and pass you, you may cause it to take to the land by putting out your arm, or holding out the whip, or by throwing a stone near it. When you approach it to disgorge, you must put away your whip, go up to it quietly and lay hold of the beak, at the same time that you must pass your two forefingers along the arch of the neck to support it and lift it gently to a stone; next, open the mouth with one hand, whilst with the other gently press upon, and a little below, the fish, so as to push it upwards, waiting for an instant for the bird's assistance, which it will give you upon finding it cannot retain the fish. After thus taking a fish from it give it a *small* fish as a reward; it encourages it to allow it to take the fish you lure it with. There cannot be a better lure than a minnow or a small dead eel. When you perceive the birds are wet and tired with fishing, place them upon stones or upon the palanquin, where they will dry themselves. Whilst they are thus resting bring out your fresh birds, and thus work and rest them by turns. After fishing feed them up, and if you have far to go you had better dry them outside the palanquin, as you move off the ground, for they cannot dry inside. About four birds is a manageable number, and for these you require an assistant to act as "whipper-in," and to carry the fishing creel. Two more men are necessary to carry the palanquin, but they may generally be engaged in "the field" before "throwing off." Of course it is easier for the birds to go down than to fish up a river or brook, and with four cormorants you may fish for some hours and for some miles, provided the water is not too cold, and all the time you keep moving on. When they come to a likely deep they will turn and fish it thoroughly, and they will frequently turn up stream after a fish, but generally when in a stream (particularly a strong rapid one) they keep moving down, striking at fish as they pass.

It is extraordinary how wonderfully active and rapid these curious birds are *under* water; and their cunning, which improves by experience, is also astonishing. You may observe them look up every rathole and under every shelving bank as they proceed down a stream. Many fish are caught in these places; but they catch fish — even grayling (which are swifter than trout), by fairly swimming or coursing them down in the open water. If they know they have a chance of getting a fish from under a large stone (no matter how deep the water is), [4] they will repeatedly dive until they have accomplished it. Fish appear to get "blown," as it were, when pursued by these birds; for they can only go for some fifteen to thirty yards. [5] The fish that escape generally do so by doubling. Upon catching a fish, which they usually do across the middle, but occasionally by the very tip of the tail, they come to the surface in order to swallow it. If it is a large fish, they work it round with the beak until the head is in the right direction, when they gulp it down head first. Should the fish be a light one, they toss it into the air, and catch it most dexterously head foremost. I have often seen fish escape that had only been caught by a fin or tail, and I have seen the cormorant dive and retake them like lightning. With the strap on, a two-pound fish is about as much as they can manage, though I once saw two cormorants in a rapid stream seize a grilse [6] of perhaps five or six pounds weight; but he escaped. Clear water is greatly in favour of spectators, as they can see every movement of the birds and fish; but it is not necessary for the birds, for some of my best days' fishing have been in dark moss-water. I have also taken a good deal of fish in water that was still muddy after a flood; but I have frequently seen it too muddy.

During the three years I kept cormorants I caught a great variety of fish with them; indeed, I might almost say that I have taken all the fresh-water fish from a minnow [7] to a pike. In brackish water near the sea I have frequently taken flooks. [8] I will conclude this chapter by giving the results of a fishing tour, and of two or three of my best days' fishings. In the summer of 1849 I made a most delightful tour [9] in the northern counties with four cormorants, upon which occasion I took in twenty-eight days 1,200 good sized fish. I was kindly invited by several fishing clubs, as Driffield, Kilnsey, &c.; and it appears from my Journal that I had some good sport at Driffield in those streams which had no weed, but the main stream was too weedy. [10] At the Kilnsey club, which I visited in the summer of 1848, I had two days' fishing. On the best day I "threw off" in the Arncliffe Brook, and fished it and the River Whalfe to the first falls. As I was anxious to know what amount of fish could be taken where they were plentiful, I fished for seven hours before the birds were completely done, when the results were forty-five fine trout, weighing twenty pounds. I obtained about this time a couple of days' fishing at Whitewell, through the liberality of Col. Townley. There had been a fresh, which had brought up the sea fish, called locally "sprods:" they are silvery fish, of about three quarters of a pound weight. "The meet" was well attended, and the success nearly equalled that at Kilnsey; but on this occasion very few trout were caught, for the birds seemed to prefer the sprods, — in which they showed their taste, for I certainly never eat more delicious fish than these proved to be, for we had them for dinner at that romantic little inn, where a large party assembled.

I will now draw these chapters to a close with a few remarks upon the otter. This animal has frequently been trained for fishing, both in this country and the East. The native fishermen on the Indus are said to employ a small species of otter for driving fish into their nets, and also to catch them. In order to prevent their biting, and consequently spoiling the fish, leather cups are strapped over their canine teeth.

An otter which it is intended to tame should be taken young, and confined in a yard well secured over both the top and sides with wirework, containing a pond, a shed with dry straw facing the sun, and a hollow trunk of a tree into which he may creep and rub himself, as they delight in doing after swimming.

The otter trainer must be careful to observe the various cries of the animal, in order not to irritate its temper, as it has three distinct modes of expressing its feelings. Thus when pleased it whistles, when suspicious of danger it blows through the valves of the nose, when vexed it growls. It is therefore only advisable to play with it when it shows itself to be amiable by its whistling. Otters are particularly playful after feeding, and it is quite a pretty sight to see them play with a ball, for even on land their activity is wonderful.

In 1848 I succeeded in taming a young otter, which I called "Diver," so perfectly, that he would follow me into the country like a dog, [11] and jump into my lap to sleep. At first he was an awkward swimmer, his early education being defective, owing to his separation from his parents, and I found it was necessary to be cautious with him, as cold water at first produced fits. Knowing that otters can scent fish under water, and even smell eels, &c. when in the mud, I taught him to dive by sinking meat with a plumb-line, which he never failed in finding. As the otter cannot eat a fish of any size when swimming, it *must* come to land to do so; its master must then approach it quietly, and taking hold of its long and strong tail (called by otter hunters "the potter"), hold him with one hand, whilst he takes the fish from him with the other, immediately rewarding him with small pieces of fish, after which he will again take the water in search of more. Otters are particularly fond of salmon, and in some waters a great many may be taken. I need hardly remark that the death-struggle of a large salmon with his foe, in a rapid stream, is a grand and exciting thing to witness.

Provided a little sawdust or sand is placed in a corner, the otter will be found a particularly clean animal, having no perceptible smell, which cannot be said of Isaac Walton and Co., who indulge so much in musk, and are not very nice feeders. They are rather delicate animals, and require to be kept warm and dry, to be well fed, and kept as fat as possible. They may be fed upon both fish and flesh, such as rabbits, [12] rats, birds, &c. Diarrhoea is a complaint to which they are liable, and their daily habit of body must be closely watched, being in a great measure an index to their health.

[1] They have not as yet been tried in the sea or upon lakes.

[2] I have frequently seen fish throw themselves upon land to save themselves from a cormorant; and upon one occasion, in the river Wear, county of Durham, I witnessed an eel throw itself a foot out of a stream, like a trout after a fly, to avoid the fatal rush of one of these birds.

[3] A little short straw should be put into each chamber of the palanquin, for the birds to sit upon.

[4] In deep water both cormorants and otters descend and ascend in a spiral or corkscrew direction, as falcons "mount."

[5] I once witnessed "Isaac Walton" exhaust a large trout by spinning round it like a top, with his neck and tail turned inwards, the better to confine the fish within the circle, the fish of course making every effort, but in vain, to escape.

[6] In January, 1850, a cormorant was shot by the Hon. W. Fraser, in Beauly River, which had swallowed a 4 lb. grilse, of 22 inches in length. Part of the fish was out of the bird's month.

[7] Trolling baits may be easily obtained by means of a cormorant; and as small fish are caught uninjured, a pond may be stocked if you disgorge them quickly and put them into water, &c.

[8] I have met with an instance of these flat fish living in a freshwater pond, into which they had been put by the owner.

[9] When travelling, cormorants may be secured by " noose-jesses" and leashes, and placed, like hawks, upon stones upon a lawn or some enclosed place, or they may be put into a loose box, the floor of which should be covered with straw, and there should be stones for the birds to sit upon; and as they are so apt to fight, it is advisable to make the place as dark as possible.

[10] In some of the deep holes at Driffield, where the water is very clear, it was curious to observe what little notice the very large trout took of the cormorant, whilst those up to a pound or more darted in all directions.

[11] I put a collar and bell upon this otter's neck, in order to hear where he was in cover.

[12] In severe frosts, when frozen out of rivers, &c, this curious animal, which so much reminds me of the weasel tribe, will take to killing rabbits, water hens, &c; indeed, there are not many rabbit holes it cannot enter.

www.ingramcontent.com/pod-product-compliance
Lightning Source LLC
Chambersburg PA
CBHW051728040426
42447CB00008B/1027